Extraordinary Performance from Ordinary People

Value Creating Corporate Leadership

Extraordinary Performance from Ordinary People

Value Creating Corporate Leadership

Keith Ward, Cliff Bowman and
Andrew Kakabadse

AMSTERDAM • BOSTON • HEIDELBERG • LONDON • NEW YORK • OXFORD
PARIS • SAN DIEGO • SAN FRANCISCO • SINGAPORE • SYDNEY • TOKYO
Butterworth-Heinemann is an imprint of Elsevier

Butterworth-Heinemann is an imprint of Elsevier
Linacre House, Jordan Hill, Oxford OX2 8DP, UK
30 Corporate Drive, Suite 400, Burlington, MA 01803, USA

First published 2007

British Library Cataloguing in Publication Data
A catalogue record for this book is available from the British Library

Library of Congress Cataloging-in-Publication Data
A catalog record for this book is available from the Library of Congress

ISBN–13: 978-0-7506-8301-2
ISBN–10: 0-7506-8301-5

For information on all Butterworth-Heinemann publications
visit our web site at books.elsevier.com

Printed and bound in Great Britain

07 08 09 10 11   10 9 8 7 6 5 4 3 2 1

Contents

Preface

This book focuses on the key value-creating activities, and the associated styles, of corporate leaders. We have identified four different ways in which corporate leaders can have value-creating roles. These four value-creating leadership styles have varying levels of sustainability and each can be more appropriate to specific types of company, the particular corporate strategy that is being implemented, and the competitive environment in which the company is operating. They can, and indeed should, also all be applied at different levels within a company. Indeed, one of the main conclusions of our research is that a value-maximizing company needs to select a specific leadership framework that will determine the levels at which each of the individual leadership styles and associated activities will be carried out. Thus extraordinary performance requires that all four value-creating styles are implemented within the same company, but not by one individual leader.

The original research that has ultimately resulted in this book considered the challenges facing corporate centres in an integrated and multifunctional way. Many leading management books and the supporting academic literature are becoming increasingly narrowly focused, even when they address the overall strategic management of organizations. This approach can create problems for practising managers as, in many cases, they face a broad range of issues and challenges that affect their whole organizations. Each of the authors has therefore progressively been broadening his individual research initiatives from his own originally strongly focused areas of expertise. Working together on this project enabled us to take a more holistic approach to the development of corporate strategies. Thus our resulting model incorporated leadership styles and cultural issues, as well as relevant control processes and appropriate performance measures, for our four value-adding corporate centre roles.

When we practically applied this configurationally based model to the potential leadership roles within a broad range of companies we found that existing leadership models and theories were too broadly based and descriptive, rather than being prescriptive. In other words they required corporate leaders to be the best at almost everything! Also many of these models merged the distinct roles of leadership and management, despite all differentiating between them at the outset. We therefore decided to develop the work on leadership that we had done for our initial corporate centre focused model into a full corporate leadership theory and practical model. In some ways therefore we regard this research as being a kind of prequel to our corporate configurations model.

We wanted to write a book that is of direct relevance and value to practising managers, but not one that is so overfull of detailed case studies that there is no room for any structured arguments. Hence this book tries, in Part 1, to set out the development of our corporate leadership model in a logically argued way before, in Part 2, discussing each of the four leadership styles in depth with a number of real company case studies. Part 3 then considers issues involved in applying the model in practice, as well as providing more background to the academic theories underpinning the model.

All the elements involved are integrated within each chapter, rather than each particular functional attribute being considered separately. This means that this book, like the original development of the corporate configurations model, has been a genuinely collaborative effort, unlike many similar ventures that are really a series of individual chapters bound together only physically by the outer covers.

We hope that you, the reader, feel that the efforts involved in producing the book have been worthwhile and that the ideas discussed can help to make corporate leadership more practical and value creating.

We would like to thank Sheila Hart for typing the manuscript and Angela Ward for helping to produce all the figures.

Keith Ward
Cliff Bowman
Andrew Kakabadse

PART 1

Developing a Practical Leadership Model

1

Redefining corporate leadership

VALUE-CREATING CORPORATE LEADERSHIP

Corporate leadership creates value because it can increase the output achieved by any workforce beyond that which can be produced by management alone.

This increased output arises as the workforce willingly increases the efforts that it inputs into the business.

These efforts are in the form of physical and psychological energy, i.e. physical or mental activity. Thus, either more energy is input or existing energy is utilized more efficiently and effectively by leadership.

MOST LEADERS ARE MANAGERS, BUT MANY MANAGERS ARE NOT LEADERS

Introduction

Corporate leadership creates value because it can increase the output achieved by any workforce beyond that which can be achieved by management alone. This increased output value can arise because the workers willingly increase the efforts that they put into the business. These efforts are in terms of physical or mental activity; we describe them as the physical or psychological energy available to the business. Alternatively leadership can enable the existing available energy to be utilized more effectively or efficiently within the business. Let us immediately be very clear that most, but not all, corporate leaders are also managers, but many senior managers in business are not leaders.

Leadership is therefore, in one sense, all about change. Corporate leaders can change a workforce from a disparate group of individuals, who are merely 'going through the motions' while at work, into a connected and aligned team that is positively committed to delivering the vision of the business.

In order to do this, leaders, by definition, need one or more followers. One dimension dictating the nature and complexity of leadership is, therefore, the number of followers that any corporate leader needs to be effective. However, true leadership requires 'willing followers', where the followers do not display either the 'forced follower' behaviour of a bull being led around by a ring through its nose, or the 'mindless followership' exhibited by a flock of sheep or herd of cattle. Thus a second dimension of the nature of corporate leadership is the 'degree of buy-in', or level of commitment, required from these followers.

These incredibly simple and fundamental dimensions have been used as the basis for our model of corporate leadership. This model, we believe, provides a practical framework for developing the key leadership roles in any size and type of organization. Before introducing this model, it is necessary to explain how we are using the terms leader, leadership and leading as these have become some of the most misunderstood terms in business and management.

A leader can be defined as someone who takes the initiative and sets the direction (i.e. takes the lead) for the organization, *and* accepts responsibility for this direction. This is exactly the role played by the 'leader' in a tree or other plant, an analogy that we like as any organization is itself a living organism. This leadership activity of setting the direction is critical to the concept of willing followers. It is illogical to think of an intelligent adult 'willingly following' someone else without any idea of where they are being led. However, there is clearly much more to leaders gaining willing followers than merely setting the direction for the business.

In common with most writers and researchers in this area, we separate leadership from management, but we will try to maintain this

separation rigorously throughout this book as it is completely fundamental to the value-creating role of corporate leadership.

Leaders have willing followers, as already stated, while managers
have subordinates. In other words, an organization can *make* someone
a manager by giving them authority over others, but only those 'others'
can make that someone a leader by becoming their 'willing followers'.
This is not a controversial statement but almost all of the vast numbers
of books and papers on leadership very rapidly start to refer to 'leaders
and their subordinates'. Like 'managing change', this is an oxymoron
and undermines the basis of most models of leadership.

However, we also strongly believe in another element of leading, which
is that it implies being the best, or at least one of the best, at doing something. Thus leaders should exhibit leading-edge abilities in some relevant
activities. In today's highly competitive environment this means, for most
companies, that its leaders will need to focus on a limited area of activities. Trying to be the best at 'everything' is a recipe for failure, even if you
believe that leaders are born, not made. This focus means that the leaders
in the organization do not try to be 'everything to everybody'. They consistently concentrate on what they believe is most important and where
their leadership can add most value. This consistent emphasis and focus
has the not surprising result of making all their willing followers realize
that these 'elements' are regarded as the most important and should be
treated accordingly. Many leadership models talk about leaders adopting
a range of very different leadership styles and associated behaviours
depending upon whom they are associating with and the business context.
This is not only incredibly difficult for the leaders to do but also, and more
importantly, will normally create confusion and a lack of trust as followers perceive these different leadership styles from one leader as inconsistency or, more sinisterly, 'participative manipulation'. The relationship
between any leader and their followers is based on mutual trust and
respect. In other words, this view of leadership styles will not generate the
true willing followers that are needed for extraordinary performance.

Our definition of leading also indicates that we regard leadership as
an activity. In other words, leaders should be judged by what they do,
or more appropriately by what they achieve. This explains the title to
the book. Organizations that already possess incredibly strong long-
term competitive advantages (such as monopoly market positions,
unbreakable technology patents, dominant brands, or total control over

key channels of distribution) can produce, for a number of years, well above normal levels of shareholder value creation without the need for real corporate leadership. Eventually any such specific competitive advantages will decay, and so will the financial performance of the business, unless the organization has developed a replacement advantage for its changed competitive environment. Such development, involving reinvestment while the company is still successful, will normally require some display of leadership within the company.

Even Great Historic Leaders Focused

Many theories of leadership discuss the concept of the 'Great Person' who was born to lead, or the traits that make a great leader. Most of the examples used to exemplify these theories are historic leaders during times of war, e.g. Winston Churchill, Alexander the Great, Joan of Arc. We are in no way seeking to diminish the achievement of these leaders but they were great leaders in only one set of circumstances or context. Our point is that the very specific context of war makes for a very focused leader.

This is particularly highlighted by the reaction of the 'deeply grateful' British population at the end of the Second World War, when they voted out of office their successful wartime leader. This leader had, of course, offered them nothing but 'blood, sweat, tears and toil' for the previous years of his leadership. Once the context had changed, these previously willing followers looked to change their leader as, presumably, they did not believe that the current one could rapidly change his focus.

However, the most value-adding impact of true leadership is where the whole workforce become really committed 'willing followers' of the corporate leaders. This is not least because the organization's consequent reputation as a really exciting, challenging place to work should, over time, attract the very best, most demanding employees. The development of a continuing supply of sustainable competitive advantages will logically follow.

This indicates two more beliefs that underpin the model that is explained and applied in this book. The most valuable, sustainable competitive advantages are developed and exploited by human effort, which therefore could, and arguably should, be represented as an intangible asset of a business. Also there is no incompatibility between the 'hard' financial results-based shareholder value-creation perspective and 'softer' people-focused leadership view of business. The key role of leadership is to create more long-term value for all the stakeholders involved in the business. This is also the only way to maximize the long-term value creation for shareholders. You cannot build a sustainable shareholder value-creating company by unfairly exploiting your employees, or your customers, suppliers, etc.

These beliefs have been deliberately stated right at the beginning of the book as we do not want to gain readers under false pretences. We have stated them here as beliefs, views, assertions for the achievement of brevity so that we can get into the more interesting aspects of our model of corporate leadership. This does not mean that we do not have very strong theoretical and research backing for these beliefs and these, for those readers who are interested, are set out in Chapter 9.

Cause and Effect

We have developed our model from first principles by building on the key requirements of business leadership. We did this in an attempt to establish a cause and effect link between business leadership and the sustained level of corporate performance. This model has then been validated by being applied to a wide range of different organizations and leaders in many industries and business contexts.

A recent trend in leadership research has been to find a number of highly successful companies (normally expressed in terms of financial performance over a number of years), and then to look for some common characteristics in their management or leadership styles.

Our concern is obviously with the attribution of a cause and effect relationship between the 'leadership' in these organizations and their financial outperformance. Clearly the strong financial performance could be caused by a number of alternative factors. These include, but are not limited to, being in an incredibly attractive industry and/or market, having an existing, well-established competitive advantage, having extremely incompetent competitors, having great management as opposed to leadership, and being extremely lucky!

Separating Leadership from Management

As already stated, a key element in this book is the clear separation of leadership from management. Even existing texts that claim to focus exclusively on leadership all rapidly fall into the trap of talking about leaders having subordinates. They do not. Leaders have followers, while managers have subordinates.

All managers can, and ideally should, be leaders as their subordinates become their willing followers, rather than unwillingly acceding to their superiors' instructions due to their organizationally granted line authority. However, the appointment of someone as a manager does not automatically make them a leader, and the current fad of renaming 'supervisors' as 'team leaders' does not magically transform their subordinates into willing followers. This trend of reclassifying managers as leaders is accelerating with the move to flatter organizational structures, seemingly because leaders can have more followers than managers can have subordinates, under span of control theories.

Conversely, not all the leaders in an organization have to be managers, as the willing followers of a leader do not need to be subordinates to their leader in organizational hierarchy terms. Individuals with absolutely no subordinates at all can still have a significant leadership role within an organization.

It is therefore important that we are very clear as to what distinguishes a leader from a manager. Managers basically have jobs to do and apply particular skills in order to accomplish goals and tasks that are probably set for them by others. Thus management is primarily about planning, implementing and controlling to achieve pre-set objectives, for which a stable environment and clearly defined, measurable outputs from both employees and business processes are desirable.

SEPARATING LEADERSHIP FROM MANAGEMENT

Management is getting 'things done' through the efforts of others, i.e. subordinates

Value-creating leadership is getting 'extraordinary things done' with the willing help of others, i.e. followers

---

SEPARATING LEADERSHIP FROM MANAGEMENT—cont'd

Management, without leadership, will normally only get the mandatory output that is specified in the subordinates' job descriptions or contracts
Leaders can gain discretionary, unspecified output from willing followers

---

Management is getting 'things done' through the efforts of others, i.e. subordinates. Value-creating leadership is getting extraordinary things done with the willing help of others. Management, without leadership, will normally get only the mandatory output that is specified in the sub-ordinates' job descriptions or contracts. Leaders can gain discretionary, unspecified output from willing followers who may not even report directly to them. This extraordinary level of performance can be achieved by leaders because they think for themselves, exercise judgement, take initiative, and are willing to be held to account even if they were never given clear specific objectives by anyone.

Indeed, we will argue strongly throughout the book that leaders must have discretion; ideally, more than 50 per cent of any leadership role should be dictated by the occupant of that role. This discretion should relate both to what they do and how they do it, in terms of direction, objectives, strategy and tactics. This means that all leaders must have a high degree of freedom if they are truly to lead. Of course, this high level of freedom includes the freedom to fail. Many managers are terrified by any such risk of failure and consequently look for roles with very clearly defined, and hopefully easily attained, expectations from their superiors. Such managers are clearly not leaders.

Focused Sporting Legends

We are great sports fans. One of us, at least, got very excited when England won the Rugby World Cup in 2003 and was severely deflated when the British Lions got whitewashed in New Zealand less than two years later.

Continued

Focused Sporting Legends—cont'd

The leaders in the victorious England team were very focused both on their objective and their personal role within the team. No great sportsperson is the best in several sports and most team players focus on specialist roles within the team. Jonny Wilkinson would probably not make a great second row forward and it's unlikely that Martin Johnson would have lifted the World Cup if he had played for England at fly-half. Even the most talented have to work very hard to become and stay the best in their highly competitive fields. In other words, they focus on specialist skills. Also, very few have ever made the transition from excellence in one sport to world-leading performance in another. Why therefore should business leaders be able to do the equivalent?

We have one further comment that reflects a danger of taking sporting analogies too far and explains why there will be very few in this book. After winning the World Cup, the England rugby team had a disastrous set of results; not surprising when half the winning team had immediately retired from international rugby. How many businesses would like to follow a record-breaking set of results with the sort of subsequent performances produced by England or the British Lions ('led', of course, by the same coach who had 'led' England to success in the World Cup)?

Another key difference is in the nature of the power base of leaders and managers, which can have a significant impact on the relationship with their followers or subordinates. As shown in Figure 1.1, managers are given power by the organization and, in most cases, this direct line authority extends to the ultimate power over their subordinates, i.e. the power to hire and fire. However, this power is really vested in the managerial role rather than in the individual currently holding that position. In other words, if the individual moves to another role or leaves the organization the managerial power is automatically passed to the next incumbent.

This is very different from the power associated with leadership. Leaders are given personal authority by their followers and the extent of this authority will depend on the level of the trust and respect

	Leader	**Manager**
Nature of power base	Personal and voluntary	Organizationally granted
Source of authority	Followers	Subordinates
Role parameters	Self-defined	Defined by organization
Key roles	Setting direction Inspiring and engaging Aligning and focusing	Planning Implementing Controlling
Value creation	Achieving discretionary outputs	Achieving pre-set objectives
Nature of relationship	'Adult to adult'	Can be 'parent to child'
Reinforcement mechanism	Mutual trust and respect	'Carrot and stick'

Figure 1.1 Separating leadership from management

generated by them with their follower group. This makes leadership power voluntary and it can therefore be taken away, sometimes almost instantaneously, if the trust and respect relationship is destroyed or damaged. As a result, leaders are highly dependent upon their followers for their continued leadership roles and this mutual dependency, as followers want a leader to follow, will affect the nature of their relationship.

Managers can, and often do, have parent-to-child relationships with their subordinates. This is not to argue that this is a good basis for a manager-to-subordinate relationship, but strong, directive managers can tell their subordinates what they require and expect. These expectations can be reinforced by the simplistic 'carrot and stick' type incentivization schemes that still abound in businesses today. The not even slightly surprising result is that subordinates often revert to childlike responses, with a complete absence of initiative and a total unwillingness to accept any level of responsibility. Leaders, on the other hand, have to earn their personal authority from their followers in a relationship of mutual dependency and this means that their relationship must be adult to adult. (This may be surprising to some readers but this is why we started by distinguishing our form of value-creating corporate leadership with its requirement for willing followers, from the forced or mindless followers associated with many other, more traditional leadership models.)

Grown-up Leadership

This adult-to-adult, mutually dependent relationship between leaders and followers highlights another important element of leadership. Leaders and followers can change roles when necessary. This role rotation is most frequently temporary but can, in some circumstances, be a permanent change that is willingly accepted by all parties involved.

The most common examples of such role reversal are where the particular skills and abilities of a particular follower make them the obvious leader for a particular task, project or process facing the organization or a specific team. A good leader will both quickly appreciate and readily acknowledge this and happily become a willing follower during this period. The open recognition that is consequently given to the skilled follower should reinforce the trust and respect within the whole team.

The true 'team leader' is simply the team member that the others look to for leadership and who they will willingly follow. This is seen very clearly in many sporting teams. The manager, coach, and even team captain may have organizationally granted authority by dint of their appointed formal role. However, the team members will look to the truly inspirational leader in times of challenge and pressure. This may, of course, be a completely different individual.

In the normal manager-to-subordinate relationship, these situations can turn at worst into very ugly power struggles or, at best, the manager very grudgingly and often belatedly defers to the subordinate who is the expert in the area. In the best business teams this rotation of leadership happens almost automatically and seamlessly. The result is that the team is constantly led by the best leader.

This adult-to-adult relationship does not mean that the leader and their individual followers should necessarily be regarded as equal parties in their relationship. What it does imply is that leaders are most unlikely to build up the required trust and respect, on which their personal power is based, unless they treat their followers with a corresponding level of consideration, trust and respect. This does not need to make leaders so soft and cuddly that they can never take the tough decisions that may be needed from time to time. However, if they have, over time, consistently shown consideration and given the required level of recognition to their followers, their personal level of trust should mean that the tough decision is accepted as being the best that is achievable given the circumstances. In other words, their personal voluntary power is not diminished by taking what is seen by everyone as a tough business decision. In practice, the reverse may well be true, an inability or unwillingness to take such difficult decisions may damage the respect felt by followers towards their leader.

In one sense therefore we can argue that leaders are created by the needs of their potential followers, a primary need being 'to have someone to follow'. This can create a problem in certain organizations, such as academic institutions, if employees feel no such need for leadership by anyone to anywhere. More helpfully it highlights that the most value-creating leadership activities will be the ones that directly impact on the specific needs of these potential followers. Those most appropriately focused leaders will achieve the greatest degree of buy-in from their followers and, correspondingly, should create the greatest change in the value of the output produced by the organization. This reinforces the need for adult-to-adult communications between leaders and followers, as the leaders must understand the specific needs of their followers so that they can correctly focus their own energy.

The quality of leadership in an organization can therefore genuinely be said to be the result of the actions of those holding the roles of leaders. If those actions adversely change the perceptions of the existing followers with regard to the leader's values, beliefs, trustworthiness, or capabilities, these followers can withdraw the voluntary authority they have previously granted to the leader. A leader without followers is, as we have already established, no longer a leader. Clearly this is not the case where subordinates disagree, however strongly, with the decisions and actions of their manager. The process of withdrawing the power and authority of any manager from below is normally neither quick nor painless for those involved.

The Value-Creating Role of Leadership

Having highlighted several significant differences between leadership and management, it is now necessary to establish why leadership is so important. Why can't organizations succeed over the long term by simply having highly professional managers? This is a particularly important question for anyone with a strong need to be in total control. As we have just established, true leaders only remain 'in control' as long as their followers allow them to.

This emphasis on control is a key component of the value-creating role of leadership. In an utterly predictable world, it *might* be possible to plan the activities of the organization in such detail that appropriate specific objectives and outputs could be established for all processes and employees of the company. If this was achieved, managers should be able to set measurable performance metrics for their subordinates that would enable the organization to achieve its overall objectives. Then, as long as all these employees achieved their pre-set objectives, this mandatory, job-prescribed level of performance should be sufficient to generate at least some level of shareholder value, as shown in Figure 1.1. After all, this is the logic behind planning and control systems; break down the overall corporate objectives into divisional, functional and departmental objectives and then allocate appropriate responsibilities to each level of management. If each of these management levels can then do the same with their subordinates, the ultimate rational business-planning process would exist.

Unfortunately, of course, the real corporate world is not like this. The external competitive environment cannot be predicted with total certainty. The increasing demands of customers, the changing legal and regulatory environment, technology developments and, most importantly, the actions and reactions of competitors create a level of risk and uncertainty for any organization that demands flexibility in its own actions and reactions. Leaders can cope with this uncertainty and volatility because, as already stated, they think for themselves and are willing to be held accountable for their actions.

In order to cope with such volatility, these leaders need the discretion that has also already been mentioned. They may need the freedom to change the strategy or tactics that are currently being employed. In even more extreme circumstances, they may need to alter the goals and objectives that are being aimed at, or even to vary the long-term direction that the business is trying to move in. Thus leaders have to cope with change. They should try to anticipate changes that will be needed in the future. If the current strategy is not working well enough, they may champion change within the organization. However, leadership is not about change for the sake of change; it is about change in order to improve or maintain the level of performance of the business.

This is another important difference between our view of leadership and the views of many other writers on this subject. Many books and papers argue that the fundamental role of leadership is change; indeed, some state that leaders should 'manage change'. We will discuss this in more detail in Chapter 8, but our view is that you cannot 'manage change' unless you already know what the changed end position will be. This means that it must be a completely predictable change and not one caused by the uncertainty and volatility of the real competitive world. Managers can manage totally predictable changes; that is what business planning systems seek to do. Leadership is required to motivate followers to take advantage of the unpredictable changes that will occur or, even more importantly, can be made to occur through positive stimulus by the business.

Thus leaders expect creativity, initiative and commitment from their followers; they demonstrate these characteristics themselves, but also expect them from others. This highlights the mutual respect and trust that there should be between leader and follower. If I trust you, then it is logical for me to expect that you will do your best; but, if I have respect for your abilities, I will expect that 'your best' will be pretty impressive. Because you have trust and respect for me, you do not want to let me down and you want to prove that you really are as good as I think; hence you will put in any extra effort needed to deliver 'your best'.

The end result is that value-creating corporate leadership can induce a truly high performance culture within the organization, where the willingly committed workforce are all giving of their best. The ideal high performance culture is self-reinforcing as employees who cannot attain the high levels of performance that are being delivered by their colleagues will find the organization too demanding and challenging. Thus they will willingly look to leave for a less challenging working environment. High performance companies are great places to work for the right people, but they can feel excessively pressurized to the wrong people. We believe that the organizational culture should achieve high performance through a process of natural selection rather than the arbitrarily imposed culling processes (such as where the bottom 10 per cent of appraisals are forced to leave) that are used by some companies.

The improvement generated by value-creating leadership can be as a result of an increase in the total energy that is input into the organization by the workforce. In most knowledge-based modern corporations the key element of this increased energy is not physical energy but the psychological energy that flows from having a positively committed group of willing followers rather than the same, or even a greater, number of merely compliant subordinates. A really good leader can ensure that employees input the vast majority of their potential energy into the organization. Negatively or neutrally committed compliant employees frequently look for alternative outlets for their underutilized potential energy outside their workplace, thus releasing the frustrations many feel as they are unable or unwilling to contribute as fully as possible at work.

However, corporate leaders also have another element to their value-creating role. It is possible for a business to have highly committed employees who are all working very hard but the performance of the business is still worse than average. This increased energy input needs to be harnessed towards a common goal; all these 'best efforts' have to be moving the business in the same direction. A critical role of the leader is therefore to ensure the acceptance by their followers of a common vision of what the organization wants to be and how it is going to get there.

The 'how' does not need to be a detailed strategy explicating 'what' the business will do. It is actually more a set of beliefs and values (often now called 'guiding principles') that actually say what the business will *not* do in order to achieve its vision. In other words, the 'how' establishes constraints on the behaviours that are considered acceptable in this organization. It is critically important that corporate leaders clearly and consistently reinforce the core values of the organization both through their own actions and behaviours and through their reactions to the actions and behaviours of others.

Walking the Talk

In some cases guiding principles can have seemingly unfair repercussions on senior managers who are new to the organization and hence may be unaware of such prevailing, very strong values. One of us worked for such a company that instantly fired a newly appointed director who had accepted entertaining from a supplier. This was never done in this company, but had been standard practice in his previous employments. The new company was so concerned to reinforce its clear position that it was prepared to

Continued

Walking the Talk—cont'd

lose someone at this level, even though there was no evidence that his decisions had been improperly affected. Indeed, there had been no time for this to have happened!

We have, however, also seen far too many instances where the significant potential benefits of a clearly articulated set of 'guiding principles' are lost due to the unwillingness or inability of the top leadership team in an organization to 'walk the talk'. Particularly unfortunate are the examples of unethical or other inappropriate behaviour by their senior colleagues that are not immediately signalled as being totally unacceptable to the rest of the workforce.

In some cases the senior executives involved may actually leave but with generous financial settlements, while in other examples the issues are not properly addressed at all as 'the person involved only has a few years to go to retirement'. However, the most worrying examples are those where no action is taken as 'the individual is too valuable to lose'. Clearly this sends a message to everyone else that the core values of the organization are effectively 'for sale'. The almost inevitable result is a sense of cynicism and mistrust regarding all the other communication initiatives started by these corporate leaders.

The idea that a key role of corporate leaders is to articulate a clear vision for the organization and achieve not only agreement from their followers but also active pursuit of this vision is not contentious. On this we are in agreement with most modern writers and researchers on leadership. By doing this, leaders can create organizational synergies within the business by getting everyone to work towards a shared vision and set of goals. Where we disagree is that there are different types and levels of corporate vision that are handled by our leadership model, whereas most other leadership frameworks incorporate only one type of vision. Further, we strongly believe that leaders are needed at all levels of an organization, and that the leaders at different levels can display different styles of leadership. These differing styles must be complementary rather than conflicting but it does not mean that the leadership within any company has to be one-dimensional.

However, for ease of explanation while we are introducing the critical leadership capabilities, our value-creating leadership activities and the resulting leadership model, we focus on the leaders within the top team of the organization. Once these elements have been set out in some detail, the implications of having different leadership styles at different levels will be more easily understood.

Who is the Real Leader?

As we have already mentioned, we are trying in this first chapter to define very clearly how we use the terms leaders, leadership and leading. It is very interesting to see how innovatively many companies define 'leading' in order to include it in their vision statement.

Many directly competing companies select different definitions so that they can each be classified as leaders in their industry, market or segment. For example, the company used as the case study at the end of this chapter faces a direct competitor that is significantly more profitable, due to its mix of business. Our case study subject therefore defines its goal in other terms such as sales volumes and market share. Quantitatively this could give a different industry leader in volume terms, sales revenue values, and total profits generated, even before ratios such as sales revenue per employee are introduced. If the softer, more qualitative definitions of leadership that include terms such as 'best' are used, the possibilities become almost infinite, so that virtually all the participants in an industry can regard themselves as being leaders in one specific metric.

It certainly makes achieving a vision slightly easier, albeit rendering it also non-motivating and pointless from a real leadership role perspective.

The key Characteristics of Leadership

Leadership involves several interlinked aspects. In order to get some clarity and consistency, we distinguish, as shown in Figure 1.2, between leadership attributes, capabilities, activities and styles. Leadership attributes are personal qualities that determine how well any particular

Leadership involves several interlinked aspects. In order to get some
clarity and consistency, we distinguish between:

Attributes: personal qualities that determine how well particular
capabilities can be implemented

Capabilities: simply anything that can be put to use in fulfilling a role
or carrying out an activity

Activities: leading is an activity, therefore leaders should be judged on
what they do and achieve, rather than what they say

Style: the term used to describe the way in which any leadership
role is carried out

Figure 1.2 The key characteristics of leadership

capability can be implemented. They include elements of personal
character that build the trust and respect that are essential to the relationship between all leaders and their followers.

Leadership capabilities are simply anything that can be put to use in
fulfilling a role or carrying out an activity. However, having said that, five
critical leadership capabilities have been identified from many years of
research into the ways top leadership teams operate together. These capabilities have varying levels of relative importance and areas of emphasis
for the different leadership activities that we have identified.

We have already stated that we regard leading as an activity. Therefore
leaders should be judged by what they do and achieve, rather than what
they say. However, leading also implies being the, or one of the, best at
whatever it is that the leader does. We believe that this requires any
leader to focus primarily on one of our four value-creating activities.
In order for the overall organization to achieve extraordinary levels of
performance, it will need to implement all four leadership activities; but
these do not need all to be done by any single individual leader. Hence
there is a need, at various levels in the organization, for leaders who are
focused on different value-creating activities.

We use the term leadership style to describe the way in which any
particular leadership role is actually carried out. Not surprisingly, each
of our leadership styles focuses on one value-creating leadership
activity, which itself emphasizes one specific key leadership capability.
We believe that this integrated focus makes our leadership model much

19

more practically applicable than more general leadership concepts that require all leaders to be great at every aspect of leadership and leading.

Leadership attributes

As shown in Figure 1.3, leadership attributes can be split into four main groups: personal will, self-confidence, personal character and communication skills. The personal will group encompasses commitment, enthusiasm, initiative and the associated willingness to be held accountable, together with a passion for results. The personal character group has integrity, transparency and consistency as important factors if trust is to be built. Also of significance is the leader's personal ability as a key driver in building the respect that is needed, as shown in Figure 1.4. The third group covers self-confidence but this must be based on a realistic level of self-awareness and of the person's impact on others. All of these personal qualities are also critical for willing followers, if mutual trust and respect is to be developed between leader and follower. This is made particularly clear by Robert Kelley in his book *Star Performer* (1998), which looks at the attributes of the most productive, value-adding employees rather than focusing on leaders. This is why our leadership model, and hence the rest of this book, does not overemphasize the importance of leadership attributes.

It is only the remaining group of attributes that are in any way unique or specific to leaders. These cover the communication skills needed by leaders if they are to convince anyone to become their follower. This communication includes actions as well as, if not rather than, words but, much more importantly, it also covers listening skills and empathy

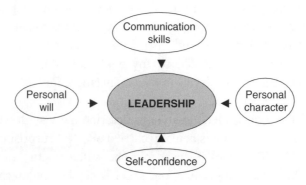

Figure 1.3 Leadership core attributes

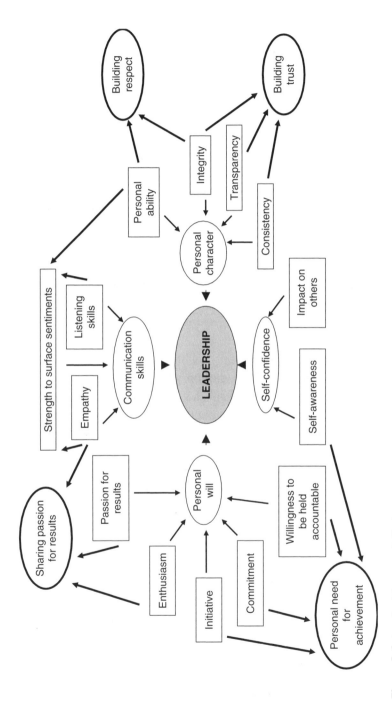

Figure 1.4 Leadership core attributes

in order to gain a proper understanding of the needs of potential followers. A true leader must have the ability to surface the real underlying sentiments that will determine whether followers will be willing to make the discretionary inputs that are required to achieve extraordinary performance from an ordinary business.

These attributes do also highlight the personality obstacles to anyone becoming a value-creating leader, which obviously include an absence of communication skills. A lack of integrity is clearly an insurmountable problem to gaining and retaining willing followers, as is a lack of personal ability, but these are not commonly found flaws. More common problems are an unwillingness to be held personally accountable and a lack of initiative. However, the most frequently observed gaps are in personal behaviours relating to learning from mistakes and openness to new ideas from followers. We have already argued that leaders need the discretion to fail but these failures must be used as learning experiences; repeating the same mistake will dramatically harm the trust and respect of followers, as will not listening and responding to their contributions.

Critical leadership capabilities
Considering the leaders within the top team of an organization raises another dynamic of leadership that is not considered by many leadership models. The tendency is to talk about 'the leader' in the singular and their followers. This means that, in the top team, the chief executive officer would be 'the leader' and all the functional directors would be regarded as followers of this leader. Once again, this perpetuates the confusion between management and leadership. The functional directors may well be subordinates of the CEO and they should also hopefully be willing followers of the CEO's leadership. However, to the rest of the organization, they are all seen as part of a single, top leadership team.

The degree of harmony and cohesion among the leaders comprising this top leadership team can therefore have a dramatic impact on the future success of the organization. This is true for leadership teams at all levels in an organization but, not surprisingly, disharmony, lack of cohesion, friction and negative energy in the top team can be extremely value destroying. Extensive research at Cranfield School of Management highlights that five critical leadership capabilities are required of today's business leaders; these are shown in Figure 1.5.

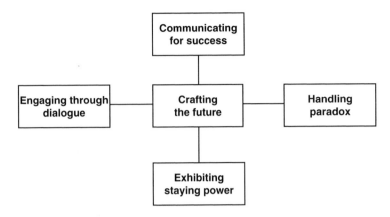

Figure 1.5 Critical leadership capabilities

These five leadership capabilities are neither mutually exclusive nor sequential, but they are applied differently and with varying levels of emphasis in each of the leadership styles identified in our leadership model. These capabilities are not fundamentally in disagreement with those identified by and used in other theories of leadership. Each leadership capability is briefly explained in the following subsections.

Crafting the future

Determining the future direction of the corporation is the leader's prime requirement; remember they cannot be regarded as a leader if nobody willingly follows the direction that they set. Just because the CEO or chairman believes that a particular path should be followed, not all of the other members of the top leadership team may agree with the direction being proposed. In any top team in a large company, it would be amazing if there were not a number of strongly held views as to the best future direction for their organization. This is borne out by the research studies at Cranfield, which show that over one-third of the world's top directors and leaders hold contrasting views from their boardroom colleagues concerning the future nature, shape and positioning of their organization.

The problem is not that different views are held initially but that they are still held once a clear vision for the organization has been articulated by the top leadership team. If it is clear to others lower down the business that some members of the top leadership team are opposed to the stated vision, there is little chance of this leadership team gaining sufficient buy-in to achieve the required 'active pursuit of the vision'. In some particularly dysfunctional top teams, such a clearly negative attitude to the corporate vision or some aspect of the core values of the business does not even result from a genuinely held different view, but is caused by personal enmity towards the individual promulgating that particular view.

Ideally the top leadership team should share a clearly stated vision for the organization and this commonly held purpose should go way beyond their personal considerations. This establishes that the leaders care more for the enterprise than for themselves. This is necessary to build the trust and respect that creates willing followers. It also creates a positive climate within this leadership team that makes the other critical leadership capabilities more possible.

This key role of 'crafting the future' also helps in defining who should be regarded as members of this top leadership team. Membership should be based on the individual's ability to contribute to the creation of this shared vision, and is not granted merely through job title or level of seniority.

This means that, in some organizations, the top leadership team can be very small while, in others, it can include quite a wide range of people from different levels in the managerial hierarchy.

Handling paradox

The shared vision normally states a long-term aspiration but, in most companies, the top leadership team is also required at least to maintain the short-term performance of the business. This can create obvious conflict between the demands of investing to achieve the long-term goals and pressures for short-term profit improvements. The leaders have to be able to handle this type of apparent paradox and ensure that the key needs of the long-term strategy are made paramount even if short-term cost savings are required.

The risk is that sanctioning investments or additional recruitment in one part of the business while other parts suffer retrenchments and cutbacks can make the leadership team seem inconsistent. This can, if not properly handled, destroy the trust and respect held by the team's willing followers, particularly among those followers suffering the lack of investment and cutbacks. The leadership team must be willing to justify its decisions where such paradoxes are apparent. After all, there need be no inconsistency in having an attentiveness to cost levels even in a business where the vision is based on creating and exploiting completely new knowledge. However, it is very easy for a 'leadership gap' to develop where leaders at lower levels in the organization pass the buck back up to the top leadership team and effectively blame them for the tough decisions that have been taken. As already stated, true leaders are not frightened to take such tough decisions, but neither should they avoid explaining why they were taken and how they fit into driving the business towards its long-term vision. They must retain their willing followers, or they lose their leadership role. This means that followers should not only know the direction in which they are heading but also what is expected of them by the leader along the journey, in terms of personal contribution, performance levels and sacrifices where necessary.

The Ultimate Paradox?

Over the years we have worked with a number of outstanding achievers in other fields who have been explaining their leadership styles to business 'leaders'.

One particular example relates to listening to the fascinating description by such an achiever to such a group of business leaders of a successful mountaineering expedition to climb Mount Everest. The members of the mountaineering team were all volunteers of course, and clearly understood the goal of the expedition. During the discussion after his presentation, the leader was asked how they would have handled a serious injury to one of the expedition members, such as a broken leg, once they were high on the mountain. Without hesitating, this leader replied that they would have made the injured person as comfortable as possible, left some food, drink and weather protection before continuing to the summit. If the person was still alive when the rest of the team was descending the mountain a few days later, they would collect the injured 'team member' at that time.

A follow-up question, as to whether this possible personal sacrifice was explicitly made clear to all those volunteers before signing up, was met with the reply that that was not necessary as it was obvious what would happen!

Engaging through dialogue

The Cranfield research studies highlight that two-thirds of the world's largest companies live with the tension that is caused by not handling paradox well. This means that the leaders are not engaging their followers fully and that the level of dialogue between leader and follower is not good enough. Even more importantly, as very few companies have actually gone bankrupt due to bad communications, there is a very strong correlation between poor quality dialogue and missed opportunities for the business. Failure to clarify important strategic issues and confront apparent paradoxes can lead to diminishing business performance.

The critical element here is dialogue as this clearly requires a two-way communication process. Far too many top leadership teams feel they have done their job if they have communicated the vision and given people the opportunity to ask questions. Unfortunately, many potential willing followers are also the subordinates of the top leadership team and may feel very uncomfortable about 'challenging' the fully developed and glossily presented corporate vision and values. This feeling will be exacerbated if the first challenging question is met with an aggressive or brusque response. Even very senior corporate executives can feel uncomfortable and become very defensive when their strongly held and carefully thought through views are penetratingly questioned, particularly if the questioner is clearly right. Managers will often respond by curtailing discussion; leaders need to find ways of encouraging adult-to-adult dialogue, even if the resulting debate increases their personal discomfort.

Communicating for success

Leaders who display their will to succeed, their passion to achieve and their personal enthusiasm can transform an organization. This transformation can only take place if these leadership attributes are powerfully communicated to all their potential willing followers. Communicating for success is a multi-fold concept. Clearly it is needed at the personal and team levels but, in a large organization, the leaders need to communicate much more widely than is possible through one-to-one or small group sessions.

Modern technology facilitates this, while maintaining some interaction and thus the potential for a degree of dialogue. However, communicating for success is much more than the formal provision of clear, unambiguous information. Leaders communicate at least as much by what they do, and what they do not do, as through the words they say and broadcast electronically. These symbolically powerful examples must reinforce the formal communications message or they can completely negate it.

This comes back to our earlier point of leadership focus and that leaders should not try to be all things to all potential followers. Consistency in action can strongly reinforce what the top leadership team states as being critical for the future success of the organization. Contradictory behaviour to the stated words, such as a total focus on short-term operating performance while espousing the long-term vision, can instil very negative feelings among previously potentially willing followers.

Exhibiting staying power

Most visions are long-term aspirations and even some mission statements will not be achieved in the normal life cycle of a top leadership team. However, if willing followers are to make the extra commitment to the organization that can produce extraordinary performance from a previously ordinary business, they will want to know that their current leaders have the staying power to drive the company toward this vision. This is particularly important at the top team level in the organization as research indicates a significant time lag before most new leaders become fully effective.

The overall vision is obviously translated into detailed strategies but this is not necessarily done by the top leadership team. Their role is to show the step-by-step determination to ensure that these selected strategies are both successfully implemented and have actually moved the business nearer to its vision. It is inevitable that there will be some failures and that some parts of the overall strategy will have unexpected and unwanted outcomes. Such setbacks also require the leaders to exhibit staying power without resorting to blame allocation or defending their own personal areas of responsibility.

The top leadership team should promote cabinet responsibility so that, irrespective of who actually made the decision, once taken the responsibility for all decisions is shared across the whole team. This stops the potential for contradictory behaviour that effectively undermines certain decisions that, as far as all the followers were concerned, had the backing of corporate leadership. Such behaviour can once again destroy the critical trust and respect for the leadership team.

Value Creating Leadership Activities

We have already argued that modern leaders need to focus in order to create value. Today's increasingly competitive environment makes it unrealistic to expect any leader to be the best, or even great, at all the aspects of the total leadership role. There are many slightly different descriptions of the total activities that can be undertaken by a leader. Many of these, in our view, confuse leadership activities with the attributes and capabilities of leaders. As already defined, capabilities make leaders more or less able to carry out the leadership activities successfully, while attributes describe personal qualities that impact on the leaders' capabilities.

Our model concentrates on the value-creating potential of corporate leaders and therefore we have defined the key value-creating leadership activities as being visioning, connecting, aligning and delivering. In order to achieve sustainable extraordinary performance, a business needs all these activities from its leaders, but each leader needs to focus on one element in order to be the best that they can be at their chosen area of focus. How these focused elements are brought together within one organization is developed in Chapter 3 and illustrated for each leadership style in their specific chapter in Part 2.

Visioning

Visioning is obviously the leadership activity that focuses on setting the long-term direction of the business. This can therefore be regarded as the core activity of a leader, as shown in Figure 1.6, where it is placed at the centre of our leadership activity model. The leader should articulate a clear and compelling vision, together with a set of core values, that describe both the reason for the company's existence and where it is going, i.e. what it is trying to achieve in the long term in fairly general terms. Ideally this vision will include more specific medium-term goals or objectives that are measurable so that their achievement can be tracked. This is now frequently referred to as a mission statement and stretching medium-term goals are called BHAGs (Big Hairy Audacious Goals after Jim Collins's work in this area). The key leadership capability is, accordingly, the central crafting the future from Figure 1.5, as shown in Figure 1.7.

The role of a compelling vision is to gain positive commitment from as many willing followers as possible, thus increasing the total energy available within the organization. Having a great vision creates no

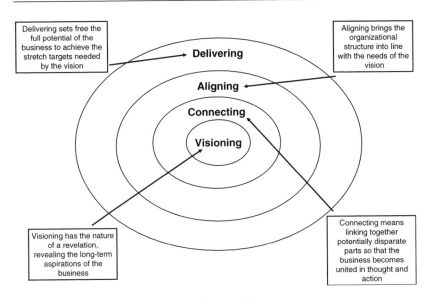

Figure 1.6 Key value-creating leadership activities

value until it has been totally bought into by others in the organization. Indeed, even acceptance of the vision and values is not enough; the willing followers must be positively committed to achieving the stretching targets set on the way to making the vision itself a reality. This means that this visioning leader must build total trust and great respect. This can be done by constantly 'walking the talk' and always being true

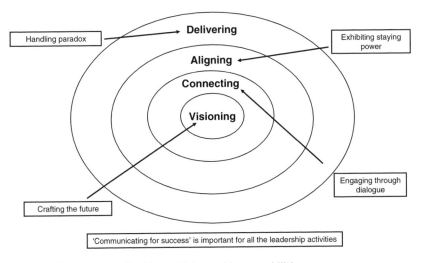

Figure 1.7 Linking leadership activities and key capabilities

to their stated vision and values. These leaders should also demonstrate their own leading abilities without excessive displays of arrogance or ego. In fact, a willingness to display their own weaknesses can increase the trust and respect of, and hence leadership authority given by, their followers. This is further enhanced by showing their personal enthusiasm for, and commitment to, the business and its long-term vision. The vision does not need to include a detailed explication of how this long-term aspiration will be achieved, but will, when taken along with the core values, indicate some 'big picture' elements of the most relevant strategic initiatives.

Connecting

The connecting leadership activity starts the process of indicating how the stated vision will be achieved. This role of the leader focuses on facilitating or enabling their willing followers to work together to try to achieve the vision that they have all bought into. The idea of working together and willingly sharing for the benefit of the total organization is key to this connecting leadership activity. The leader can, where necessary, cut across the formality of organizational structures to drive changes in the way people work and think. Hence this also requires people leadership skills but these changes are more focused and less fundamental to people's beliefs than for the visioning leadership activity.

A key element in this activity is therefore communicating in order to connect internal groups across the organization but this communication is by no means exclusively in one direction from the top down. Communication can be needed both up and down the organization, as well as sideways across the business in order to enable willing followers to improve their contribution to value creation. A classic example of how this works is through the sharing of knowledge across the business so that people in other parts do not waste effort or miss opportunities by not knowing about what already exists within the organization. Not surprisingly therefore a key leadership capability to implement the connecting activity successfully is engaging through dialogue, as confirmed in Figure 1.7.

Aligning

The aligning leadership activity is more specific about how the long-term vision and short-term objectives are to be achieved, at least in specific areas within the business. Its main emphasis is on improving the cost efficiency of these areas, normally by removing duplication of effort and generating economies of scale. Thus this potentially releases physical energy in some parts of the business but this is often taken as a direct cost-saving benefit rather than being redeployed into other value-creating activities. The aligning leader stimulates changes, particularly in the organizational structure, but these are primarily transactional changes as they affect not what the business does but how and, frequently, where it is done.

Whereas the connecting and visioning leadership activities emphasize shared responsibilities, with a consequent requirement for a high level of trust and respect between leader and followers and among followers, the aligning activity tends both to allocate and focus responsibility in the single centralized source of the activity. A common example of this leadership activity is the move towards specialist shared service centres within large groups, such as customer call centres, global accounting centres, etc. The focused responsibility and accountability for delivery of these centralized services is made possible through the implementation of service level agreements between the single source provider and their internal customers within the business. This results in a more formal relationship between these specialized centres of expertise and the rest of the business. As many of the changes initiated by this style can affect the organization structure quite fundamentally, these leaders need to exhibit staying power as their key leadership capability.

Delivering

By themselves, these first three leadership activities of visioning, connecting and aligning do not guarantee extraordinary performance from the business. They should result in a highly motivated workforce that is willing to share knowledge with colleagues and is organized, where appropriate, to work in specialized activities very efficiently. What remains is a focus on actually delivering the improved results that should flow from these other activities. This is clearly the role of the delivering leadership activity. Even more than the aligning activity, delivering seeks to associate direct responsibility and accountability with control over performance. The delivering leaders set stretching, but credible and achievable, targets for their followers that are not confusing in terms of trade-offs, e.g. between short-term profit and long-term growth; between cost efficiency, product quality, and customer satisfaction. This means that the delivering leader must be strong in the leadership capability of handling paradox so that these issues are not passed down to their followers.

Interestingly, the delivering leadership activity focuses on the level of performance that is required rather than the way in which it is achieved; i.e. the what rather than the how. This is not an issue if the 'hows' have already been addressed by the other leadership activities. However, as is discussed in Chapter 3, if what we describe as the out-to-in leadership framework is being used, these specific targets are set before any clear leadership on the 'hows' has been established.

Introducing the Model

As stated at the start of this chapter, our corporate leadership model is based on the number of followers needed by a leader to be effective and on the degree of buy-in required from these followers. These dimensions are shown diagrammatically in Figure 1.8, from which it can be seen that we are distinguishing four styles of corporate leadership. However, as both dimensions actually represent continuums, this segmentation has to be admitted as a slight simplification but one that practically represents the alternative leadership roles within organizations.

The lowest level of corporate leadership is seen in organizations where only a few followers are required and even these few followers do not need to buy in fully to all of the leader's vision, values and views. It is important to register that although the horizontal axis in Figure 1.8 starts

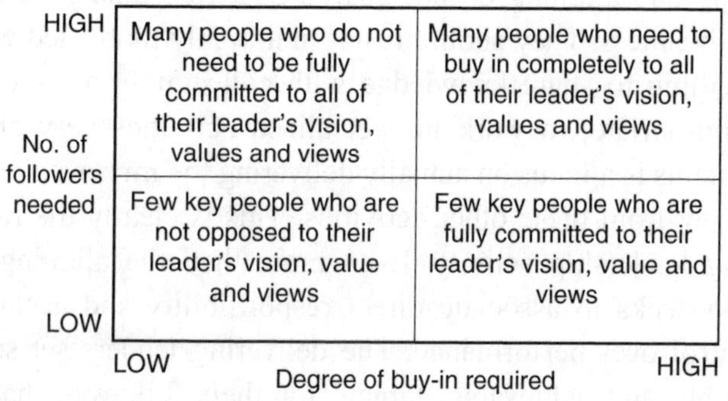

	LOW	HIGH
HIGH	Many people who do not need to be fully committed to all of their leader's vision, values and views	Many people who need to buy in completely to all of their leader's vision, values and views
LOW	Few key people who are not opposed to their leader's vision, value and views	Few key people who are fully committed to their leader's vision, value and views

No. of followers needed

Degree of buy-in required

Figure 1.8 The leadership model

32

at the low level of buy-in, few leaders can be highly successful with a really low level of commitment from their followers. Managers can be quite successful with such low levels of commitment from their subordinates, but we are focusing on leaders who seek to obtain discretionary inputs from their followers. Hence a medium level of commitment represents the real start point for acknowledging someone as a true leader. However, as long as the followers are not actively 'opposed' to the leader's aspirations for the business, some types of leader can still be relatively effective. To achieve effectiveness in this type of corporate leadership, these leaders need to motivate their very limited band of followers and this is normally done through personally tailored incentive plans.

(Although we have already stated that leaders can, and should, exist at all levels in the organization, it is still easiest to introduce our leadership model by concentrating on leaders at only one level. Not surprisingly therefore, for the rest of this chapter we will focus on leadership at the very top of the organization as represented by the top team or even the chief executive officer. In Chapter 2, the model is developed in much more detail and the focus remains on the top leadership team but, in Chapter 3, where leadership throughout the organization is discussed in depth, the restrictions introduced here are removed.)

A classic example of this limited corporate leadership is seen at the centre of a decentralized conglomerate group, where the corporate centre sets financial targets for each business division within the group. The top management of each of these divisions is normally highly incentivized financially to achieve these targets and, in many cases, will leave if they fail to perform. Beyond this very focused level of commitment to the performance of their own business unit, even these senior people have very little buy-in to the vision and direction of the overall group. Below these divisional board members, there is normally a total lack of involvement or interest by employees in the overall group or the corporate leaders who are normally based in a physically and psychologically distant head office. The total identification of the divisional employees is with their own business unit and they regard their divisional top team as their leaders. Thus it is important that these 'leaders' adopt an appropriate leadership style that turns these employees into their willing followers.

The leaders at the centre of this type of group are normally only interested in the financial performance of the individual businesses within the group. Accordingly a significant part of their role is concerned both with acquisitions and divestments to change the portfolio of businesses and tax and treasury planning so as to maximize the financial returns remitted to the centre. Given the emphasis already mentioned on financially incentivizing their followers who are in charge of the decentralized business units, it is not surprising that we normally describe this style as incentivizing leadership, but we also use the term 'shareholder style' leadership, as shown in Figures 1.9 and 1.10. We prefer to use descriptors for each style that reinforce our strong view that leading is an activity and therefore leadership is not in any way a passive role within any organization that wants to achieve extraordinary performance from ordinary people.

There is one other leadership style that only requires a few followers but needs these limited followers to be fully committed to the vision and values of their top leadership team. A common example of this type of leadership is where the vision is built around centralization or standardization, normally as a means to reduce the total costs incurred by the total group. The few, fully bought-in followers are not only those obvious managers who will run the centralized facilities or services for the group but also the divisional managers who have lost one or more areas that were previously under their direct control. If they do not buy in to the changes proposed by the top leadership team, they could in some circumstances make the new set-up either completely unworkable or not financially cost-efficient. There is often considerable pressure

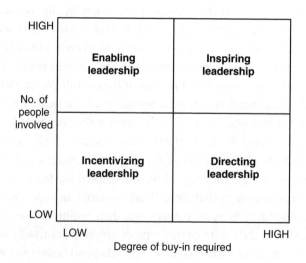

Figure 1.9 Corporate leadership styles

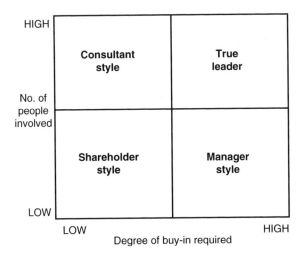

Figure 1.10 Corporate leadership—alternative descriptors

on those managers responsible for implementing the first phases of centralization to deliver the promised cost savings as quickly as possible in order to motivate the divisional managers to accept willingly the next round of proposed changes. This is a leadership style that often therefore looks initially for 'low hanging fruit' and seeks 'quick wins', even in a long-term strategy.

This style of leadership could be described as the 'manager style', as it involves more managerial control being exercised on behalf of (if not directly by) the top leadership team. However, as this style also actually involves more direct intervention by these leaders in terms of deciding and then telling their limited group of followers what will change within the organization, we normally describe this as 'directing leadership'. Clear 'direction' from this style of leader can avoid ambiguity, wasted activity and effort, so that the organization becomes much more efficient. For those followers who like certainty, it enables them to focus their energies on clear tasks. With the exception of those employees directly affected by the centralization, this style of leadership often has very little impact on most of the employees in the group. They are likely also to identify primarily with their own business unit and to look for leadership to their divisional management. However, they may be aware that these divisional managers are now less fully in control of their own business units, and hence have less discretion.

The employees who are directly affected by the change will normally now be expected to regard the centralized management team as their new leaders, rather than their previous divisional head. This can often be difficult to do, particularly when they are physically remote (which can occur when the centralized processes remain located within the divisions) and the change immediately results in significant headcount reductions. Remember that the centralization is often justified on the grounds of cost savings. As a consequence of the problems of developing these new leader-to-willing follower relationships, many such projects now involve relocating all the centralized processes to a completely new physical location. In extreme cases, a completely new workforce is also hired to staff this new location.

Our third leadership style involves many people across the organization but these people do not need to be fully committed to the vision of the top leadership team. An example of this style is where the top team believes that there is knowledge within the group that is not being fully exploited as it is not properly disseminated across all the businesses. The role of this leadership team is therefore to act as facilitating consultants (hence the alternative style descriptor, the 'consultant style') to the businesses in spreading this knowledge.

In many cases this first requires that what is known and used very successfully in one part of the group is codified, so that it becomes usable by other businesses that do not possess the tacit know-how of the originators. It is also critical that the leaders utilizing this style have sufficient understanding of the similarities and differences among the businesses within the group. This style is often applied by large groups that seek to leverage common sources of competitive advantage or core competences across what otherwise appear to be quite different businesses. Thus specific knowledge regarding reducing costs or differentiating the levels and quality of customer service could be disseminated across other businesses in a group where such knowledge could be applied to increase the value created by the business. This highlights that the key value-creating role of these leaders is to enable the organization to work more effectively, therefore we call this style 'enabling leadership'.

A key element of this enabling leadership is that it does not require the leaders actually to develop the knowledge that is being more fully exploited. They have to find out about the existing knowledge across the group, identify where else it could be applied and then facilitate making the knowledge practically usable by those business units or support processes. This is why a lot of people across the group need to be involved but is also why they do not need a high degree of buy-in to the group's vision and values.

These followers need to be motivated to make the group's leaders aware of any potentially valuable knowledge or know-how that they possess and to be willing to implement similar knowledge that is made available to them, from elsewhere in the group. Apart from these 'interferences' from the top leadership team, these business units will largely be left to run their own affairs. However, in many groups that implement this leadership style, the shared and transferred knowledge tends to be concentrated in one area, such as marketing or research and development.

This can tend to have greater implications for the people working in these areas. Over time they may come to identify more closely with their functional colleagues across the group than with their fellow employees within their business unit. This can increase if people are transferred around the group in order to accelerate the knowledge transfer. The result can be to make this group-wide team look to their functional leader for their sense of direction and vision, rather than to the business unit leadership team.

The remaining leadership style could be described as being the 'true leader' as it requires a high degree of buy-in from most of the people, which fits with our earlier description of leaders effectively winning the hearts and minds of their willing followers. However, we believe that the essence of these leaders is that they truly inspire their followers and thus we describe this style as inspirational or inspiring leadership. Not surprisingly this is the most difficult style to achieve in practice, particularly across any large, multi-business unit group.

The 'inspirational leaders' at the top of this style of group focus on articulating a clear corporate vision and set of values that are relevant to all the businesses within the group. They then seek to gain buy-in to this vision and commitment to try to achieve it while adhering to the group's set of values. If this is achieved so that most employees become willing followers, they will automatically identify more closely with the group than with their current business unit. This enables a higher level of transfers of people around the group because the values and organizational cultures are basically the same everywhere. There is a high level of trust between leaders and followers under this style and the resulting openness and transparency make people willing to move as they see it both as a development opportunity and as a chance to make an increased contribution to the group.

Illustrating the Need for the Model

A key objective of this chapter was to define clearly how we use the terms leaders, leadership and leading. This should have clarified where our approach to corporate leadership both agrees and disagrees with the other modern views of leadership. Such clarity is necessary before we delve more deeply into our leadership model and its implications for the leaders needed at all levels in an organization, as is done in Chapters 2 and 3.

Our basic leadership model highlights four different styles by combining the number of willing followers required to make a leader effective with the level of buy-in or commitment required from those followers. We believe that each of these leadership styles has significant implications for the followers involved and that inappropriate combinations of leadership behaviour within one organization can create significant confusion among these followers. As this is very important, it may be helpful to illustrate how this can arise with a real-life case study that we have seen replicated by many top teams.

This case study is based on the group executive team of a very large multinational single product group in the fast-moving consumer goods sector. The chief executive of the group is very clear about his key leadership role (unfortunately, but not atypically, all of the group directors that we refer to in this case study are male). This is to provide a clear vision and set of corporate values for the large number of operating businesses within the group. The corporate centre has established an overall objective for the group, which is to become the No. 1 international player in its industry but, in recent years, its internally generated organic growth rate has been lower than the existing industry leader. Thus the CEO's emphasis in all his communications is on building a winning culture across the group and stimulating innovative new ways to compete; he believes that the group is currently very good but that it is not yet a 'great' company.

Beyond this focused leadership role for the corporate centre, he believes that the group should be based on a decentralized philosophy but where the primary identity and loyalty should be to the overall group rather than to the individual business units, thus giving a clear example of our inspiring leadership style.

The chief financial officer of the group, whose office is not surprisingly down the corridor from the chief executive, agrees wholeheartedly with the idea of decentralization and the resulting freedom and responsibility concept that is central to the group's guiding principles. To him, responsibility is the same as accountability. Thus his focus is on setting specific annual profit targets for each business unit that, once agreed, should be regarded as firm commitments to the centre by the divisional heads. After all, he effectively has to give a commitment to the stock markets to achieve the expected earnings per share growth for the overall group.

Further, partly because of the lack of organic growth but also because he strongly believes that there are still excessive levels of cost within the group, these annual profit targets include an element of cost reduction for virtually all business units. Tax and treasury management are largely centralized within this group and in the past few years have contributed significantly to the overall earnings per share growth of the group. This is also a clear example of one of our leadership styles, but this time of the incentivizing leadership style.

The group operations director also feels that it is quite practical to reduce the cost levels within the group. He is seeking to achieve this by centralizing significant parts of the supply chain. This started by looking at the plethora of third-party suppliers that were used by the group. A major cause of this was the amazingly wide range of component specifications that were in use for what was supposed to be the same product produced and sold in different markets. The next stage was to rationalize the number of manufacturing plants, thus moving away from each end market being relatively self-sufficient. As several smaller factories were closed, the supply of product became a more centrally driven activity. Indeed, this centralization was being extended into other aspects of the supply chain, including raw material sourcing and logistics. Thus many end-market business units are now dependent upon this centralized supply chain process for the timely and cost-efficient supply of their finished products. Their line management responsibilities are consequently focused on the sales and marketing of these products. Indeed, in one geographic region this whole supply chain, including all the remaining factories, is now managed by a separate, centrally reporting operations management team. Therefore the operations director provides a good example of our directing style of corporate leadership.

The group marketing director has a different view from his colleagues, which comes as no surprise to any of them. He believes that as a consumer products company the future success of the group is dependent upon its brand portfolio and its trade marketing effectiveness. In fact, as the group starts with the significant corporate disadvantage of not having the dominant global brand in this category (not surprisingly, this is owned by the industry leader and accounts for half of their global sales volumes), a particularly key marketing issue is how well the company understands its consumers. As a result, the corporate centre has identified some leading-edge marketing segmentation techniques that enable consumers to be grouped together by relevant values, lifestyles and behaviours, so that specific brands can be appropriately targeted. The central marketing team has also identified some best practices around the group (e.g. to do with evaluating new brand launches and creating trial through different distribution channels) and is looking to leverage this knowledge as widely as possible. In addition they have identified a limited number of key brands that they believe have almost global potential. These 'drive brands' are being pushed very strongly to the business units and each is supported by a centrally reporting brand management team. However, it is also well accepted that the successful development of any of these brands in a highly competitive marketplace requires a consistent and significant level of marketing investment over several years. Once more a clear leadership style but, this time, an example of enabling corporate leadership.

Each of the leadership roles in the top team of this group is clearly aimed at adding value and is focused on what, to each individual group director, seems to be the key issue facing the business. However, the result at the divisional manager level and within their management teams is a great sense of confusion and loss of focus. This corporate centre stimulates such a massive number of group-wide initiatives and demands so much information that the supposedly decentralized business divisions find it hard to run their own businesses properly. There is a strong view across the business units that any centralizing initiative actually ends up costing them more than if they had done it themselves. Many of the business unit heads do not believe that the centrally sponsored brands are relevant to their end markets and pay, at best, lip-service to their development by investing the minimum that they can get away with each year.

Also, as the achievement of this year's profit target is the most important driver of their managerial bonus scheme, even this level of expenditure may come under threat if their business unit's performance falls below that included in the annual plan. In other words, the complete freedom of the business units to implement their specifically tailored long-term strategies to achieve the group's vision, while complying with the group's core values, may be somewhat constrained by the conflicting leadership styles being implemented by the top team located at the corporate centre. It is difficult to see how the high level of mutual trust and respect that is critical to the inspiring leadership style can be achieved in such a complex and confusing set of relationships. Not surprisingly, the conflicting requirements have demoralized many of the senior business-unit managers and increased their level of cynicism. This is clearly not helping the group to achieve its already challenging growth and long-term shareholder value-creation targets.

Indeed, as is quite common, this top team is not behaving as a 'leadership team'. Each member is acting as a functional leader (i.e. leading their own specific function) without considering how these functions need to interact in order to create a successful business. A key challenge of corporate leadership is to integrate together all the differing leadership roles that are needed across any modern complex business.

We will return to this case study at the end of Chapter 3 with some suggestions as to how all of these leadership styles could be positively accommodated within the group. This will be after we have developed our leadership model in Chapter 2 and discussed the implications of having leaders at all levels of the organization in Chapter 3.

Summary

Some readers may have been surprised that this chapter did not begin with the normal set of attributes described as being required by leaders. This is not because we disagree with these but because we believe that these 'attributes', and their relative importance, are driven by what leaders actually do and the consequent capabilities that they need. Hence we prefer to concentrate on the activities that leaders undertake, rather than attributes they possess. Our leadership capabilities then indicate how well any leader is able to carry out each of these leadership activities.

Thus, in an ideal world, a corporate leader would obviously be brilliant at visioning, would inspire and energize the total workforce, would support and show confidence in these people so that they feel totally enabled or empowered (the first and last time we use this term!), and would clearly focus attention on the key areas of the business. However, we do not live in an ideal world and have yet to meet a leader who can do all these things well, let alone perfectly. Our leadership model copes with human frailty and allows leaders to focus on a more limited range of activities. This focus also means that the normal leadership 'attributes' have very different levels of importance depending upon the leadership style that is being adopted, as is the case for the leadership capabilities. Also, and more importantly, we strongly believe that almost all these 'leadership' attributes are as applicable to the role of followers if they are to make their full potential contribution to the business. The one differentiating area of attribute in the case of a leader is the 'communication' of these attributes to others so that they become followers.

If we take the Emotional Intelligence view of leadership as clearly stated by Daniel Goleman in *The New Leaders* (Golema et al., 2002), leaders need personal competences and social competences. The personal competences refer to how you manage yourself and encompass self-awareness and self-management, which are fairly self-explanatory. The social competences deal with how you manage relationships and include empathy, inspirational leadership, teamwork and collaboration, among others. We do not disagree with any of these laudable attributes but all leaders do not need each of these attributes to be developed to the highest level possible. This is tacitly accepted by many leadership models as they identify various leadership styles that emphasize or minimize particular attributes. However, they then argue that leaders should have the capability to switch from one style to another, and then back again, according to the requirements of the situation or group of followers they are dealing with.

This is where we fundamentally disagree. A key element in building any level of trust is consistency in behaviour. If followers observe leaders behaving very differently with different groups of people, they are likely to be very suspicious of the motives of their leaders; the phrase participative manipulation comes to mind again. It is in any case asking virtually the impossible of the leaders to do this. We want you to be affiliative with this group in order to build a unified team but to adopt a pace-setting style setting aggressive targets and being achievement focused with this group! It is well known that as soon as people are placed in a pressured situation they will revert to type; in other words, they go back to their normal, ingrained behaviour. Corporate leaders do not lack pressure in today's competitive environment. We strongly believe that leaders will, and should, behave as themselves. We also believe that there are certain behavioural characteristics that are incompatible with leadership because no one will become and remain your willing follower. We agree that it is possible to moderate some of these behaviours to remove the very worst aspects and bring some people back towards the rest of the human race. Personally we still have doubts about willingly following someone whose behaviour has been significantly 'modified'.

2

Focused leadership styles

As we stated in Chapter 1, we regard leading as an activity. This means that leaders should be judged by what they do and what they achieve, not by what they say or how they appear. The achievements of value-creating corporate leadership can therefore be expressed in terms of the improved performance of the business. This improvement in performance could be benchmarked against previous achievements, current expectations or what could be achieved by a top team comprising good managers but without true leadership capability. In our terms, corporate leaders have the potential to achieve extraordinary levels of performance from businesses employing perfectly ordinary people.

This obviously raises the question of how our focused leadership styles can achieve such improvements in performance. We have already argued that leaders can provide two major benefits to an organization. By improving the level of commitment of the workforce, leadership can increase the total energy, both physical and psychological, available within the business. Also, through the focusing of this total available energy, leaders can increase the efficiency and effectiveness with which it is applied. As discussed in this chapter, our four leadership styles each improve performance through impacting on the different elements in this relationship.

All leaders need followers but our model of leadership accepts that the level of commitment to individual leaders of different groups of followers will vary. It is unrealistic to assume that all corporate leaders have the ability to generate total commitment from their entire workforces. Neither is it necessary to achieve this in order for leadership to create value. What is common to all forms of leadership is that the associated authority is personally granted to the leader by their followers. This means that leaders have to earn their personal authority, whereas managers are granted authority through their position in the organizational hierarchy. Personal leadership authority is earned through the trust and respect that develops between leaders and their followers. We have already highlighted an important difference from many leadership models because trust is developed through consistency in behaviour over time. Our focused leadership model allows each style of leader to behave very consistently.

Respect can be built by being recognized as being the best, or one of the best, in some particular area, so that colleagues become willing followers. In this chapter, we explain how the potential ways of developing respect can be linked to the types of power in a relationship and how this relates to the level of follower commitment that can be achieved. These ideas then allow us to illustrate the different ways in which strategic leadership and people leadership fit into the leadership styles. Once again, our leadership model does not require corporate leaders to be all things to all people.

Comic Book Hero Leaders

A key objective in developing our leadership model was that it should be practical. This meant that it had to take account of the limited abilities of any individual or group of individuals comprising a leadership team. Many of the existing leadership frameworks require corporate leaders to be excellent at all the possible activities undertaken in a leadership role. We strongly believe that superheroes only exist in comic books, films or computer games.

It is also worth commenting that several of these fictional superheroes seem to have some personality characteristics that would make them very unsuitable as corporate leaders.

Corporate leadership roles are determined to some extent by the environment in which the organization operates. Thus transactional leadership seeks to make the existing organization work more efficiently and effectively. There is an increasing transactional leadership role as an organization moves from the incentivizing style to the directing style. A corresponding move from the enabling style to the inspiring leadership style shows an increasing role for transformational leadership, as the organization seeks to change itself, its external environment, or both.

However, the main thrust of this chapter is to examine in much greater detail the focus of each of our leadership styles. There are almost as many variations in describing the key value-adding activities of leadership as there are books and papers on the subject. We have already defined the key value-adding activities as visioning, connecting, aligning and delivering.

Visionary leadership does not mean something speculative, fanciful or dreamy. However, we are using visioning as 'having the nature of a revelation', in that the leader reveals the long-term aspirations of the business through the vision and its associated core values. By the connecting activity we literally mean linking together potentially disparate parts of the organization so that it becomes united and associated in thought and action. This connecting activity may affect what activities are carried out within the organization. Aligning simply means bringing the organization into line with the vision, possibly by rearranging the organizational structure, changing where specific activities are carried out, or modifying how these activities are carried out.

The delivering leadership activity appears to be the most self-explanatory as it relates to achieving both the long-term and short-term targets and goals of the business. However, it really means delivering in the sense of 'setting free' the full potential of the organization so that the goals are the stretch targets agreed to by the positively committed workforce. It should be clear that any organization that has leaders who carry out all these four key leadership value-adding activities fully should have a very good chance of achieving and sustaining extraordinary levels of performance. The obvious challenge is to find *a* leader who can be great at all these activities. Our argument is that no single person can be, or needs to be, the best at all these activities.

Each of our leadership styles therefore focuses on only one of these activities. As already stated, in order to keep the initial explanation of these new elements as clear as possible, we will concentrate in this chapter on leaders at the top of the organization. Clearly, an organization does need to implement all the key leadership activities if it is to achieve, and sustain, extraordinary performance. How this is achieved is discussed in Chapter 3 where we look at leadership at different levels in an organization.

Leading means being the Best

Right at the start of the book, we stated that we use the term leading to mean 'being the, or one of the, best'. The reason for this is that it is vitally important in building the respect that transforms compliant employees into willing followers. Thus prospective leaders need to gain respect for being 'great at something' if they are to be given personal leadership authority by willing followers.

Obviously there is a wide range of 'things' that leaders could be great at, but they can be grouped into three main categories. At one end are leaders who are brilliant at 'getting things done', 'making things happen', 'generating momentum', etc., as shown in Figure 2.1. We define this as transactional leadership. At the other end are more cerebral leaders who are respected for their intellectual capabilities or specialist knowledge. Such knowledge may be business specific, strategic or technical but it should be sufficiently relevant to the organization that it stimulates willing followers. These 'thinking' leaders tend to have a transformational impact on the organization as they can radically change the existing business model.

In the middle, we would place potential leaders who have great people skills. These may be in people development, building relationships with others, influencing skills, etc. Of themselves, such people

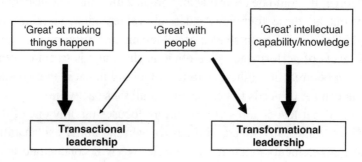

Figure 2.1 Leadership 'greatness'

skills do not necessarily make a value-creating corporate leader. Clearly it helps any leader to have great people skills, but respect in this area must be added to respect for the leader in another category. People skills enable leaders to carry people with them, but the key question is where are all these people going. As discussed in Chapter 1, the benefits of leadership are an increasing level of commitment allied to a clearer sense of direction. As a result, our leadership model highlights that great people skills are more relevant to transformational leaders than those who are best at making things happen.

The level of commitment that can be achieved is determined by the nature of the power that exists in a leader-to-follower relationship. This power is granted to the leader by their followers and could be caused by their perceived dependence on, or sense of obligation to, the individual leader. This type of power would normally result in, at best, a neutral level of commitment by the followers and, at worst, a negative level. Genuine belief in, and respect for, a leader's expertise could generate a much more positive level of commitment. This could be further enhanced if the followers personally identified with the leader, such as could happen with a leader with strong people skills who has defined an exciting aspirational vision for the company. As already stated, even strong people skills by themselves would normally create only a neutral level of commitment.

A negative level of commitment means that followers may stay in the organization but they do so because of a lack of opportunities outside or a fear of the unknown. This means that the organization may already have lost its best people and those that have been retained are keeping their heads down and doing as little as possible. The neutral level of commitment describes compliant employees who will do what they are told to do but no more. They are passive followers who are not really committed to the organization but, equally, are not necessarily looking to leave. In many managerially dominated companies without good leaders such negatively and neutrally committed employees can comprise the vast majority of the workforce.

It is only the positively committed followers who are really willing to put in discretionary, extra effort towards achieving the organizational vision, goals and objectives. Where great corporate leadership has created a truly high performance culture, the majority of these positively committed willing followers can create such a strong momentum through their willingness to put in extra effort and exceed required outputs that the negatively and neutrally committed employees will either change or leave.

Measuring the Right Things

There is a commonly used employee climate measure that tracks labour turnover but this needs to be applied very carefully. The normal logic is that lower employee turnover is better, but it really depends on who is leaving.

Obviously, if a company is losing its potentially highly committed best employees something is very seriously wrong. However, there may only be a limited number of these, so the overall turnover measure could still be low. Also the labour turnover could be low as the company is retaining some negatively committed but fearful employees, together with many neutrally committed and merely compliant employees. Hardly the recipe for a world-beating workforce.

The company may want to stimulate a higher turnover of people who do not fit the organization's values and expectations or who cannot 'hack it' in the more positively committed environment instigated by real corporate leadership.

This is a clear example of true inspirational leadership increasing the total energy input into the company from a positively committed workforce. However, there are other ways for corporate leaders to improve the performance of the organization without increasing the total energy input, as shown in Figure 2.2. The incentivizing style achieves this by refocusing the existing energy on those areas with the greatest performance impact; what can be described as 'making the most of what you have got'.

The directing style reorganizes the workload across the organization so that certain activities or processes are carried out more efficiently, normally through some form of centralization or standardization. This effectively releases physical energy within the business that either can be redeployed to improve overall performance or, very commonly, can result in cost savings with a similar financial performance improvement.

The enabling leadership style seeks to leverage existing knowledge more widely across the business so that all relevant areas have access

Enabling style	Inspiring style
releasing psychological energy	increasing total energy
Incentivizing style	**Directing style**
refocusing existing energy	releasing physical energy

Figure 2.2 Energy source of improved performance

to best practices. This releases psychological energy that would otherwise be spent 'reinventing the wheel' and this can also either be redeployed or result in cost savings. Interestingly, while many businesses tend to take the benefit of any released physical energy in the form of cost savings (e.g. through people reductions), most redeploy the psychological energy released under the enabling style of leadership. This newly available psychological energy is commonly the input of the more highly skilled, and hence potentially more value-adding, knowledge-based workers within the organization.

Strategic versus People Leadership

Most modern leadership frameworks put more emphasis on the people leadership elements within a leader's role rather than the strategic leadership of the business. As any organization is a living organism, it is clearly important that the corporate leader motivates the workforce but the role of the leadership team must balance the needs of the people within the business and the business itself, which includes the interested and involved people outside the business. We believe, once again, that it is both unreasonable and unrealistic to expect a single leader to be brilliant at providing both people and strategic leadership.

People leadership clearly involves inspiring and engaging employees so that they become positively committed willing followers. This can be achieved, in part, by setting a personal example of excellence that gains the respect of followers and through consistent leadership behaviour that displays the highest integrity. Clear, constant communications, a display of personal enthusiasm, and transparent trust and belief in the people in the business also build the level of employee commitment. However, the mutual aspects of the trust and respect that are so critical to leader-to-follower relationships mean that the leader should also expect a high level of performance from this trusted and very capable workforce. This puts an increased emphasis on leadership support for and feedback to the key teams and individuals that are critical to achieving an extraordinary level of performance.

Not surprisingly, as shown in Figure 2.3, the higher physical number of followers needed for the enabling style and the inspirational leadership role mean that people leadership is more important here than for the other two leadership styles. As seen in Figure 2.3, there is an increasing need for people leadership as a business moves across from the enabling style to an inspiring leader role. This does not mean that the incentivizing style and directing style can ignore the needs of their fewer followers but it means that they should focus more on the issues associated with strategic leadership of the business. There is also an increasing importance of this strategic leadership as an organization moves from the incentivizing style to the directing style, due to the need for an increasing level of buy-in from the limited number of followers involved.

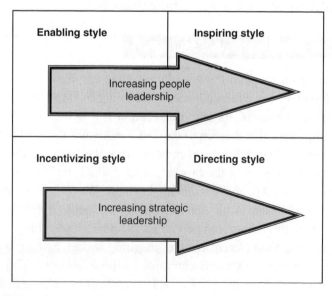

Figure 2.3 Strategic versus people leadership

The emphasis of strategic business leadership is on providing a clear sense of direction and focus. This includes an emphasis on delivering the results expected in the short term while still moving towards the long-term goals and objectives of the organization. Focusing the business on improving performance may require changes in organizational structure, but strategic leaders will make the decisions that are in the best interests of the business. The emphases on clear performance measures and alignment in organizational structures should also minimize the paradoxes that need to be handled by followers.

Transactional versus Transformational Leadership

In this chapter we are trying to explain some key differences among the various leadership roles and styles that are needed by any business that seeks to achieve extraordinary levels of value creation. However, there is another element that is particularly relevant while we are still concentrating on the leaders at the top of the organization. Our research has highlighted some significant mismatches between the leadership philosophy and the more specific leadership role at the top of many large businesses.

The leadership philosophy of a corporate top team relates to the belief that they have about the nature and impact of their leadership within their business. This belief includes the relative importance of their leadership, as well as the style and manner in which this leading activity should be carried out.

Hopefully, this philosophy completely matches the actual leadership role that is both felt to be required by the potential followers within the business and is being fulfilled by the top team. Unfortunately this is not always the case. The top team may feel that their leadership role is both appropriate and is being fulfilled, but their followers may feel that either the philosophy is inappropriate or that it is not what is actually being implemented by the top leaders.

A simple example may make this clearer. Many top teams believe that their organizations need strong leadership and that it is their role to supply such leadership, in both strategic and people leadership terms. The first critical question is whether the top team has sufficiently strong leadership capabilities actually to deliver its philosophy. However, it may also be that such strong leadership from the top is rejected by most of the people in the business as they are already positively committed willing followers of leaders from lower levels in the organizational hierarchy. This frequently happens in decentralized multi-business groups where the individual business unit top teams may be providing strong leadership for their own businesses. It may be more appropriate for the corporate top team at the centre of such a group to focus on our lower key incentivizing style of leadership. This would involve them leading only these divisional top teams and this could be achieved through a focus on these divisional teams improving the financial performance of what they perceive as *their* own businesses.

It is possible to distinguish between transactional leadership and transformational leadership. A business needs both if it is to remain successful over time, but they do not have to be delivered by the same leaders. All leadership philosophies and roles involve elements of both transactional and transformational leadership, but it is their relative importance, as shown by the time and effort spent on each, that classifies leadership as one type or the other.

Transactional leadership seeks to make the workplace work better, whereas transformational leadership tries to make the business different. An oversimplistic comparison would be between efficiency gains and effectiveness improvements. A better distinction is that transactional leadership looks for continuous improvements in the way the business operates. Transformational leadership often involves some degree of discontinuity as these leaders may change more fundamentally how the business does things. An even clearer distinction is that, in shareholder value terms, transformational leadership seeks to create new value by changing the industry value chain in some way. Transactional leadership focuses on capturing more of the existing value that is available within the industry. Transactional leaders focus on control processes and are often results-oriented. They are often interested in the organizational structure and whether it can be better aligned to the goals and strategy of the business. Transactional leadership tends to be formal and can be short term in its time-frames, particularly with regard to improvements in financial performance.

By contrast, transformational leadership focuses on the long-term vision and direction of the business and is more informal as it is more concerned with the people in the business. Also it is more means-oriented rather than concentrating on the end results produced by the business.

Transformational leaders therefore establish visions and core values for their businesses and through these influence the mindsets and beliefs of their followers. Consequently they are far more likely to develop a large number of positively committed willing followers than transactional leaders.

If these attributes are applied to our leadership styles model, as is done in Figure 2.4, there is clearly an increasing transformational leadership input as we move across the top of the matrix from the enabling style to an inspiring leadership role. Similarly there is an increasing transactional leadership role on the lower level of Figure 2.4 in the move from the incentivizing style to the directing style. The challenge is to put together complementary, rather than contradictory, leadership styles so that a business gets the benefit of both strategic transactional leadership and more people-focused transformational leadership.

Focus in Order to Create Value

In Chapter 1, we articulated four value-creating leadership activities: visioning, connecting, aligning and delivering. We also stated that each of our leadership styles should focus on only one of these activities in order for the leaders to be the best that they can be at this activity.

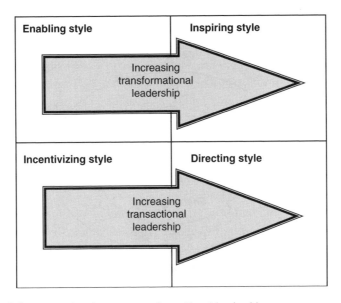

Figure 2.4 Transactional versus transformational leadership

Visioning is clearly the activity that sets the long-term direction for the company but, if it is to be value creating, this leadership activity requires both acceptance of this vision and active pursuit of it by a large proportion of the workforce. This normally involves a high level of people and transformational leadership. As shown in Figure 2.5, the visioning leadership activity fits very tightly with our inspiring leadership style, with its own need for a high level of buy-in from a wide range of followers. Therefore this is the value-creating activity that the inspirational leadership style should focus on. As shown in Figure 2.6, the source of value creation is an increase in the total energy input by this large number of willing followers. Hence this style can be described as 'increasing what you have'.

The connecting leadership activity facilitates the willing followers working together, often across the formality of the existing organization structure, to change the way people work and think in order to achieve the agreed vision. Thus the connecting leadership activity represents the main focus of our enabling style of leader. It emphasizes building relationships across the organization with sufficient trust and respect that followers will willingly share their existing knowledge with others where it

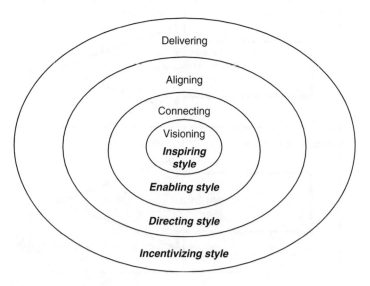

Figure 2.5 Leadership styles, focus on leadership activities

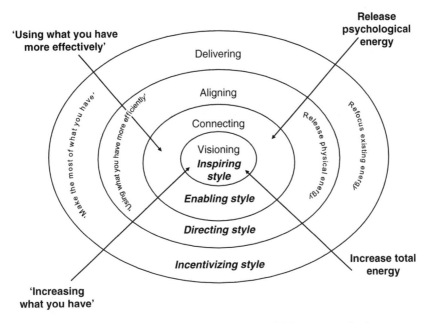

Figure 2.6 Leadership styles, focus on leadership activities: source of value creation

is relevant and can add value. Therefore these connecting leaders do not necessarily need to develop such shareable knowledge but they must know where else it can be used to create value and must make it readily transferable. One way of facilitating these transfers is to increase the level of shared responsibilities among followers with similar areas of expertise, even though they may be physically and/or organizationally located in discrete parts of the business. The benefit is clearly in generating economies of scope by releasing psychological energy that can then be more productively redeployed; what can be described as 'using what you have more effectively', as is shown in Figure 2.6.

The aligning activity concentrates on removing duplication of effort and generating economies of scale. This leadership activity can be described as 'using what you have more efficiently' and is clearly a very tight fit with our directing style of leadership. Hence the directing style leader should focus on the aligning leadership activity. The delivering activity focuses on the actual level of performance that is required rather than how it is achieved. This strong emphasis on business performance makes this delivering leadership activity the obvious focus for our incentivizing style leader. The source of value creation is refocusing existing energy within the company and therefore this style has already been described as 'making the most of what you have'.

Focus of Corporate Top Team Leaders

The direct association of one main leadership activity with each of our four leadership styles enables us to specify what each of the types of corporate top team leaders should focus on. This focus depends somewhat on the context of the business and the environment in which it is operating and the level at which each leadership style is being implemented. That said, each style has a different focus and a consequently different skill at which these leaders should be seen as being the best.

For the incentivizing style, the focus of the top corporate leaders is on improving the financial performance of the business through the setting of stretching performance targets for their followers, as is shown in Figure 2.7. This means that, as shown in Figure 2.8, these leaders require expertise in corporate governance and financial performance measurement and control so that their followers respond positively to the targets set and their associated incentivization programmes.

Enabling style	Inspiring style
Leveraging existing knowledge	**Creating new knowledge**
Incentivizing style	Directing style
Improving financial performance	**Centralizing standard processes** (to reduce total costs)

Figure 2.7 Focus of corporate leaders

Enabling style **Systems/process skills**	Inspiring style **Vision/values communication**
Incentivizing style **Corporate governance/ finance**	Directing style **Supply chain skills**

Figure 2.8 Key skills that corporate leaders should be the best at

The consequence of this focus and expertise is that these incentivizing style leaders, when found right at the top of a company, are often financial experts who exert influence on their business through their governance expertise and the active management of the portfolio of businesses within the group, i.e. by acquisitions and divestments; this is shown in Figure 2.9.

The focus of directing style leaders is markedly different in that they seek to centralize standard processes and activities in order to release

	Enabling style	**Inspiring style**
Type of leader	Process expert	Visionary leader
'Leading at'	Systems/ process skills	Visioning
Key leadership challenge	Achieving buy-in to sharing philosophy	Creation of new know-how
	Incentivizing style	**Directing style**
Type of leader	Financial expert	Supply chain expert
'Leading at'	Controls/governance	Technical skills
Key leadership challenge	Actively managing portfolio to add value	Gaining acceptance of changes

Figure 2.9 Leadership roles and challenges

duplicated resources and reduce total costs. Consequently these leaders require supply chain skills so that they can identify opportunities for significant cost savings and efficiency improvements through standardization that does not detract from the effectiveness of the previously tailored processes that were being applied across the business.

These 'technically skilled' leaders need to gain acceptance of their proposed changes, particularly from those most directly affected by the change; remember, the directing style needs a high degree of buy-in, but from relatively few people. Gaining this acceptance can be particularly challenging as the centralization or standardization often removes some, or all, of the power base and authority of those most directly affected, e.g. the people who were in charge of the activity that is to be centralized. This can be particularly challenging when these potential 'followers' are more senior in the hierarchy than the leader who is proposing the change.

The enabling style of leader focuses on leveraging existing knowledge more widely across the business by connecting different parts of the organization together more effectively. Effectiveness is a key term for this style of leadership while the directing style is more interested in the efficiency of what is done. This means that enabling style leaders need very strong process and systems skills. As shown in Figure 2.9, they should therefore be regarded as leaders in this area of process expertise. In those multi-business organizations that still have strong functional areas across the whole business, this would alter the role of the functional director significantly. The enabling leadership style requires more of a facilitator who gets people to work together and willingly share their knowledge, rather than the more traditional line management head of the function who thinks that they know best and tells subordinates how things will be done.

The key leadership challenge facing the enabling style leader is achieving sufficient buy-in from a wide range of employees to the concept of sharing knowledge across the business for the benefit of the business as a whole. As already mentioned, this leadership role does not necessarily have to create the knowledge that is to be shared; value can be created by exploiting existing knowledge to its full potential. Ensuring that all such current knowledge is properly packaged and communicated, so that it can easily be adopted by other parts of the business, clearly requires employees to go beyond the normal requirements of their own job specifications. Hence value-creating leadership is needed to achieve this.

The visioning leadership activity is the most obvious and traditional example of leadership but its source of value creation is often confused. The true visionary leader establishes the compelling aspirational aim of the company and achieves a high level of buy-in to this vision from the vast majority of the workforce. This leadership activity does not set out the detailed 'hows' that are involved in achieving the vision. Indeed, the associated set of core values and beliefs establish a range of constraints on how the vision can be delivered. However, the challenge generated by such a vision should inspire the positively committed followers to find new ways of working together so that the business moves towards its long-term goals that form part of the vision. Thus the key leadership challenge for the inspirational leader is to stimulate the creation and exploitation of new corporate know-how that can be used to achieve the vision.

This ultimate achievement therefore depends upon the other leadership activities of connecting, aligning and delivering, but in our model these other activities do not have to be carried out by the inspirational leader.

Impact on Organizational Culture

These different leadership roles and styles can have significantly different impacts on the culture within the total organization, or the part that is most affected by a specific leader. We define organizational culture as the sum of the shared values and beliefs of the people within the organization: the 'norms' to which these people relate and which bind them together. Some companies have very strong 'cult-like' cultures where new employees go through what is effectively an indoctrination process. Most of these very tight cultures will reject any new people who are not a good fit, with the result that such misfits will rapidly leave the organization, one way or another.

The inspiring leader style, with its focus on the visioning activity, needs to develop a high degree of trust between the leaders and the entire workforce that represents their potential followers. Such a strong level of buy-in and commitment should mean that the primary identification of these followers is with the visioning leader at their level in the organization. This means that for an inspirational style leader at the top of a very large global group, the geographically spread workforce should all identify with this potentially remote leader and the overall group, rather than with the individual business units in which they are physically located. Clearly this represents a massive leadership challenge in these large organizations and ways to break down the problem are discussed in Chapter 3.

By way of contrast, the incentivizing leadership style requires a much lower level of trust between the leader at the top of the organization and their followers. This results in most employees identifying most closely with the business unit, or even a smaller profit centre or other financially accountable subdivision of the business, that they actually work in. As shown in Figure 2.10, this level of association is reinforced by the communication style used by these different styles of leader. The incentivizing style tends to use formal communications based around the planning, budgeting and reporting process. This means that financial underperformance can result in immediate, direct and challenging communication from the otherwise remote leader. The inspiring leader style normally uses a much more informal, continuous form of communication in an attempt to ensure that their vision is not only properly understood but also fully accepted and bought into by their many followers. This is often done by the leader willingly debating how the vision can be achieved; in other words, the vision is communicated downwards once it has been established but the strategy to deliver it is developed through much more participative debate.

	Enabling style	Inspiring style
Trust	Medium to high	High
Identification	Process/function and group	Leader and total business/group
Communication style	Up-down-sideways	Informal/ continuous debate on how to achieve vision
	Incentivizing style	Directing style
Trust	Low to medium	Medium
Identification	Smallest business unit (profit centre)	Activity/role/business unit
Communication style	Formal/budgets, results	Formal/commands or instructions

Figure 2.10 Impact of leadership style on organizational culture

The directing style of leadership also often uses a relatively formal method of communication that emphasizes instructions, sometimes bordering on commands, from the leader *down* to the followers. This is normally an assertive leadership role where the level of trust is only at the medium level and is based on the specific technical expertise of the leader. The technically expert leader seeks to align the organization as efficiently as possible, with the result that employees directly identify with the level at which they are most closely aligned. This could be with a centralized activity that they are associated with, the particular functional role that they fulfil, or the business unit in which they are located. The classic example of the directing style of leadership is the very efficiently structured manufacturing operation like the original Model T Ford, where the entire process is broken down into its smallest elements and then arranged so as to maximize operational efficiency. Each specific area therefore has direct responsibility for only their own activities, and they identify most closely with this area and their co-workers in this area.

There is a significant contrast between this and the enabling style of leadership where the value creation is dependent upon the network of relationships that develop across the organization. While there is still a degree of specialization in terms of skills and, particularly, knowledge, the value of these specialists is enhanced if their knowledge and skills are deployed as widely as possible within the business. This makes the dialogue up, down and across the organization so important. It also means that there is an increased need for trust between leader and followers, and among followers. If another part of the business is expected to change the way they do things by adopting a practice used elsewhere in the organization, they need to have respect for and trust in both their enabling style leader and the source of this purportedly 'better practice'. The common 'not invented here' mindset makes leveraging existing knowledge extremely challenging.

Where it works well, the result is often that the affected employees identify most closely with their specialist peer group, even though they may be widely dispersed across the group. This identification is increased if job rotations and project teams are used to accelerate the dissemination of particularly valuable knowledge. The consequence is that these followers feel a lower level of identification with the business unit or profit centre in which they are physically located.

Summary

This chapter sought to set out the main elements in our leadership model, in an attempt to indicate the differences among the four styles of leadership. Each leadership style focuses on one potentially value-creating leadership activity and has its own blend of strategic or people, transactional or transformational emphasis. This results in a variety of organizational cultural factors being dependent on the leadership style that is being implemented.

We believe that most leadership models and theories ask too much of any corporate leader by expecting them to be the best at all these leadership activities. Consequently most senior managers fall short of these excessive demands and thus remain as merely managers. Our model tries to take into account human frailty by actually requiring leaders to focus on one key activity. This raises the obvious question of how should a leader identify which activity to focus on, and hence which leadership style they should adopt. The answer is in two parts. The first is based on playing to strengths and uses a fundamental building block of leadership that is self-awareness, both of who you really are and how you are perceived by potential followers. A truly honest sense of self-awareness includes an accurate self-assessment and an understanding of your emotional strengths and weaknesses. This should result in a sense of self-confidence based on reality rather than wishful thinking.

This self-awareness can enable an individual to develop self-management capabilities, which is how any potentially dramatically damaging flaws can be modified. However, the major benefit is that it indicates the relative level of the key leadership attributes that this person possesses at present. As already stated, attributes are the personal qualities that determine how well the key capabilities will be implemented and, thus, what leadership styles and focused activities this potential leader is likely to be best at. However, we do not overly emphasize the importance of attributes as most of the attributes that are important for leaders are also critical for their followers if they are to maximize their contribution to the business.

The second element of the answer is that it depends on the context of the organization. We have already said that a leader's focus is determined by the needs of their followers. It is also affected by the needs of the business that they are leading and, in many cases, this is driven by the context in which that business is operating.

Leaders clearly cannot maximize their value creation unless they address the needs of both the organization and their potential followers within the organization; what we have described as strategic and people leadership. If there is no overlap between these sets of needs and the leadership strengths of a particular leader there will be no value creation, as shown in Figure 2.11. The leader will normally be regarded as failing. This explains why many previously successful leaders subsequently fail when either they move companies or the environment of their existing business changes substantially. A leader may be able to change their style but this can take time and has significant associated risks. Similarly leaders can adapt to completely different business contexts and consequent leadership needs but this also has risks. Not least of these is a total lack of credibility if the change of leadership style is significant unless, that is, the leader moves to a new organization.

Therefore it can make sense for a business to import, from outside, a new leader if its context has changed dramatically. No existing internal leader may have the appropriate leadership skills and credibility that are needed for this new environment. If an external potential leader can be identified who has already proved that they have these skills and have previously implemented what is perceived as the right leadership style, the associated risks may be much less of bringing that individual, or team, into a new organizational culture than of hoping that an

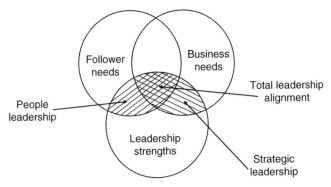

Overlaps between leadership strengths and needs of both followers and the business create the opportunity to create value

Figure 2.11 Leadership value creation

existing, internal leader can identify and make the required changes to their leadership style.

A Practical Model

A brief case study example may make this clearer. In 1993, IBM was facing financial meltdown. Its share price had collapsed to $40 from a peak of $175 and its credit rating had been downgraded disastrously following a series of record reported losses of $2.8 billion for 1991 and $5.0 billion for 1992. Newspapers and analysts were openly discussing the possibility of financial liquidation for the company that led the world's computer industry. This industry was still growing strongly but the major source of IBM's very high profitability ($6.0 billion in 1990) was its dominance of the mainframe market. The problem for IBM was that this was one sector that was no longer growing. Increasingly computer systems were moving to client-server networks. Mainframe sales were largely for replacement machines for existing customers and when the US economy went into recession in 1990 for the first time in ten years many of these replacement purchases were simply deferred.

IBM's current top management team had been home-grown with virtually no external experience among them. Thus they had known only growth and success and had built an organization of 400,000 employees to support more of the same. The financial downturn came as a great shock and $18 billion was provided for headcount reduction costs as the total number of employees was reduced to 300,000 by the end of 1992. In 1914 Tom Watson Senior had been brought in when the fledgling company was in trouble and he really created the IBM that grew to dominate its industry. Now the group turned to an outside leader for the second time.

Lou Gerstner was appointed Chairman and CEO on 1 April 1993. For the previous four years he had been running RJR Nabisco following its highly leveraged takeover by KKR. In this leadership role, his focus had been on driving out costs and generating net cash inflows to both service and repay the $25 billion of debt that resulted from this famous deal. Prior to that he had been President of American Express where cost-cutting had also been quite high on the agenda. However, he had joined the Travel Related Services division of American Express several years earlier, having worked with the business as a McKinsey consultant before that. TRS could easily have been classified as a mature or even declining business as both its travel division and its card operation faced increasingly stiff competition. Gerstner conducted a radical strategy review that resulted in significant market segmentation with consequent new product introduction. He changed the organizational culture, and many of the people, by cutting bureaucracy and bringing in several innovative incentivization programmes. The business, and its people, responded with a dramatic growth in profitability over the next decade of Lou Gerstner's leadership. With this track record, he joined IBM.

Quite rapidly he brought in other complete outsiders to key top jobs at IBM and initially they focused on cost-cutting, including more people reductions. The next priorities started to reposition the group away from being a product focused, technology driven, hardware supplier that did software, consultancy and other services in order to sell boxes, back into the 'global solutions' company that it had really been during its first period of success. He urged the internal business units to cooperate, collaborate and share rather than compete with each other and made some strategic acquisitions of software and service businesses, such as Lotus Developments. This was a major cultural shift for IBMers, which was reinforced by doing away with the famous dress code. The stock market had regained its faith in IBM by the second half of the 1990s and the shareholder value created during Lou Gerstner's leadership was quite amazing; not surprisingly, the stock option packages granted when he joined meant that he personally shared substantially in this increase in value.

Such a success story should make readers keen to become leaders at the top of such major businesses. This is obviously never easy but without leadership experience at lower levels it is impossible. The important issue is that our research has not indicated one particular style of leadership at the top of organizations, nor that experience of any one style is the best route to the top. What is clear is that experience of, and exposure to, leadership is critical and this should be gained as early as possible in a career. The good news is that leaders are needed at all levels in a business so that opportunities for getting this leadership experience are quite possible. These multilevel leadership roles are considered in Chapter 3.

3

Most leaders are also followers

Leaders, by definition, need followers. More importantly, in order to achieve extraordinary levels of performance, leaders need positively committed followers who willingly try to deliver discretionary outputs over and above the mandatory levels required by their line managers. Thus, ideally, all employees should be positively committed to *a* leader. However, it is not essential that all employees are positively committed to the same leader.

Indeed, in the majority of today's complex modern corporations it is not logical to expect any single leader to achieve such a high level of required buy-in from every employee. This is illustrated by the matrix in Figure 3.1 that plots the level of perceived inclusion of followers against their level of internalization. Internalization means both full understanding and individual acceptance. This is important because shared understanding by leader and followers does not necessarily mean acceptance by these same followers; therefore the communicating for success leadership capability must aim for complete acceptance of the message rather than merely understanding it. In the case of our incentivizing style leadership, with its less challenging requirement of fewer followers who need a relatively low degree of buy-in, there can be some variation in the levels of understanding and acceptance among these followers. However, where lots of followers need to have a high

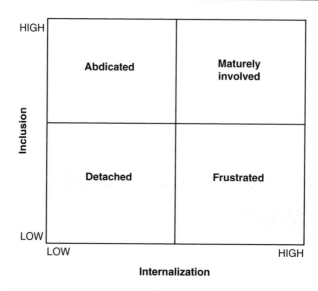

Figure 3.1 Nature of follower involvement

degree of buy-in, such as for the inspiring leadership style, the same level of understanding and acceptance must be shared across all these followers.

Clearly, where followers do not feel that they have been included in the development of the vision, values, goals or objectives of the business *and* have not internally understood or accepted them, they will feel detached from their leaders. If they understand and accept the leader's message but do not feel included in the development or implementation process, these followers are likely to feel frustrated. If they were included in the process and their inputs were taken into account but they do not either understand or accept the actual outcome, these followers have abdicated any responsibility for their potential leader's decisions. In other words, these potential followers are unwilling to accept the principle of cabinet responsibility. None of these categories of followers is likely to have any level of positive buy-in to their leaders.

Positive commitment is generated from followers who feel maturely involved in their leader's actions because they have been included in the process and they both understand and accept the outcome of that process. Expecting any single business leader in a large organization to generate this maturity of involvement from all their employees is, in our view, being completely unrealistic and impractical.

Our leadership model avoids this problem as it accepts that leaders can be found at any level of the organization. Managers, not leaders, have to have subordinates and they want control over these subordinates. Leaders seek buy-in from their followers, who can come from any level of the business. Thus these followers can themselves be leaders with their own groups of followers. Bizarre as it may seem, in other circumstances these followers can even be the leaders of their own leader. An important advantage of having leaders at all levels is that each level of such leaders should be much closer to their own followers and should therefore be more able to achieve positive buy-in.

This highlights yet another significant difference between our leadership model and most existing models. These state that leadership cannot be delegated; we argue that several of the key value-creating leadership activities both can and should be delegated to the most appropriate level of the organization. This 'most appropriate level' is where the highest buy-in can be obtained from 'maturely involved' followers. Our concern is not with delegated leadership but with inappropriately detached or absent leadership, as is diagrammatically illustrated in Figure 3.2.

Leaders should stand back, but not necessarily stand apart, from their followers, particularly if these followers are themselves leaders with

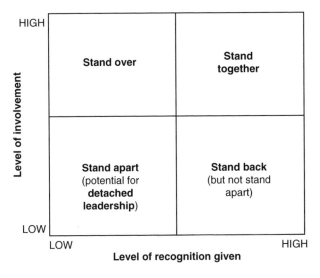

Figure 3.2 Nature of leader involvement

their own followers from lower levels in the organization. The dimensions for this framework are the level of involvement of the leader and the level of recognition provided by the leader to their followers. If the involvement is low but so is the level of recognition, the leader is standing apart from their followers. This can easily become detached or absent leadership, if their followers have a high need for recognition.

Where the involvement is high but the level of recognition is low, the leader is acting as a manager not a leader as they are 'standing over' their subordinate. It is important to remember that recognition is not the same as praise, where the praise takes the form of a pat on the head in a parent-to-child relationship. If the level of involvement is high and the level of recognition is high, it is impossible to distinguish who is the leader and who is the follower. All are standing together as one team without a visible leader.

Leaders often need to provide a high level of recognition to their followers. This is particularly true when recognition is a key need of these followers. They equally need to grant these followers the ability to exercise their initiative if they are to fulfil their value-creating potential for the business. This 'standing back but not standing apart' from their followers thus means allowing small 'controlled' failures by these followers as learning processes.

This reinforces the mutual dependency that exists between leaders and followers, because leaders themselves need the freedom to fail. Leadership requires discretion that means the freedom to act. This must include the freedom to fail as long as this failure is a learning failure. Also learning failures that happen to leaders from lower levels in the organization are normally far less expensive than if leadership, and the corresponding freedom to fail, only starts right at the top of the business. Thus leaders who genuinely have the discretion to exercise their initiative can impact value creation from any level of the organizational hierarchy. It should also be clear that the *only* difference between such a leader and their maturely involved follower, who is fully exercising their own initiative for the good of the organization, is that the leader has followers.

It is very interesting that career development progressions normally lead through a period of narrower specialization, where an individual acquires functionally based expertise, to a broadening out as more senior, general management roles are taken on. In many organizations, it is only these more senior roles that are viewed as leadership roles. This is not logical. People need to learn to lead. This includes learning to take risks, learning to take the initiative, learning truly to set the direction and the pace of movement in this chosen direction, and *learning to fail*. Thus potential top corporate leaders need leadership challenges early in their career so that they can develop both their leadership capabilities but, equally importantly, the self-awareness and social awareness that are the foundation of these leadership capabilities.

Complementary versus Contradictory

We have already argued that leaders at the top of the organization need to focus in order to maximize their value-creating potential. This is also true for all leaders at any level of the business. Leading is still about 'being the best' and this requires focusing on one leadership activity and hence one of our leadership styles. The relevant leadership style is dictated by the particular needs of their followers as well as the context of the particular business and the overall leadership framework that it is implementing.

The key is that the leadership exercised at different levels in the organization must not be contradictory. If it is, the different levels can cancel each other out with the result that the business does not realize the potential value created from leadership. Even worse, these contradictions can cause such confusion that they create battling sets of followers within the organization, where each set is positively committed to the directly conflicting leadership styles within the competing 'baronies' of the leaders in the business.

Leaders at the top of the business either set a clear leadership agenda for the whole organization or they abdicate certain leadership roles to lower levels. Remember, we believe in delegating specific leadership activities to the right level but we do not believe in either abdicated followers or abdicated leaders. This means that the top corporate leaders should ideally develop a clear leadership agenda that has complementary leadership styles at each level of the organization. Such an agenda should make it clear what leadership activity is to be the focus of each level. There are several possibilities but the one most commonly found in practice is one that often does not work and is what we describe as the amplifier leadership technique.

Amplifier leadership acknowledges that, in a large company, the single leader at the top of the organization cannot obtain a high level of buy-in from all the widely dispersed employees. Accordingly the business uses the normal communication cascade process down the organizational hierarchy, i.e. through management levels, in an attempt to ensure that the leader's message is understood. This amplifies the message and may even ensure that it is received by all employees. Unfortunately, the communicating for success leadership capability involves much more than repeating the message until it is received by everyone. The leader's message has to be reinforced by actions of this leader that are totally consistent with it. Maturely involved followers need to feel that they were included in the development process that resulted in this message. They also need both to understand the message and accept it, which means understanding and accepting the implications for themselves and their areas of the business.

Clarity in Communications

The authors are all old enough to have, as children, played the party game known as 'children's whispers'. A line of people is set up and the first child is given a message to pass back down the line. This is done by each child whispering the message to the one behind them. The result, not surprisingly, is that the message is completely garbled by the time it reaches the back of the line. The apocryphal example is from the First World War when the original message sent was 'send reinforcements, we're going to advance', but the message finally received at Headquarters was 'send three and four pence, we're going to a dance'.

Leaders cannot take the risk of their message being misinterpreted, whether deliberately or not, by intermediaries placed between them and their potential followers.

Another silly example we like is of the comparison with an Englishman abroad, particularly in France. When locals appear not to understand the message, our Englishman speaks louder and more slowly but still, of course, in English. The French element adds in the bit that the recipient may actually understand what is said perfectly, but is not going to admit it. Understanding the message is not the same as accepting it.

This normally requires some level of dialogue so that a full understanding of such implications can be gained. Clearly this can be difficult in a tiered communication process, particularly if the dialogue is with someone who was no more involved in the development process than the potential follower to whom the leader's message is being passed down. This is exacerbated when the direct communicator is a manager without any leadership capabilities, or is a leader who has not bought in to the message themselves.

However, the major problem with the amplifier leadership framework is that it does not necessarily allow these tiered potential leaders really to act as leaders in their own right. Leadership requires discretion, but these lower levels of the organizational hierarchy are often merely passing on someone else's vision, etc. and are acting in a purely managerial capacity. Second-hand leadership is not real leadership, and this is what most models mean when they assert that leadership cannot be delegated. Specific leadership activities *can* be delegated as long as it is clear to both potential followers and leaders at each level what the delegated powers are. Thus a much lower level of leadership could communicate the overall vision for the business and then, using the visioning leadership activity, develop a specific vision for their own part of the business that is totally complementary to the group vision.

However, this still means that the same leadership style is being implemented at each level of the business and leaders need to focus their energies.

Developing the Model

We have already argued that leaders' roles should be determined by the needs of the business and of their potential followers. It is helpful to examine the leader/follower interchange in some detail, as is done diagrammatically in Figure 3.3. The satisfaction of followers' needs, in terms of achievement, affiliation, recognition and self-esteem can be regarded as their outputs from the leader/follower interchange and this results from the energy inputs made by the leader. Remember, leading is an activity and so is following. These inputs are the leadership strengths, possibly offset by specific weaknesses or leadership gaps, which we describe through our terms style, capabilities and attributes.

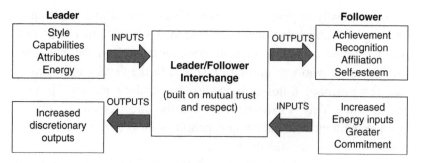

Figure 3.3 Leader /follower interchange

Depending upon the perceived level of satisfaction of their needs, followers respond by increasing their energy input back into the leader/follower interchange. This generates the increased discretionary outputs that cannot be obtained from the business without this voluntary interchange. The whole interchange is built on the foundation of mutual trust and respect between leader and follower. This foundation, combined with the satisfaction of their needs, generates greater commitment on the part of these followers. A stronger level of trust and respect normally means a shorter time lag between the satisfaction of followers' needs and their increased energy input into the business.

This focus on the needs of potential followers indicates that the most appropriate style of leadership will be the one that most closely fits with any particular combination of followers' needs. If we use the normal needs analysis format, we can distinguish between followers who have a high need for recognition from others and those who have a greater need for self-esteem, so that the opinion of others is less important to them. Similarly, there are individuals with a high need for achievement, while others have a larger need for affiliation, i.e. a sense of belonging to something that is greater than themselves. If we now consider the potential combinations of these needs, as is done in Figure 3.4, there are four possibilities that reflect quite importantly different types of followers' needs. Some followers' main need is for a strong sense of personal achievement. These people do not need a high level either of recognition or of affiliation as long as they feel that they have been challenged and that they have risen to the challenge. They are likely to respond very positively to being set stretch targets by our incentivizing

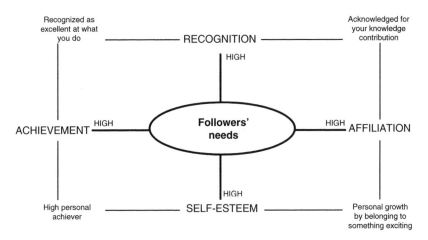

Figure 3.4 Followers' needs

style leader, as shown in Figure 3.5. Equally importantly, they will not react adversely to this leader's potentially more limited abilities in people leadership as they are themselves normally quite self-confident and self-contained.

Another combination of needs is for a high level of achievement but with this achievement being overtly recognized by the organization. In other words, these people are willing to put in the extra effort to do a great job, but they also need to know that others appreciate that they have done a great job. This recognition can come from the relatively

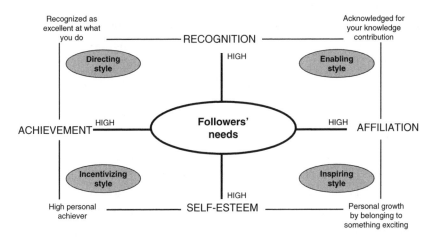

Figure 3.5 Matching leadership styles to followers' needs

small group of people whose opinions they consider to be important. These important others are likely to be closely linked colleagues with similar types of expertise, such as those working directly with them or in related areas of the business. This combination of achievement and recognition can be facilitated if the individuals are allowed to concentrate on a more limited range of activities, such as results from the standardization of tasks and consequent specialization that our directing style of leader seeks to implement. This type of potential follower should therefore respond positively to the directing style of leadership.

Potential followers who have a high need for recognition together with a high need for affiliation will appreciate the sense of professionalism and belonging that can result from the enabling leadership style. Its emphasis on sharing knowledge across the organization, without regard for the formal hierarchy, means that people are valued not just for their personal knowledge but for their contribution in facilitating the way in which this knowledge is used to its maximum potential across the business. Recognition is accordingly given to value-creating, knowledge-sharing contributions in order to encourage others also to willingly share their knowledge.

The remaining combination gives the most interesting result in terms of our leadership model. Potential followers with high needs for both affiliation and self-esteem will want to make the best contribution they can if they personally value being part of this organization. This puts the onus on their leader to make these people really want to be regarded as committed members of this team; clearly a role for our inspiring leadership style. At first sight this may seem surprising because it means that our inspirational leader style does not necessarily need to give a high level of recognition to all their followers. However, on closer consideration this is quite logical because this leadership style requires that most of the company's employees become positively committed followers. It is not possible for this leader to give meaningful recognition to everyone for their individual contributions towards the achievement of the vision. It is therefore important that these followers get sufficient personal satisfaction from knowing that they have made the greatest contribution that they could towards the achievement of the exciting vision that they already feel personally committed to.

This analysis indicates that leadership should be delegated to the level at which the leader/follower interchange will work most efficiently and effectively. This is determined by the ability to have maturely involved followers, following leaders who both understand the specific needs of these followers and are implementing an appropriate leadership style. The result should be positively committed followers of this level of leadership, but this is affected by the context of the business and alternative leadership frameworks are therefore most appropriate in different contexts.

In-to-out leadership

The most obvious framework for delegating leadership activities can be described, using our leadership styles and activities diagrams from Chapter 2, as in-to-out leadership. In this leadership structure, the top leadership team focuses on the visioning leadership activity. Their objective is to craft a future for the business that gets employees at all levels excited about working for the company. This means that the vision, and associated set of core values, must be relevant to everyone involved in the organization. If it needs significant tailoring to make it relevant to major parts of the business it will not generate the required high level of buy-in from enough followers across the company. The critical followers, in terms of their level of buy-in, are those people who will themselves be leaders at lower levels in the organization. They must not only both fully understand and accept the vision but also feel that they were included in the development process. In other words, they are maturely involved as positively committed followers of the 'inspiring leadership' style being implemented right at the top of the business.

We have already mentioned the issue of who is regarded as part of a particular leadership team and this is a clear example of this perception problem. These critical followers are themselves leaders with their own followers. The trust and respect that they have hopefully generated with their own followers should mean that, if they state that they felt they were involved in the development of the vision and fully buy-in to the resulting vision, their followers will also accept the vision as being appropriate for the business. Their followers will regard them as part of the top leadership team that developed the vision. These 'indirect' followers cannot be regarded at this stage as being positively committed to the vision but using the amplifier leadership technique will not make them maturely involved.

However, this can be achieved by their own leader focusing on another leadership activity by implementing a complementary leadership style.

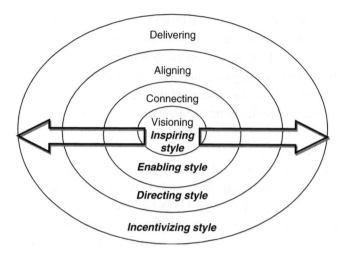

Figure 3.6 In-to-out leadership framework

With the in-to-out leadership framework the next level of leadership focuses on the connecting activity by using the enabling style, as shown in Figure 3.6.

This enabling style of leader is not constrained by their position in the managerial hierarchy and often cuts across the formal organizational structure. These leaders seek to make the organization united behind achieving the vision that they are personally fully committed to. Thus their initiatives, which are focused on linking together otherwise disparate parts of the business, must be fully congruent with the vision and values of the total business. This congruence with the overall vision must be made very clear to the enabling style leader's followers: such as, by doing 'this', we will assist the business in moving significantly closer to *our* vision in these 'specific' ways. Consequently if they achieve positive commitment from their followers, who may be spread right across the company, they will effectively reinforce the overall commitment to this vision. However, their own followers will obtain greater value from their leader/follower interchange as they can associate much more closely with this leader. This leader should also be much more able to address their specific needs as followers, due to the mutual trust and respect on which their relationship is based.

Not surprisingly, in many in-to-out leadership frameworks this enabling style leadership is found in those functions of the business that are spread across all the business units, e.g. marketing, research and development, IT and sometimes even finance.

The next obvious leadership focus is on the activity of aligning the organization so as to make achieving the vision either feasible or more likely. As already stated, the directing style of leader often has to restructure the organization in order to achieve the improved efficiencies and release of physical energy that is being sought. This requires a high buy-in but only from those most affected by the changes. Once again, locating this leadership role as close as possible to those critical followers whose very specific needs and concerns must be addressed should maximize their eventual level of buy-in. The directing style leaders also face the challenge of placing their initiatives in the context of the overall vision and values, which they are personally positively committed to. If this is achieved, they should be able to achieve a high level of buy-in from their followers, who will then become leaders for this change within their own areas of the business.

It should by now be clear that these various levels of leadership are not really hierarchical, except for the key decision as to what is the leadership role at the very top of the organization. Once that is decided, the other leadership roles and styles must be complementary to this leader, rather than contradictory. How these different styles and their corresponding initiatives complement and are congruent with the top leader's style should be clearly explained to each group of followers. This enables these followers to be positively committed to their appropriate, i.e. most value-creating, leader without worrying about being disloyal to other 'more senior' leaders in the organization. Many organizations now try to ensure that they achieve transparency or clear 'line of sight' in terms of their objective-setting and/or their management reporting lines. The same concept is even more important in terms of leadership levels within the business.

The remaining leadership style in the in-to-out framework is the incentivizing style with its focus on the delivering activity. Suppose that the top leader in a large, multi-business organization has established the vision and core values for the group, having involved all the potential lower-level leaders in this process. The key functional support areas have implemented the enabling style and have successfully connected the various parts of the business so that all existing knowledge is being leveraged as widely as is relevant. The supply chain and finance areas of this group have adopted the directing style in order to align the organization with the requirements of the vision. This has led to the standardization of many activities, several of which have been either centralized or outsourced. What remains is for the business unit leaders to focus on the delivering leadership activity so that the long-term vision is actually realized. The challenge, of course, is to move towards this vision while still achieving at least the required level of performance in the short term. This is why the incentivizing, or shareholder, style leader has to be excellent at the handling paradox capability. After all, shareholders are very demanding. They want good future growth, plus strong current performance.

However, the key element in this framework in such a group is that the leadership role at the business unit level is very clear. We do not need, or want, these leaders to put their energy into developing a vision and set of values for their business units. They should have been involved in, and be positively committed to, the group's vision. Consequently they need to agree with both the top leadership team and their own leadership team how their business unit should contribute to the achievement of this vision.

These business unit leaders should regard themselves as fully responsible, and be held accountable, for the performance of their business. Yet the vision and medium-term objective of their group will determine precisely what form this desired performance should take. It may be that their mature business unit has the role to generate profits and cash flows that can be reinvested in the more rapidly growing parts of the group, or they could be the more rapidly growing part with the key requirements for the launch of new products and the penetration of new market segments. Clearly a growth objective to double the size of the overall group in five years does not mean that every business in the group has to grow at a rate of 15 per cent per year for these five years. This is another reason why the incentivizing style leader has to be able to handle paradox, rather than letting their followers figure it out for themselves, if they can.

In some cases, this may result in a differently worded vision for the business unit, but their leadership role to their followers involves communicating how this sub-vision is complementary to, and congruent with, the group's vision. Their followers should therefore feel an integral part of the larger group and quite a few of them will already be positively committed to other leaders within the group, i.e. the enabling style and directing style leaders who have an impact across the organizational structure. The leadership role at this level is therefore effectively constrained by the other leadership roles carried out elsewhere in the business. It is quite possible for leaders at this level to implement a totally contradictory style of leadership that negates the potential value added at the other levels. By focusing on the remaining leadership activity, their leadership style should be complementary, not contradictory.

Obviously there are potential leadership roles at many other points in organizations implementing any multilevel leadership framework. Our objective in this section is to illustrate how a complementary leadership framework can be implemented.

Out-to-in leadership

An obvious alternative framework would be to start from the outside of our activities model, as shown in Figure 3.7. A key requirement of the in-to-out framework is that the top leader can articulate a vision that is meaningful for everyone in the business. This normally means that there is quite a lot of common context across the whole organization, so that employees can identify with the overall business rather than just with their own physical location or functional area. In many large businesses, such a group-wide vision would be relatively meaningless and not something that would generate positive commitment from anyone.

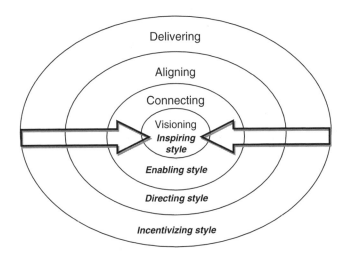

Figure 3.7 Out-to-in leadership framework

As a result, the top leaders in such organizations may decide to focus on the delivering leadership activity. The appropriate incentivizing style of leadership therefore concentrates on setting challenging, stretching targets for the component parts of the business. Not surprisingly, this out-to-in framework is commonly found in decentralized, highly diversified, large groups where the top leadership team focuses on improving the performance of the portfolio of businesses comprising the group. Some businesses can be sold simply so that new ones can be acquired where the governance expertise at the top of the group may be able to create value. Quite often this value-creation period is quite short and, once the potential improvements have been achieved, this now highly performing business may be sold so that the cycle can be repeated.

This extreme culture means that even senior executives in the underlying operating businesses identify much more closely with their own business unit than with the group's top leaders. However, the incentivizing style only requires a few people to have a moderate level of buy-in to these leaders. This can normally be achieved by linking these stretching performance targets to very high incentive payments for the business unit leaders. This is why incentivizing style leaders must set stretching, but achievable targets; if they are immediately perceived as completely out of reach by their followers, the incentive schemes do not act as motivators for these potential lower-level leaders.

The very top leadership team in this incentivizing style-led group can be very small, as it can for the visioning-led group using the in-to-out framework. The key difference is that in this out-to-in structure, these few leaders do not need to involve many others in their leadership discussions, while the inspiring leadership style needs to get mature involvement from all the lower-level leaders in the organization. If this is not obtained the leadership value-creation potential of the in-to-out framework is unlikely to be realized.

The delivering activity focused leaders should state very clearly what they expect from their followers and what, normally in financial terms, will be delivered in return. This makes their leader/follower interchange very specific but passes a significant leadership challenge to these followers. Obviously, these followers are themselves potential leaders of their own parts of the group and, if they are to deliver the stretching targets set for them by the top leadership, they will need to realize the full potential from their businesses. This could be significantly helped by developing a positively committed workforce that is willing to increase its energy input level so as to achieve the discretionary output that follows from value-creating leadership. At the business unit level in this incentivizing style-led group, there can therefore be a need for an inspirational style of leadership with a corresponding focus on the visioning activity.

Having this leadership activity at this much lower level in the organization is not contradictory in this framework as no meaningful group vision has been developed by the top leadership team. They have effectively delegated this leadership activity to the level where a higher level of follower buy-in can be achieved. Obviously this can result in many significantly different visions, and even associated sets of core values, being developed within the same group. Owing to the lack of integration and coordination across most such diversified groups, this is not normally a major problem. The inspiring leadership style in each business unit can address the specific needs of each relevant group of potential followers, so that each business unit develops its own strong level of identification and culture, but they can be quite different from each other. The only thing that binds such a group together is their common ownership, and this could rapidly change. A change in ownership should not necessarily impact on the leadership style and related culture that is in place within such business units.

The real leadership challenge in this out-to-in framework is where and how to implement the other two value-creating leadership activities. In our extreme example, the connecting and aligning leadership activities would have to be implemented within the individual business units, i.e. below the specific visioning activity carried out by the business unit leader. This can miss out on possible group-wide synergies, even in a diversified set of businesses. Consequently, many incentivizing style top leaders accommodate this by accepting the need for leadership roles that cross over more than one business unit.

This can most easily be achieved with the enabling style and its associated focus on the connecting activity as this can readily cut across formal organization structures. One problem for enabling style leaders in these types of groups is gaining sufficient buy-in from their potential followers who are physically located in, and closely identify with, the individual business units. Another issue is for these leaders to develop adequate information themselves about the relevant knowledge that already exists around the group and where else within the group it may be useful. They can overcome at least part of these problems by taking a more proactive role in the knowledge transfer process. Each new acquisition into the group can be analysed for relevant knowledge that it either possesses or needs and a project team can be set up to transfer the knowledge, when suitably codified if necessary, out to other business units or into the new acquisition as rapidly as possible. The window of opportunity for value-creating action can be quite short if the portfolio of businesses in the group is being dynamically driven by the top leadership team.

There is a larger problem for the aligning activity focus of any directing style leaders in this environment. The aligning activity often changes the organization structure on a long-term basis in order to realize the greatest possible economies of scale. This is questionable where the composition of the group can change rapidly. If a major shared service centre has been set up on the financial justification of the current portfolio of businesses, this can act as a constraint on the freedom of the top leadership team to change this portfolio.

However, even this apparently significant problem has been overcome in several such groups. These directing style-led activities are established as stand-alone business units within the group and given their own stretching financial performance targets. This is quite possible due to the formal service-level agreements that often accompany this directing style of leadership activity. Equally important in these groups, given the focus of the top leadership team on improving financial performance, having visible profit responsibility and accountability raises the leadership profile of these previously cost-centre status areas of the business. The benefit to the top leaders is that the subsequent disposal of other business units that are customers of the new profit centre does not necessarily mean that these sales revenues and profit contributions are lost to the group. The newly profit-accountable leaders in such shared service centres have a strong personal interest in retaining their customer despite the lack of shared ownership.

Changes in context

We have asserted that the appropriate leadership framework is at least partially dictated by the context in which the business operates. A brief case study can illustrate this. For many years, under the leadership of Sir Patrick Sheehy, BAT Industries had an out-to-in leadership framework.

The corporate centre actively ran the portfolio of businesses that had been widely diversified from its original core businesses in tobacco. At its peak, the group had several businesses in each of financial services, retailing, paper and packaging, as well as significant equity interests in other large diversified groups. Indeed, even its tobacco interests were structured as four independent businesses that actually competed against each other in certain countries.

The resulting incentivizing leadership style at the centre of the group was complemented by the inspiring leadership style at the top of most of these, individually large, business units. The potential leadership gaps were in the connecting and aligning activities as these did not really take place above the business unit level. This was felt to miss out on potential value enhancements due to synergy opportunities across several businesses, but most particularly among the tobacco businesses.

Once Sir Patrick had retired, the new leadership team, headed by Martin Broughton, carried out a full strategic review of the group. This resulted in a significant change in direction as the group was refocused on its tobacco interests. The other businesses were either sold or demerged and significant acquisitions and mergers in the tobacco industry took place. The four tobacco divisions were merged into the single global business that British American Tobacco had become. Accordingly, a unified and meaningful vision for the group was articulated and group-wide functional responsibilities were developed.

In terms of our leadership framework, this necessitated a change from the old out-to-in structure to an in-to-out one where the top leaders not only establish the vision, but also gain buy-in from at least all the potential lower-level leaders. These other leaders then implement the most appropriate complementary leadership style depending upon the needs of their own followers. Making such a significant change in leadership styles throughout such a vast organization, when it is also going through such dramatic dynamic changes in its structure, represents a massive leadership challenge. At least, achieving clarity of the changes that need to be made through our leadership model and framework helps to break the challenge down into identifiable elements that can then be tackled systematically.

In-and-out leadership
We have argued that high context businesses can normally use the in-to-out leadership framework with the top leaders articulating a

compelling vision. Their critical followers who are lower-level leaders themselves focus on those complementary leadership styles that are most appropriate to the needs of their own followers. In highly diversified groups with virtually no internal context, a logical alternative framework is from out-to-in with the top leadership team focusing on improving the financial performance of the disparate businesses making up the group.

Of course, many businesses sit somewhere in between these two extremes but it is still true that the leadership framework flows from the style required at the top of the organization. The leadership style that is most appropriate at the top of these organizations depends on the common factors that actually bind the group together. Another related brief example should make this clearer. Altria Inc. is a large US-based group that, among other things, owns Philip Morris, which is BAT's largest international competitor. However, unlike BAT, there has consistently been a common theme running through all the businesses in the Altria portfolio. Consequently its top leadership style should be neither that used by the old BAT Industries nor that required by the new, much more focused BAT plc. Altria's businesses involve selling branded consumer products, primarily through indirect channels of distribution such as wholesalers and retailers. Even more interestingly, as this applied to a large number of originally US-based companies that are now global, their international businesses have mainly been built on the back of a very successful domestic strategy. This option was not available to the UK-based BAT group as it did not have an original domestic business on which to base its strategy.

The consequence of this context across the group is that the logical focus for the top leadership team is on leveraging the extensive and very relevant knowledge that exists within the group, but is particularly located in the USA. This even extends to identifying suitable acquisitions for the group as these would already be successful US-based branded product businesses, in which Altria's leaders could leverage their knowledge of how to globalize such products. The enabling style of leadership with its focus on the connecting activity can create substantial value at the top of this type of group.

There still remains the selection of complementary leadership styles at other levels in this type of business. If the top leaders are implementing the enabling style, there is a need for the visioning activity at some lower level. It is the inspirational leadership style that achieves the highest level of buy-in from the largest number of followers but the leadership role must address the common needs of this large group of followers. This indicates that the most appropriate level for the visioning activity is at that level where all the potential followers can most closely identify with, and hence commit to, the vision.

In Altria's case, this is likely to be at the product group level globally as everyone working in the cigarette businesses fully understands their particular vision, in the same way as do people within the food businesses around the world. So, in this sense, Altria's cigarette business will be implementing the same leadership style as BAT. However, the connecting activity can cut across these product-based organizational sub-divisions when leaders believe that to do so would create value. Similarly, there may be significant aligning activity opportunities in specific areas of the world. Thus directing style leaders should not only operate across the overall global organizational structure, but also on a lower regional, national or even local basis.

The delivering activity will be the focus of the specific business unit leaders for each product group, i.e. with their own visions, in each geographic area (this is still normally a country, but that is changing with new technologies and trade agreements). It is important to note that, as in the case of the in-to-out framework, the discretion of these incentivizing style leaders can be significantly constrained by the impact of the leadership styles being implemented elsewhere in the business. Thus, in many cases, their brand strategies may be driven by the top leadership team and their specific role within their global vision will have been agreed with the inspirational style leadership at the top of their global product group-based division. They may not even have control of all the activities in their own geographic sphere of influence, as some of these may have been centralized or outsourced at the behest of the directing style leaders with possibly a regional remit. However, these leaders should still strive to improve the performance of those areas of their business where they can exercise discretion. Not surprisingly, we describe this as an in-and-out leadership framework, as shown in Figure 3.8.

There are also some groups where the common factor keeping the business together is the opportunity to generate economies of scale. In these cases the top team should focus on the aligning activity by implementing the directing style of leadership. The key leadership role is to ensure that

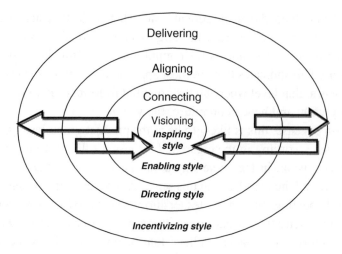

Figure 3.8 In-and-out leadership framework

the organization maximizes its potential scale efficiencies by, wherever practical, only carrying out specialized activities in one area of the business. This can therefore be regarded as improving performance by specialization, and releasing physical energy that was being wasted by previous duplication of effort.

In the era of mass production, this leadership style was very popular as large companies sought to break down the total manufacturing process into its smallest component elements. This enabled separate, relatively small work groups to concentrate on their particular subdivision of the total process, such as individual component manufacture, assembly of pre-manufactured components, etc. The key objective of such specialization is to standardize these activities so that constant repetition by employees increases their efficiency.

The associated risk is that this specialization on a completely standardized small set of activities leads to boredom and frustration. Bored and frustrated employees are unlikely to try to input any discretionary effort into the business. They are more likely to seek to find ways to achieve their specified output levels with the minimum possible effort, which can clearly have significantly negative impacts on the quality of this output. However, a positively committed workforce in this environment can generate a substantial number of improvements in these standardized activities; after all, their specialization and constant repetition makes them highly expert in each activity. Thus leadership is very important to motivate these separate groups of employees operating in such environments.

The directing style leadership skills have now been applied at very high levels in the service sector and in support functions within manufacturing industries, such as in establishing the call centres and shared service centres that have already been mentioned. It is important to remember what the role of this aligning leadership activity is. Directing style leaders improve the efficiency of what is already being done by the business. They are primarily transactional leaders who only need a high level of buy-in from those people most directly affected by the changes they initiate. Thus they are also mainly strategic, rather than people, leaders; this is normally reinforced by their strong technical skills and highly analytical approach.

This means that there is a great need for people leadership at the level of the very specialized, potentially bored work groups that result from such aligning leadership activity. These genuine 'team leaders' can provide the tailored vision for these groups that they can strongly identify with. This cannot be done at the very top of such businesses because there is nothing at this level that such highly specialized employees would identify with. Once again, the leadership role of followers, when they become leaders themselves, can be very different from that of the leader to whom they are themselves positively committed.

Interestingly, the other value-creating leadership activities are implemented in a variety of ways in directing style-led organizations. In most large groups, the focus of the aligning activity is on the supply chain (i.e. the buy, make, move) activities within the business. In many cases, these activities have been broken down into highly specialized subdivisions that service the needs of the entire group. This places significant constraints on the final business units that actually market and sell these goods and services to external customers. Their need is for leaders who focus on delivering the group's objectives, given the constraints under which they operate. Thus an incentivizing style of leadership is appropriate.

However, within these highly specialized subdivisions and in the individual sales and marketing-focused business units, new knowledge will probably be developed that is potentially relevant, and applicable, more widely across the group. These individual areas need a process that makes it possible and practical for this knowledge to be shared.

This is obviously the role for the enabling style of leadership where its primary connecting activity can work across the formal organizational structure. These leaders need to access knowledge developed both within the specialized 'production' areas and the frequently geographically organized sales and marketing business units. As before, this may mean that the enabling style leaders in the organization are functionally orientated, so that these functional leaders' roles are more facilitators than line 'managers'. In these organizations, the 'manager' style of leadership is right at the top.

Leadership without a Leader

In the last sections, we tried to show how alternative leadership frameworks through an organization can take into account having different leadership styles at the top of the organization. Indeed, we have argued that the required framework is largely dictated by the leadership style implemented at the top. However, it is possible for an organization to show leadership at many levels without having a discernible leader with a particular style at its head.

We have already stated that leaders may also be followers in different circumstances. Indeed, great leaders automatically become positively committed, willing followers of others when appropriate. Thus, in a truly team-based organization, or part of an organization, leadership rotates among the team members depending upon the needs of the team at any specific time. At the beginning of this chapter, as was shown in Figure 3.2, we mentioned the combination of highly involved leadership and a high level of recognition as being one where it is impossible to distinguish who is the leader and who is the follower. There is one team standing together, possibly without a leader, but also potentially with a rotating leadership role among its members. Clearly there is a need for an extremely high level of mutual trust and respect among the team members for this to work. However, more importantly, there is also a need for complementary leadership styles among these team members. Rotating leadership from one enabling style leader to another adds no value to the team; the best enabling style leader should lead whenever this style is appropriate. If leadership can rotate from the visioning-focused leader through to the delivering activity-focused leader as the needs of the business change, then the team may get the best leadership at all times. This explains our earlier comment that, in some circumstances, a follower can become their leader's leader. This can work with a closely knit team, built on solid foundations of trust and respect and with a clear acceptance of each team member's leadership strengths and weaknesses. The challenge is to communicate what is happening to the less closely connected followers who look to this team for clear, consistent leadership.

Summary

In this chapter, we have sought to set out how leaders at different levels in an organization can adopt complementary styles that reinforce, rather than destroy, the value-creation potential of leadership at the top of the business. At the end of Chapter 1, we said that we would now revisit the case study of our fast-moving consumer goods-based multinational in an attempt to indicate how its currently contradictory and competing leadership styles could be made mutually compatible and complementary.

The chief executive is clearly implementing an inspiring leader style with its focus on the visioning activity. We have now established that a key issue for this style is the high level of buy-in that is needed from a wide range of followers. A critical group among these required followers is all the lower-level leaders who need to be seen as being positively committed to the group's vision by all their own followers. As discussed in Chapter 1, it does not yet appear that even all the centrally located top team have fully bought in to their leader's vision. However, the CEO's leadership challenge is significantly greater than just gaining full acceptance from this small group. The key business unit leaders also need to feel that they were maturely involved in the development of this vision and the associated core values. Only if this is achieved will they be likely to achieve any level of positive commitment from their own followers towards the group vision.

The inspirational leadership style of the CEO requires a very high level of mutual trust and respect between the leader and these key followers, who are themselves also leaders. The CEO acknowledges that all employees should identify primarily with the group rather than with the business unit in which they work. In this type of geographically spread business, this can be achieved only through reinforcement by the lower-level leaders. Yet these lower-level leaders must implement a complementary style, rather than trying the amplifier framework discussed in this chapter. The group marketing director and the group operations director have potentially complementary styles, but their initiatives are significantly curtailing the freedom and flexibility of the business unit heads in what is supposed to be a decentralized group.

These business unit leaders should implement the incentivizing style of leadership themselves by focusing on the delivery of the specific performance objectives of their business units within the group's vision. In order to do this, they each need to be able to link their tailored objectives back to this overall vision and explain clearly to their followers why their own targeted level of performance is important to the group. This linkage to the overall vision is also important for the enabling style of the group marketing director and the group operations director's directing style of leadership. All of these individuals also need to understand the implications of implementing their specific leadership styles in the context of a top leader who is acting in the inspirational leadership style. To their own followers, they will all be regarded as part of this top leadership team and thus must exercise cabinet responsibility for all the major decisions taken at this top level.

However, the most significant problem is caused by the incentivizing style being implemented by the group financial director. This style of leadership is contradictory and destructive from someone perceived as a member of a top team that is itself implementing an inspirational leadership style. The top team is not itself handling any of the paradox between the long-term vision and the pressure for short-term performance improvements; it is effectively passing it down to the business unit leaders. Unfortunately, by trying to implement all four value-creating leadership activities right at the top of the organization, they are at the same time not granting these lower-level leaders any discretion. Discretion is necessary for any leadership role. This group should be utilizing an in-to-out leadership framework as its top leader is focusing on the visioning activity. The lower-level leaders can therefore focus on the delivering activity, although their flexibility is constrained not only by the group's vision and core values but also by the activities of the enabling style and directing style leaders within the group's top team.

The business unit heads therefore need the discretion to set their own stretching targets for their businesses if they are to be seen as leaders. If it is known by their potential followers that these tough targets are also set by the corporate centre, these business unit heads may seek to develop an alternative leadership role by focusing on the visioning activity and develop their own visions for each business unit. This would be counter-productive in such a group but might be preferable to them becoming detached or frustrated followers, without any leadership aspirations at all.

In Part 2 we consider each of the leadership styles separately and in more depth.

PART 2

Identifying the Right Leadership Style

4

Value-creating inspirational leadership

In this second part of the book, we consider each leadership style in much more detail and with some in-depth examples of each style being applied in practice. It is important to register that, in doing this, a new leadership model is being retrospectively applied to these case studies, with the not surprising result that some of the well-known companies cited do not comply with all of the recommended facets of the model. As our value-creating leadership activities framework has the visioning activity at its centre, it is logical to commence this more detailed consideration with the inspirational leadership style.

The inspiring leader style also sets the most challenging standard as it requires a high level of buy-in from nearly all the workforce if it is to be really effective and value creating. In very large, geographically widely spread groups, visioning activity-focused leaders right at the top of the organization can be effective by achieving a very high level of buy-in from a substantially smaller proportion of their total employees, as long as the resulting highly positively committed, very willing followers include all the significant lower-level leaders across the business. If these lower-level leaders themselves then implement their own appropriate and complementary leadership styles, their followers should also become committed to the associated vision for the overall business that emanated from the potentially still remote, to them, leader at the very top of the group. This does not mean that these lower-level leaders should merely try to repeat and amplify the visionary message of the top leader. They can, however, reinforce this vision through their own leadership activities. Alternatively, they can have a strongly negative impact, if their leadership actions are contradictory to this vision and its associated core values.

As shown in Figure 4.1, our inspirational leadership style creates value by increasing the total energy that is available within the business. This is achieved by the development and clear communication of an aspirational vision for the company, that sets out what the business wants to look *and feel* like at some unspecified point in the future. In other words, it should include the core values and business principles that must be accepted and adhered to by all employees, even though they may appear to act as a constraint on the future performance of the company. However, it is not enough that everyone in the organization has heard or seen the vision. It is not even enough for them all to understand the vision. The visioning activity, if it is to create value, must achieve both positive commitment by employees towards the vision and personal discretionary action by them that seeks to attain the vision.

This requires a vision for the company that really motivates and inspires the workforce, so that employees are enthusiastic and excited about being part of this organization. Such employees are then willing to put in extra, discretionary effort in order to move the company

Number of followers required	Many (most of workforce)
Level of buy-in needed	Very high
Source of improved performance	Increase in total energy
Type of leadership	Strong people and transformational
Key value-creating activity	Visioning

Figure 4.1 Overview of inspiring leadership style

towards this compelling vision. Rather than being satisfied with 'doing slightly better' than the minimum required, or even just 'doing what they can get away with', these positively committed followers really want 'to do their best' so that they do not 'let their leader down' and they can feel proud of their own personal role in the future success of the business.

The inspirational leadership style therefore has a strong need for people leadership in order to generate this high level of buy-in. However, most really inspiring visions also emphasize the creation of new value, rather than capturing more of the existing value within an industry. Even where the emphasis is on capturing value, this leadership style usually requires a radically new business model in order to achieve the level of step-change in performance that is incorporated in the vision. This means that our inspirational leader also must be outstanding at transformational leadership if the vision is to be achieved. In other words, the company envisaged by an aspirational vision will normally look and feel very different from its current appearance and state.

One key consequence of this type of energizing vision is that there is often a strong common culture within such companies. The objective of a visioning leader at the top of a business is to create a positive 'can do' feeling right across the business, where all employees are willing to contribute to the best of their ability, and in whatever way they can, towards the *common* vision. As is shown in Figure 4.2, this should result in the primary identification of all employees, even in a vast organization with

Primary identification of followers	Overall business as represented by the visioning leader
Minimum level of trust needed	Very high
Minimum level of respect required	Very high
Source of respect	Intellectual capability/capacity to transform the business
Communication style	Continuous, informal debate on how to achieve the vision

Figure 4.2 Cultural implications of inspiring leadership style

over 100,000 workers, being with the overall group rather than with the particular business unit, function or department in which they are physically located. With incentivizing style leadership, which is discussed in the next chapter, it is very common for employees' primary identification to be with the lowest level of grouping in which they are involved. Indeed, in some such groups, many employees are completely unaware that their business unit is actually part of a much larger entity. Such lack of identification and affiliation with the total group is not necessarily a bad thing with incentivizing style leadership if it results in a close and positive identification with a smaller subdivision of the business.

However, leaders implementing our inspiring leader style rely on their vision and associated core values to stimulate the desire by employees to be part of their envisaged future. The aspirational vision is what binds these individuals together giving the business a common purpose and sense of direction. It is therefore vital for the success of a visioning activity-focused leader, at whatever level in the organization they operate, that their potential followers closely identify with the business as represented by this visioning leader. For such a leader right at the top of a global group, this clearly means that the overall global group should have primacy in employees' minds. Where the visioning leader is running a business unit in a larger group, which is itself led by an incentivizing style leader, the followers of our inspiring leader should identify primarily with this business unit and its specifically tailored, and hence relevant, vision.

The voluntary leader-to-follower relationship is, as already established, fundamentally based on mutual trust and respect. Where, as is the case for the inspirational leadership style, the required level of buy-in from followers is very high, there is a corresponding need for a very high level of trust and respect between the visioning leader and their followers. Such a high level of trust can only be built through the leader's personal attributes of integrity, consistency and transparency. Thus, the inspiring leader must continually reinforce the vision and the underlying core values through not only their words but also their actions; there really is a need for this style of leader to 'walk the talk'.

Importantly the focus on the visioning activity does not imply that this style of leader has also developed a detailed strategy that will deliver the vision. An aspirational vision sets out the grand 'where we want to get to' for the business but normally lacks any detail on the 'hows' involved in getting to this 'where'. Indeed, the explicit core values and business principles stated as part of the vision may restrict the choice of 'hows' that are available to the business. This means that continuing dialogue is required between these leaders and their followers as to the best way of achieving the agreed vision. The total trust that is required by this leadership style means that the leader must be open to real debate about the strategies that should be implemented within the organization. If such debate is unnecessarily restricted or curtailed, it is unlikely that consequently disaffected followers will maximize their discretionary inputs to the business, i.e. they will revert to being frustrated followers rather than maturely involved ones.

The inspirational leadership style also needs to generate a very high level of respect from their followers and this also is built on a foundation of the very highest integrity. The other key basis for building respect is the leader's personal ability. For this style, an inspiring leader must have the intellectual ability to develop and then articulate a compelling vision for the organization together with the capacity, to the extent necessary, to transform either the internal business or the external environment in which it operates. This means that, of our critical leadership capabilities, two in particular are very important to the visioning activity focused leader, as shown in Figure 4.3.

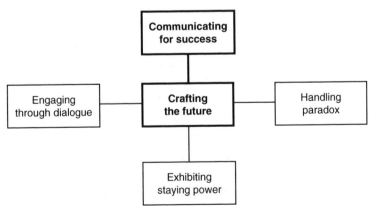

The visioning leader ideally needs all the critical leadership
capabilities but the most important are crafting
the future and communicating for success

Figure 4.3 Critical leadership capabilities: the visioning leader

The Implications of Focusing on the Visioning Activity

Crafting the future is fairly obviously the most important leadership capability for this style of leader. However, the aspirational vision, with its associated core values and more clearly measurable mission, must be developed while taking into account the needs and desires of influential potential followers. A visioning leader who insensitively powers forward in an attempt to force through a totally personal view of the future is likely to be met with substantial resistance. Even more likely is that the best, most independent-thinking and creative people will leave the organization, rendering the achievement of the aspirational vision impossible.

This means that the communicating for success capability is also very important to the inspirational leadership style. We have already stated that this capability is important to all the leadership styles, but that it has different emphases in each style. For the visioning leader, this emphasis is on surfacing the sentiments and views of potential followers so that the final vision will stimulate their enthusiasm, loyalty and positive commitment, i.e. it will inspire them to input discretionary energy to achieve this vision. Emphasizing the unique know-how-based values of the organization and the innovative ideas that will be needed to achieve the vision can help to craft a future that others will enthusiastically follow. Benchmarking the proposed vision against past and present creative heroes, and their ability to emerge with innovative solutions to complex problems, can be very powerful symbols for this style of leader.

Potential paradoxes and unwelcome challenges should be positioned as hurdles that can be overcome through the energy and ability of loyal followers. Placing emphasis on the freedom of these followers to make decisions, exercise their own initiative and try out innovative ideas is also highly motivating. Conversely, any tendency to adopt formal processes to find ways through complex problems and challenges is likely to be interpreted as an infringement of this freedom and as unwelcome bureaucracy.

Whatever challenges arise in seeking to achieve the company's vision, the inspiring leader must maintain the total trust and respect of the workforce; this style of leadership tends to be highly personalized. Thus the leaders' networks and their intensive listening skills are important. However, the style of communication is even more important as these leaders do need to engage their followers through dialogue. Any such leader who attempts to stage-manage major communication events, and does not expose themselves to the cut and thrust of real debate, is unlikely to achieve the required level of commitment, irrespective of their skills at presentation. Informality normally facilitates more effective communication, and therefore visioning-focused leaders are expected to be comfortable with informal interactions with their followers.

Informal, unstructured open communications are an ideal opportunity for these inspiring leaders to reinforce not only their vision for the company's future but also their personal knowledge and professional expertise, but not to massage their egos. Personal power that is granted on the basis of knowledge rather than dexterity with administrative processes is very valuable to this leadership style. The exhibiting staying power capability in this style means staying to see the business through the challenges that it faces as it transforms itself to achieve the vision. This depends upon their continued acceptance as the 'true leader' by their key followers. We have already argued that leaders are vulnerable because they are highly visible, at least to their followers, and they have only the personal authority that is granted to them by their followers. The visioning-focused leader is consequently potentially the most vulnerable as they need such a high level of commitment from such a large number of followers.

Key Challenges Faced by the Inspiring Leader

This requirement for a high degree of buy-in from a large proportion of the workforce is the most obvious challenge faced by a prospective inspiring leader. However, they can still be highly effective as long as they achieve very strong, positive commitment from all the significant lower-level leaders in the organization.

A more interesting challenge is that this leadership style creates value by increasing the total energy input into the business by this very broad cross-section of the workforce. This makes it very difficult, if not impossible, to give meaningful recognition to all these people; recognizing everyone's contribution can seem like recognizing no one's. Equally there is a danger associated with highlighting a limited number of specific contributions in that this can be demotivating for others who have also given freely of their best. This problem is less significant if the most important

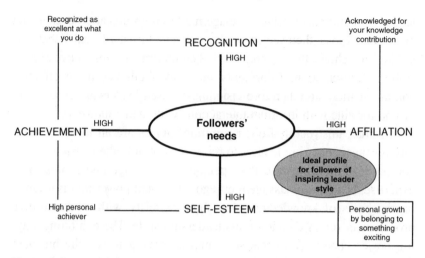

Figure 4.4 Implications of inspiring leader style for followers

needs of the key followers are for self-esteem and affiliation, as shown in Figure 4.4, with recognition and achievement being correspondingly less significant to them. Such followers will often be very satisfied simply by being part of, and particularly being enabled to make a positive contribution to, the exciting organization that the visioning leader has created.

Another key challenge for this leadership style is that the source of sustainable value creation is very commonly the creation of genuinely new know-how by the company. This does not mean that these leaders personally create the new know-how but they create the environment in which such new know-how is much more likely to be developed. This type of environment is clearly facilitated by the strong transformational and people leadership skills that are required by these leaders. Not surprisingly therefore this style of leadership is most frequently, but very definitely not only, found in highly innovative businesses that depend on the creation of new know-how for their continued survival, let alone their success. It is therefore to such an industry that we turn for our first case study of this inspirational leadership style in practice.

The Founding of Microsoft

Microsoft was founded in 1975 by Bill Gates and Paul Allen with an amazingly challenging and aspirational vision for what was initially a tiny business. This vision was 'to make software that will permit there to be a computer on every desk and in every home'. Initially they hired their brightest friends plus four experienced programmers and a key objective, even from the outset, was to hire only the very best people. Fundamental to their perception of the company's future was the ability of its people to think creatively and to use their own initiative, rather than the existing knowledge that they had when they were hired. Thus the new company rapidly developed an incredibly intensive recruitment process that involved up to ten interviews, tests of problem-solving capabilities and thought processes, and the individual's work habits.

This was formalized after 1989 when Steve Ballmer joined Microsoft and took over the coordination of recruitment; he wanted 'people who are smart, who work hard and who get things done'. In the early years, these employees all worked very long hours and developed a very strong corporate culture. The company quite deliberately recruited less people than were really needed: what was known as the 'n-1' factor. Salaries and benefits were not excessive, but staff were financially motivated by getting shares in the company with the result that many became paper millionaires following the Initial Public Offering of Microsoft shares in 1986. This made Bill Gates a billionaire at the age of 31 and subsequently a number of other Microsoft employees have achieved this level of wealth as well.

However, the first major products of the company were very pragmatic solutions to major opportunities. The first personal computer kit product was launched in 1975, the Altair by MITS, and Microsoft adapted BASIC to create a condensed version called PCBASIC, for this new product. However, the licensing rights were owned by MITS so that Microsoft could not itself sell its PCBASIC product to any of the clones that rapidly appeared on the market. Eventually, after a legal battle, Microsoft regained its product rights and walked away from the Altair product.

This move was important as it signalled the start of Microsoft's drive to make software independent of specific computer manufacturers. Up until this point, the power in the industry had been with the hardware manufacturers as software was customized to optimize the performance of the hardware. Microsoft set out to create an industry standard software product that would run on anybody's hardware. This had great appeal to applications programmers as they would not have to rewrite completely all their applications software for all the different manufacturers.

Achieving this common platform meant that the software was not efficient in its usage of computing resources, but hardware costs were now starting to fall rapidly and computing power was increasing exponentially. Thus Microsoft's timing was right. By 1979 Microsoft had contracts for PCBASIC from around 50 original equipment manufacturers (OEMs) and annual sales revenues were over $1 million.

In 1980 IBM decided to enter the already rapidly growing PC market and it was in a hurry. Consequently it outsourced the processor to Intel and wanted an external supplier for both the software languages and the new concept of an operating system for its PC. Microsoft offered both products to IBM within its one-year launch time-frame, even though it did not have an operating system. It bought a system called Q-DOS (Quick and Dirty Operating System) that was really a clone of Digital Research's market-leading system, CPM. The redeveloped system was named MS-DOS but, this time, Microsoft retained the third-party licensing rights and made MS-DOS an 'open' system so that programming specifications were published. This was done to encourage applications developers to write MS-DOS-based products. By the end of the 1980s Microsoft had locked in virtually all the major global players and had very high sales revenues from MS-DOS with incredibly strong gross margins.

Microsoft was therefore then able to implement in full its long-term corporate strategy for dominance of the software industry. A key element in building its initial leadership position was its emphasis on 'get the customer first, deliver the technology later', as shown by its first two major products. The next stage was that the product must deliver for all the potential customer groups, even though their requirements were different. Previously software providers had normally focused on only one group rather than embracing OEMs, application developers, systems integrators, distributors and end-users. If this total coverage could be achieved, then Microsoft's products could become the industry standard, around which all the other elements making up the industry would have to fit. This was helped by a very aggressive marketing strategy that included flat-fee pricing to encourage OEMs to incorporate Microsoft's software in every machine that they shipped. Once established as the industry standard, the pricing was switched to a per machine rate.

With each new development in the industry, Microsoft has looked for ways to further strengthen its position as the industry standard: by linking its products, by linking with other leading players such as SAP, and by continuing to use its aggressive marketing strategies.

Potential problems

At the time of the group's flotation in 1986, Microsoft had around 1,200 employees and it moved to its campus site in Redmond, 10 miles east of Seattle. Each employee had a standard small office that they could decorate as they wanted and the site had a subsidized cafeteria, free coffee, etc., as people still spent a lot of their time at work. Bill Gates kept reorganizing the business into small work groups and he personally monitored 100 bi-weekly status reports from project and program development teams. He still had an immense personal impact on the business through his high energy, challenging involvement at many levels. He was a classic visioning activity-focused leader of the group during this period. The management process during this period was therefore flexible and informal, although the company always used specific quantifiable objectives that were reviewed every six months: SMART objectives–specific, **m**easurable, **a**ttainable, **r**esults-based and **t**ime-bound. Reviews focused on learning from mistakes and the culture (fuelled by Bill Gates) was that the feedback was blunt and to the point.

By the mid-1990s, the company was scanning all 25,000 US-based computer science graduates to get 400 new hires, but it needed many more than this. It needed to hire several thousand people as the group continued to grow rapidly and it had 300 full-time recruiters to fulfil its aim of hiring only the best; this was restated as 'hiring better than they already had'. Inevitably, as the total employees grew to over 20,000 the organization went through many changes and lost its original small company feel.

In 1996 Robert Herbold joined Microsoft as Chief Operating Officer after 26 years with Procter & Gamble. As discussed in Chapter 6, Procter & Gamble is a very good example of an enabling style of leadership. He defined recruitment as being Microsoft's No.1 Core Competence, and made identifying future leaders into a more formal process. Thus the group moved to a key people review process that sought to achieve early identification and career planning. The objective was to create a group of better leaders and managers who would be capable of 'clearing the obstacles, making decisions quickly and defining clear goals'. This meant that Gates, Ballmer (he was made President in 1998), and Herbold would need to allow these new leaders to lead. Bill Gates then had 16 people in his Business Leadership Team and the process identified three waves of high potential future leaders.

However, this meant that the group had to review its employee feedback and development process. What about all the significant contributors to the company who were not identified as future leaders? How were these people to be developed, motivated and retained? To long-term employees, it was crystal clear what it took to succeed at Microsoft but this was not true for the vast majority who had joined a much larger group in the more recent past. The Microsoft 'Competency Model' identified six success factors: taking a long-term approach to people and technology; getting results; individual excellence; a passion for products and technology; customer feedback; and teamwork. These factors were turned into 29 individual competences, with four levels of performance for each, so that performance reviews could be more formally compared across the organization.

Unfortunately, such formality is not an adequate substitute for the much earlier 'meetings with Bill', which had quite rapidly identified those employees who fully matched up to Microsoft's competency model. This problem was acknowledged by the group when it started to lose very good people. In-depth employee interviews highlighted complexity and bureaucracy as being major problems and the company sought to give its employees a new way of setting priorities, objectives and understanding what leadership in the group should mean. Very importantly, this was encapsulated in a new corporate vision that replaced the almost achieved 'a PC on every desk and in every home'. 'Giving people the power to do anything they want, anywhere they want, and on any device' should be a sufficiently aspirational and challenging vision to motivate the business units to cooperate together to find completely new ways of moving forward.

To facilitate this, Steve Ballmer was appointed CEO and the group was reorganized into eight new groups that are attuned to customers' needs rather than around technology issues. These new business units have more delegated authority, with Ballmer acting as a 'leader of leaders' in the company's words. In our words, he is acting in the enabling leadership style, with the business unit leaders focusing on the delivering activity. These business units have very recently been reorganized once again to try to achieve even more clarity and focus for their own leadership teams. The group is also seeking to influence the working culture, with Steve Ballmer publicly stating that he does not work weekends any more. This new structure has enabled Bill Gates to become exclusively Chairman of the group and has freed him to revert to the original visioning-focused leader role that created the business. He can challenge the business unit leaders, and can also get involved in specific projects from time to time, but his main value-creating role is to be the personal embodiment of the vision and set of values that underpin Microsoft.

Reinventing the group

This refocusing of Bill Gates as the overall inspirational leader of the group, but now supported by other senior executives who are also acknowledged as having significant and complementary leadership roles, should reinvigorate the long-term sustainability of the business. The group is operating in a very dynamic environment and needs to develop new group skills to compete successfully once end-users no longer buy software but download it as and when they need it. The visioning activity-focused leadership style is suited to such a dynamic environment as its informality and flexibility enable the positively committed followers to exercise their own initiative to find the radically new ways of working that are required as the external environment changes. The risk for all such companies is that, as they grow into much larger organizations, their processes become over-formalized and bureaucratic.

Effectively, the group is moving to an enabling leadership style with its focus on the connecting activity. This is better suited to a more stable environment where knowledge developed in one part of the business can be leveraged elsewhere. In Microsoft's case, the perceived need to formalize and codify the critically important people management processes started to lead to the standardization of processes and skills that is more relevant to the enabling leadership style. The visioning leader focuses on standardizing the values that underpin the aspirational vision that makes employees want to be value-creating contributors to the business. It is all too easy for rapidly growing companies unwittingly to change the leadership styles at their top, particularly when senior executives join from outside groups that are themselves very good examples of a different style of leadership.

However, it is also possible for a large group to make these transitions when its management is completely home-grown. Indeed, as was discussed in Chapter 2 in the case of IBM, it took an external appointment to take the group back to its origins with a visioning activity-focused leader at its head.

The Origins of IBM

In 1911 a merger of two small companies created the Computing, Tabulating, Recording Company but by 1914 the new company was in some trouble. It therefore recruited an outsider, Tom Watson Senior, to sort out its problems. He took over a business making mechanical devices for processing data and, from it, eventually created the modern IBM. The company had some further financial problems but, in 1924, Watson changed its name to the extremely aspirational International Business Machines and started to build the core values that were to be so important to IBM's later growth. He felt very strongly that beliefs come before policies, practices and goals, and he wanted to bring out the full energy and talent of the company's employees. In fact, Tom Watson openly admitted that he wanted to create an organization of zealots, who would all totally buy in to the vision of 'meeting the emerging needs of our customers' through 'selling service'. The company motto became 'Think', and everyone should 'go the last mile to do things right and seek superiority in all we undertake'.

The world-famous IBM culture was therefore built up in this period: well-groomed men wearing dark suits with white shirts and dark blue ties, no smoking, no alcohol, and marriage was encouraged. Watson instituted a 'promote from within' policy and liked IBMers to socialize together to reinforce the culture. In the 1930s, by which time IBM was market leader in tabulating machines, the company had its own 'schoolhouse' where employees sang IBM songs and stories about 'heroes' were told so that the company's beliefs were truly institutionalized.

A key element of this vision and set of values was that it was focused on the customer rather than being product-centric. This made it easier for IBM, in the post-Second World War period, to adapt to the rapid growth of the typewriter market. In the 1950s, as a result, IBM had 72,000 employees and sales revenues of over $500 million.

Although IBM did not pioneer the computer revolution, it embraced it so emphatically that it rapidly came to dominate the new industry. Using its size, sales-force muscle and marketing skills it had taken an 80 per cent share of the US computer market by the end of the 1960s. IBM's customer focus led it to move internationally as its major customers did, and from this existing customer-led strategy it then built leading market shares in many other countries as well.

The growth in sales revenues was very impressive (from $7 billion in 1970 to $40 billion in 1980), but the profits growth was even more impressive. In 1980, IBM had a 38 per cent share of the global computer industry's sales revenues but a 60 per cent share of its profits. This enabled the group to reinvest vast sums in research and development, massively outspending its competitors. At the end of the 1980s IBM was spending $9 billion a year on R&D.

Problems set in

John Akers, a lifetime IBMer, took over as Chairman and CEO in 1985 and publicly predicted that IBM's sales revenues would grow in ten years to $180 billion from their $46 billion level in 1984. This would still have been a slower annualized rate of growth than in the previous ten years. As a result of this growth expectation, IBM built an infrastructure capable of coping with this size of business so that the group had over 400,000 employees by the end of 1986.

Although IBM's sales were growing in several areas, its major source of profits was much more focused. As already discussed, IBM was late into the PC market but very quickly became market leader. Unfortunately, even with $10 billion of sales revenues this business unit was not shareholder value enhancing. Mainframe computers contributed the vast majority (60 per cent) of IBM's profits, due not only to their high share of total sales revenues but also to their very high gross profit margins (over 50 per cent). This was a market that IBM totally dominated, having a 44 per cent global market share and an 85 per cent share in the USA of the compatible mainframe market.

The problem for IBM was that this was one sector in the computer industry that was no longer growing. Increasingly computer systems were moving to client-server networks rather than the very large mainframes in which IBM excelled. This trend started in the mid-1980s but had grown dramatically as personal computing power and networking capability mushroomed. By 1994 client servers accounted for 50 per cent of total applications in the USA. What is particularly interesting is how closely IBM had been involved in these technological developments.

For example, Reduced Instruction Set Computing (RISC) is considered absolutely key to high performance work stations. RISC was invented by an IBMer, John Coske, but was initially exploited by Sun Microsystems and Hewlett Packard. In the early 1990s both these companies launched microprocessor-based multiple parallel processor computers that were the equivalent of mainframes. This increased the competitive pressure that had been started by Digital Equipment Corporation (DEC) in 1989 with the launch of its first line of mainframe computers; these were priced at half the level of IBM's existing products. By 1993 it was estimated that traditional mainframe computing power was 5–8 times more expensive than these newer technologies.

The financial impact of this was dramatic. IBM's hardware gross margins were slashed from 55 per cent to 38 per cent on sales revenues that fell 20 per cent in two years. This meant a $10 billion fall in actual gross profits, from 1990 to 1992. The published financial results were also heavily impacted by the very large provisions that were made for headcount reductions ($6.7 billion in 1991, $11.6 billion in 1992); total headcount was back down to 300,000 by the end of 1992. The net results were that IBM reported losses for 1991 and 1992 of $2.8 billion and $5.0 billion after a profit of $6.0 billion in 1990.

Not surprisingly, the share price went into free-fall hitting around $40 early in 1993, having peaked at $175 in the mid-1980s. At the same time Standard & Poors, the credit-rating agency, downgraded IBM from AAA (as good as it gets) to AA– (a significant fall). Indeed, there were several leading newspaper and magazine articles that openly discussed the possibility of IBM going bust. It was into this situation that a second outsider was to be introduced on 1 April 1993. Lou Gerstner's leadership impact has already been discussed in Chapter 2 but there are clearly parallels with the previous visioning-focused leader role of Tom Watson Senior.

IBM's initial vision under Tom Watson Senior was to 'sell service' and to 'meet the emerging needs of our customers' and its initial dominance of the computer industry was achieved employing exactly those ideas. It was an expert at 'relationship marketing' before the term had been invented. Its sales force had unrivalled access to the key strategic decision-makers in the major US corporations and they acted almost as strategic consultants rather than computer sales people. Not surprisingly, IBM focused primarily on the largest customers and these were the companies that needed big mainframe computers to process the mass of data that was critical to their businesses. Thus the product and the specific technology were driven by the customers' needs.

It should therefore have been relatively easy for IBM, with its very close relationship with these customers, to have identified 'their emerging need' for distributed processing and networking before its competitors. Given its huge R&D expenditure levels it should also have been quite possible for it to have developed the technology before anybody else. (Remember that, in fact, IBM did develop a lot of this technology but did not itself bring it to the marketplace.)

However, by this time, IBM's business units were being run by technologists and the leaders at the corporate centre had seemingly lost sight of their key role within the group. In Lou Gerstner's words, 'the company started to believe that it knew what was best for customers, rather than finding out what customers wanted and then giving it to them'. Also, unfortunately for IBM, at this time competitors were becoming much smarter and the external competitive environment was changing rapidly.

Competitors had gradually realized that they could not compete head-on with a company as dominant as IBM. Therefore most existing competitors started to focus on specific segments of the IT industry, but equally specialist competitors were being attracted to enter the new, very high-growth areas. IBM was facing 'death by a thousand cuts' rather than a knock-out blow by a single competitor.

Customers were also becoming more knowledgeable about the technology that had become so vital to the continued success of their own businesses. In the early years of the computer industry, IBM's brand name had stood for the low risk, reliable solution to your computing needs: it even used the maxim 'no one ever got fired for buying IBM'. The strength of this reputation enabled IBM to obtain premium pricing even for 'me-too' technology. Yet its massive volume meant that its costs were the lowest in the industry, hence it generated incredibly high margins. Customers eventually became unwilling to pay a premium for the IBM name on the blue box. They were also much happier to have a range of computer suppliers, preferring to pick the best company for each particular element of their IT requirements.

Again IBM's dominant position in the industry should have given it fore-warning of these changes but it had obviously stopped looking outside of itself to predict the future. As already discussed in this chapter, visioning-focused leadership is most suitable for such a dramatically changing external environment. Unfortunately for IBM, its top team was not operating in this leadership style when its industry went through this dramatic upheaval. The good news is that the second coming of an outsider re-established this inspiring leader style and enabled the group to recapture its previous focus on creating new know-how that is relevant to its customers.

The 3M Example

Visioning activity-focused leadership is the most sustainable way for a top team at the corporate centre to create shareholder value. The continuing creation of new know-how can enable a group effectively to reinvent itself as its external environment changes, so that there is no reason for the group's value creation to cease.

Having said this, establishing and then maintaining a value-creating inspiring leader style at the corporate centre is also much more difficult than all the other styles of leadership. The need to get a high level of buy-in to the group's vision and values from the vast majority of people in the business creates a significant challenge for any corporate centre, let alone one that is inevitably physically remote from its underlying business units. This can be particularly difficult during a transitional period where the leaders at the top of the organization are, of necessity, also having to force through other changes. Lou Gerstner's need to continue with the severe cost-cutting programmes made it even more problematical to establish a credible new vision for IBM.

However, sending out tough messages should not be seen as being incompatible with inspirational leadership. Value-creating leadership in really innovative companies is not vague and fuzzy. These leaders are very demanding, set stretching visions with tough values standards that have to be lived up to, and they are totally focused on creating value. This can be reinforced by considering the development, from a very unpromising beginning, of the 3M company, as to many people it represents the archetypal innovative group.

3M was founded in 1902 as a corundum mine, but the quality of the output from the mine was so poor that only 1 ton was ever sold to the original target customers. The company struggled for several years, using the poor quality abrasive output to make sandpaper before, in 1914, it developed its first innovative product, a cloth abrasive. The general manager, William McKnight, was an accountant who had become a sales manager but, fortunately for the group, he had an insatiable curiosity and great leadership ability. Following the near collapse of the company originally dependent on a single product, McKnight was also determined to build a diversified portfolio of products. Hence he encouraged experimentation, along with the associated learning failures. An early example of such a failure was a move into car wax and polish in 1924 that had to be abandoned. However, the contact with automobile paint shops generated another opportunity that was to be spectacularly successful. There was a need for a foolproof masking tape for this market and 3M invented one. Later, when customers wanted a waterproof packaging tape, the group developed its masking tape technology to what ultimately became the Scotch tape range.

Similar stories abound in the history of 3M, including the world-famous development of 3M's 'Post-it Notes', but the critical element is that 3M institutionalized the evolutionary process that resulted in these innovations very early in its life cycle. From 1925 onwards, its technical manual specified that 'every idea should have a chance to prove its worth' so that the group had an ideas 'generating and testing' process. These ideas had to be genuinely new and they had to meet a demonstrable human need.

In order to generate new ideas the group has its 15 per cent rule, under which technical staff are allowed to spend 15 per cent of their time on projects of their own choice. Staff can also receive a technology-sharing award when one of their ideas is shared with and taken up by another business unit. 3M has always kept the group broken up into small autonomous divisions with an ideal size of around 100 people and $250 million in sales revenues. This means that most new ideas will have a significant impact on the business unit, while this may not be true at the group level given that there are now over 40 product divisions and over 60,000 internally developed products ranging from roofing granules through various types of tapes to bioelectronic cars.

Group structure
Each business unit has its own laboratories that are essential to the future of the division and the group; thus there are nearly 200 laboratories

working on well over 1,000 new product developments at any point in time. These are coordinated by the central technical function that identifies and then disseminates new technologies. There is a very strong culture that products can belong to the business unit but the technology belongs to the group and should be shared. This is facilitated by regular technical forums to discuss new ideas and there is an annual technology fair where marketing and production staff can see what is being developed.

Indeed, 3M's technical employees are heavily linked into the marketing process and many marketing managers started their careers in research and development. Sales and marketing are meant to understand in depth exactly how products are used by customers and to feed this back to their technical colleagues. Also the technical director at each business unit acts in a customer liaison role, as understanding specific customer problems has created many new product opportunities for the group.

Each product division is meant to fund its own growth by investing in R&D but the corporate centre can get involved in particularly high-profile projects. These are those identified to have both the potential to generate significant levels of shareholder value and to change the basis of competition in the specific marketplace, i.e. the new product should continue to produce super profits for several years as competitors will take time to catch up. For these projects, the corporate centre can provide ring-fenced funding and a dedicated business team, including technical and financial support from the centre where necessary. It is quite possible that the new product may lead to the creation of a new business unit if it is very successful.

Thus the corporate strategy stresses new product development through a decentralized structure but with the emphasis on business unit performance.

Performance measures used
One way of keeping the emphasis on new products and technological innovation is to set targets regarding the proportion of sales revenues that must come from new product launches. In 3M the objective for all business units is that 30 per cent of sales revenues should be derived from products launched in the last four years. The group also looks for a 25 per cent rate of return on sales revenues, as its products should be

in the early stages of their technology life cycles when selling price is not the critical basis of competition.

The group has also been gradually introducing the concept of economic profit in order to get a more direct linkage into shareholder value at the business unit level. This financial discipline is achieved by having financial analysts integrated into every business team. Their role is to educate all the team members in the key financial risk and return relationships for this innovative group. In reality 3M is relatively risk-averse in that it is very happy to experiment and have failures as long as these failures are on a small scale. It also emphasizes acknowledging when something isn't working and closing it down, rather than keeping it going to see if it will somehow turn itself around. Also cost management is inbuilt into the culture and reinforced by the team-based financial analysts. With this financial knowledge and culture spread throughout the business units, corporate leadership at the very top of the group can focus on stimulating the creation of new know-how, confident that its business units have the competences and incentives to translate this know-how into shareholder value.

Embedding this financial focus within the business units enables the inspirational leadership style at the top of the group to concentrate on developing and communicating the critically important vision and set of values that bind the group together. The incentivizing leadership style centre focuses on the financial performance of the business units, and normally their short-term performance. It does this because there is no overriding group vision or common set of values, other than making more money, that justifies the business units remaining as part of the group. As discussed in Part 1 and developed in Chapter 5, this makes it much easier for the incentivizing style leader dramatically to change the portfolio of businesses comprising the group than it is for a visioning-focused one.

This eventually places a strain on the inspiring leader style as the core business units compete in increasingly mature markets. In 3M's case, 75 per cent of the group's products use technologies that coat something with something else. The group has lots of patents and other forms of protectable technology and deliberately markets many niche products, although most are sold in office products, automotive and metalworking markets. It prefers to be No.1 or No.2 in each market where it competes; if the niche market is quite small, 3M can dominate it while still keeping its business units small. However, as these markets mature, selling price is likely to become a more important factor and this will increase the pressure to realize economies of scale in manufacturing. If this happened 3M's smaller business units could become a disadvantage. To date, of course, the group has avoided this pressure for change by continuing to create innovative new products that do not compete primarily on selling price. There is another even larger group that has also used the inspirational leadership style to avoid becoming forced to compete primarily on price.

Another Inspiring Leader Role

This style of leadership is normally critically important to the success of the company in which it is applied as it should have a transformational, rather than transactional, focus. The inspiring leader is seeking to change what the group does, rather than merely make it more efficient at doing what it does already. Interestingly this is often achieved in a seemingly tangential way due to the indirect involvement of the leader at the corporate centre in the day-to-day operations of the business units. However, although the involvement may be indirect, a 'true' leader can have a dramatic impact on the underlying businesses through the establishment of the group's vision and underpinning set of values. These can be established at such a challenging level that the business units have to revolutionize their ways of doing business if they are to have any chance of achieving the vision set by their corporate centre. This makes the business units much more likely to cooperate with each other to try to find new ways of working, or new products, etc., that may make the challenge achievable.

Of course, the leaders in this corporate centre must be able to win the total commitment of the business unit managers to the group's vision. This is the ultimate test of their leadership capabilities and a successful, continually innovative group needs visioning leaders who can win the hearts and minds of most of the people in the group. With the 'shareholder' style of leadership the grudging acceptance of, and reluctant compliance with, the targets set by the corporate centre is almost all that is required, but this would be completely unacceptable to an inspiring leader. Hopefully, the examples already used have demonstrated how this inspirational leadership style can create value in growing companies and changing external environments.

It is now very common for companies to have a very general vision that can never actually be achieved and to motivate employees by establishing very stretching but just about achievable missions. These stretching missions must be measurable and should have a completion date, which makes it easier for the leader at the corporate centre to move the target as this completion date gets closer. Thus, although the inspirational leadership style emphasizes the corporate vision and accompanying set of values, this leadership is not soft and cuddly. In successful such groups this leadership style sets very demanding standards, both for itself and the business units within the group. GE, under Jack Welch as Chairman and CEO, is an excellent illustration of such a demanding inspiring leader style being successfully implemented at the corporate centre of a vast business empire.

Jack Welch took over a very successful company in 1981 that had already had a succession of very highly regarded chairmen and CEOs. Indeed, a critical element in GE's continued success was the emphasis that the group put on developing the best general managers. For example, the selection process that ended with Welch becoming Chairman and CEO began in 1974 when a number of internal candidates for the job were identified. Virtually all the losing candidates went on to become CEOs of other major companies.

Jack Welch implemented the concept of 'integrated diversity', which meant 'the drawing together of GE's different businesses by sharing ideas, by finding multiple applications for technological advancements, and by moving people across businesses to provide fresh perspectives and to develop broad based experience'. This constant focus on innovation across the group was brought into stark focus through a series of very challenging group-wide mission statements from the corporate centre.

The first of these was made in 1981 and was 'Be No.1 or No.2 in your industry, or get out'. This was done to refocus the group after a period of very diversified growth in the 1970s, and resulted in a high level of divestments and acquisitions soon after Jack Welch took over. In some cases the challenge to improve a business unit's industry ranking necessitated a dramatic change in its way of working and resulted in cross-divisional initiatives as radically new solutions were sought.

In the second half of the 1980s Jack Welch identified another group-wide challenge that was to cut through the bureaucracy within the group. A 'work-out' initiative was launched across the group that was literally designed 'to take work out of business processes', i.e. to re-engineer business processes in the business units. The key is that this initiative was stimulated by leadership from the corporate centre but implemented by the business units themselves. The process was started in 1988 and by 1992 over 200,000 employees in the group had been through work-out training. Each business unit's employees were able to propose 'bureaucracy busting' initiatives and the business unit's top management had to give an *immediate* 'Yes or No' response. This created a dramatic change in GE's organizational culture from its previously centre-driven 'command and control' to a much more participative style that tries to realize the full potential of all employees. An important element in this mission was to transform the group internally so that it 'developed the sensitivity, the leanness, the simplicity and the agility of a small company'.

However, the biggest change was stimulated by Jack Welch's third major initiative. In order to avoid becoming forced to sell increasingly commodity-style products to ever more powerful customers, GE sought to move into selling total solutions to a customer's problems. This involved building much closer relationships with many customers and understanding the 'total cost in use' to the customer rather than merely the selling price gained by GE as a supplier. As a result GE moved much more into the provision of services than it ever had before and this was only practical if its business divisions worked closely together. Thus GE Capital, which had previously focused almost exclusively on consumer finance, became involved in offering financing deals on many of GE's big-ticket technology products. For example, in 1993 GE Capital became the largest aeroplane leasing company in the world following its deal with the financially troubled GPA group. GE did not stop at financing and, in jet engines, the group manufactures, provides financing, performs maintenance for the airlines and sells spare parts. Following its acquisition of airline overhaul facilities, it also maintains jet engines produced by its competitors. The divisions still work in a highly decentralized way and develop their own competitive strategies that, in the case of both GE Capital and Aero-Engines, can clearly involve significant acquisitions. In addition they share ideas and work together to find new applications for technical innovations.

The next major initiative was in improving quality through its now famous 'Six Sigma' quality programme that aimed to eliminate defects by the year 2000. Once again, the visioning-focused leadership specified the scale of the challenge and the business units had to create the know-how to achieve the required improvement in quality. A critical element in this is the sharing of ideas across the group so that the idea can be developed and improved by other divisions. This is greatly facilitated by the group's internal business school that uses ideas from within GE and both develops and disseminates them. The role of Crotonville, which is where the business school is located, is therefore to accelerate the process of spreading existing knowledge around the group, so that it can be improved and transformed into genuinely new know-how. Jack Welch was a frequent visitor to, and speaker on, the programmes being run at Crotonville, using the opportunities to reinforce the group's vision and values. The regular rotation of senior managers around the business units further reinforces this concept of redesigning the business before it is broken.

Yet GE also believes in delivering results in the short term as well as transforming itself to be more competitive in the future. Throughout Jack Welch's 20 years in charge of the group, its earnings per share grew in every year and indeed in every quarter of every year. Obviously there can occasionally be a conflict between 'delivering the numbers and sharing the group's values', particularly where the values are as clearly stated as they are for GE. The group states that it believes in 'honesty and integrity, individual responsibility and opportunity, and an interdependent balance between responsibility to customers, employees, society and shareholders'. As Jack Welch himself might have put it, 'If you make the numbers and share our values, that's great; share the values but miss the numbers and you get a second chance; miss the numbers and don't share the values and you leave. Those who make the numbers, but do not share the values cause the biggest problems to the business as it agonizes over whether they can be made to buy into the group's values.'

Continually Creating new know-how

As already stated, the most obvious examples of the inspirational leadership style would appear to be those that are totally dependent upon the creation of new know-how for their survival, let alone continued success, e.g. technology-led groups.

A brief consideration of the Canon group and the role of its 2,000-strong corporate centre may reinforce this. Canon was founded in 1933 as the Precision Optical Research Laboratory, from which it developed its base in precision mechanics to fine optics. It has been producing lenses in-house since 1939 and developed an X-ray camera in 1940. From here, it moved into new technologies such as medical equipment, semiconductors and microelectronics producing calculators, copiers, word processors and computer peripherals. The group has always retained the manufacture of key value-adding components in-house.

The top leadership team sees its main role as the development and constant re-emphasizing of the vision of the company. It believes that technological leadership is critical to its future success and that this depends upon innovation across both technologies and existing product groups. This explains the centralization of basic technology research that may have relevance to more than one business group. Canon is organized into global product divisions with local sales units, so that its primary strategic drivers are the product groups with the geographic regions and functional disciplines playing a secondary role. Consequently, the centralized Research & Development and Marketing resources are accountable to the individual product groups. This means that while *all resources* are seen as belonging to the group, they are effectively 'loaned out' to the business units to work on cross-functional projects. These task forces have the authority to make their own decisions and have been responsible for several major new product innovations.

The creation of this large 'virtual' corporate centre allows most managers to pass through it at least once in their career and this creates a very strong identification with the group, rather than with their original business unit. As was shown in Figure 4.2, this is very important to the organizational culture needed in the inspirational leadership style-led organization, where employees should identify with the group before their own division. If most managers 'pass through the centre' and realize that they still retain a great deal of managerial discretion and authority when working there, there is likely to be the high level of trust between the corporate centre and the business units that is also essential in this leadership style.

However, this process also provides the top leadership team with the ability to challenge the performance of the business units, particularly with regard to innovation but also regarding cost structures. This should result in a healthy and constructive debate between the centre and the business units about the strategy that is required to deliver the centre's challenging vision. In a successful group such as Canon, the business units should consequently view the visioning activity-focused leadership at the corporate centre as being value creating and, indeed, essential to the continued success of the group.

Visioning Leaders at Other Levels

In this chapter we have concentrated on examples of visioning activity-focused leaders operating right at the top of their organizations, even though we have already argued that this inspirational leadership style can also be value creating at much lower levels in any hierarchy. This emphasis has been for two main reasons. First the value-creation impact of this leadership style at the top of the company is, not surprisingly, normally far greater than when the role only impacts upon a part of the total business. Second, hopefully, readers can relate much more readily to the case study examples of well-known companies and, in some cases, their equally famous visioning leaders, than to an example of a specific business division or support function within a much less well-known organization.

However, this is in no way meant to downplay the potential importance of the inspiring leader style at these other organizational levels. One very common example of this is where the corporate centre of a group adopts an incentivizing style of leadership, thus effectively delegating the visioning activity to the leaders of the decentralized business units that make up the group, as shown in Figure 4.5. As already stated, this requires that the business unit leaders obtain a much higher level of buy-in to their business unit from the vast majority of their direct employees than is needed towards the overall group.

They can achieve this by developing, for *their* business unit, a very specifically tailored, aspirational vision to which employees can directly relate. Thus, these employees are much more likely to become positively committed to their business unit-based leader than to the incentivizing style leader located at the top of the overall group. In this type of group, this can result in a range of differing visions being implemented at these lower organizational levels. Indeed, in some extremely decentralized groups, some of these tailored visions even

125

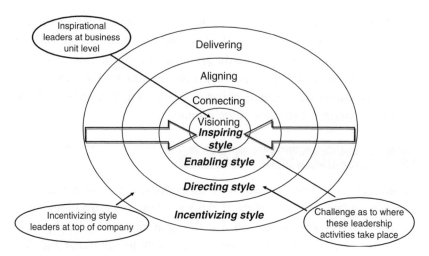

Figure 4.5 Out-to-in leadership framework: inspirational leaders at business unit level

have their own specific core values that also differ from others in use across the other business divisions.

What is particularly interesting is what happens when these leaders change their management roles. They have, over time, developed a successful inspirational leadership style at the business unit, divisional or regional level in an incentivizing style-led group. One possibility is that this leader is then promoted to the top job, i.e. CEO, in the group. Do they then continue with their own proven leadership style, which involves a dramatic change for their new potential followers right across the group? This is, in effect, what Jack Welch did when he was made Chairman and CEO of the whole of GE. Prior to his appointment, GE had been famous for its structured and relatively formal planning process that was administered from the corporate centre with stretching targets being passed down to the otherwise decentralized business units. The group was becoming ever more diversified through a vast array of acquisitions in seemingly unrelated industries. In the terms of our model, we would have regarded GE, at this time, as implementing the incentivizing style of leadership.

This was to change rather emphatically with the promotion of Jack Welch as he imposed his own preferred style of leadership on the group. As already mentioned, most of his rivals for this top job at

126

GE went on to become CEOs of other major groups. They were also mainly visioning-focused leaders when they were running decentralized business divisions within GE. Therefore, they also had to choose whether to stick to this successful style, and to try to apply it not only in a completely different business context, but also at a different level in the organization. The alternative in any situation is obviously to alter their current leadership style to the one which is already being applied at the top of their new organization. Of course, where the new leader is recruited from outside the organization, it is possible that there is no conflict between their current leadership style and the style of the leader that they are replacing. As is discussed in more depth in Chapter 8, this is much less likely when the potential new leader is promoted from within the business. The consequence is that there is risk associated with a change in leader, even from within the organization. Either the promoted leader has to change style to fit with the existing style at this level of the organization or the potential followers have to adjust to and accept their new leader's different style.

Another increasingly common example of the inspirational leadership style below the top of an organization is within the shared service centres and other centralized support areas that now exist in many large groups. This initiative to change the organization structure in order to achieve the economies of scale that can result from such standardization of activities involves our directing style of leadership, with its focus on the aligning activity. However, once set up, these centralized activities need both managing and leading. The directing style emphasizes strategic leadership and only requires a high degree of buy-in from those very few people who are most directly affected by the proposed change.

However, a much larger number of people, i.e. all those who work in these new organizational structures, are also affected by these changes. They may no longer have a strong sense of affiliation with the business unit of which they used to be an integral part but the overall group leadership may be too remote to generate any positive commitment from these potential followers. This is, of course, particularly true if the group top team is implementing the incentivizing style of leadership. There is a possible inspiring leader role within such focused subdivisions of the organization. The inspiring leaders at this level can develop a tailored vision so that their employees can achieve a genuine sense of belonging and affiliation to each of these areas that can be much stronger than to the overall group of which they are now part. There is, however, a challenge for these potential 'true' leaders who are, themselves, followers of a 'manager' style leader; this challenge is considered in Chapter 8.

Conclusion

The inspirational leadership style, with its focus on the visioning activity, is potentially the most value-creating style of leadership and the most difficult to sustain. This is because it requires a very high level of buy-in from the greatest number of people across the organization. If this is achieved, these willing followers should increase the total energy input into the organization, so that extraordinary results can be achieved by the business.

This requires a vision that really motivates and inspires the workforce. The focus of the inspirational leadership style is therefore on people and transformational leadership. The high level of buy-in demands complete trust and respect between the visioning leader and their followers. This is true irrespective of the level in the organization at which this style is being implemented. Ideally all employees should be positively committed to one leader; this means that the inspirational leadership style will be needed at some level in all organizations.

5

Focusing on the delivering leadership activity

The inspirational leadership style discussed in the previous chapter is found at the top of our most commonly found 'in-to-out' leadership framework. The other very common framework is described within our model as 'out-to-in' and this has the incentivizing style of leadership right at the top of the organization. Therefore this is logically the next style to be considered in depth.

An incentivizing style leader at the top of an organization is often located in a small, financially-focused corporate centre physically removed from the group's portfolio of relatively independent business units. Such a leader is primarily concerned with the end results both promised and delivered by these autonomous units rather than with the detailed competitive strategies implemented by each business. The best examples of this leadership style develop world-leading expertise in the corporate governance areas of financial management and planning and control so that stretching, but not completely unrealistic, targets can be set and appropriately tailored, but mainly financial, performance measures are established for each of these underlying businesses.

The alternative 'shareholder' descriptor for this style of leadership was selected because it encapsulates the idea of the leader acting as a well-informed controlling shareholder in the underlying businesses, and this represents one of the major differences of this leadership style.

This implies a predominantly financial attachment to any of these businesses and hence a willingness to sever the attachment if it ceases to be value creating. The focus of this leadership style is quite simply on improving the financial performance of these businesses. If this can no longer be achieved for a particular business unit, this delivering activity-focused leader should consider divesting this particular business and acquiring a new one where its leadership capabilities can once again create value.

Thus, as shown in Figure 5.1, the key skills required by shareholder style leaders include corporate finance so as to facilitate the acquisitions and divestments that may be needed in order dynamically to change the portfolio of businesses comprising the group. Indeed, this ability actively to manage their portfolio of businesses represents the key challenge to this leadership style if it is to sustain its creation of value. A very clear example of this is provided by a quote from Lord Hanson, the founder and leader of the Hanson plc group that is used later in this chapter as an example of this leadership style. He said of his group of companies, 'everything is potentially for sale, it is just a matter of price'. In other words, if Hanson received an offer for any of its businesses that was above its internal assessment of the ongoing value of the business to the group, it was willing to sell it; and it frequently did. It did not therefore have anything that it regarded as a core business. Such a sale would be most likely to occur once Hanson had

Key value-creating activity	Delivering
Focus of leader	Improving financial performance
Key skills required	Corporate governance/finance
Key leadership challenge	Portfolio management

Figure 5.1 Focus of incentivizing style leaders

improved, as far as it could, the financial performance of this business, so that the future potential growth in profits and cash generation was expected to be much less dramatic.

This highlights the other key skill required by these delivering activity-focused leaders, which is corporate governance skill or expertise in planning and control. We use the delivering activity in the sense of setting free a business to deliver its full potential and this is achieved through the establishment of stretching targets by these corporate leaders. These targets must be established with agreement from the managers heading up the underlying businesses within the group if they are to be positively motivated by them. This motivation is normally stimulated by attaching very high incentive payments to their achievement, which obviously gives rise to the style descriptor of incentivizing leadership. In order to achieve such stretching targets, these business unit managers must themselves become leaders with their own followers, who are willing to increase their energy inputs into the business unit. As discussed in the previous chapter, this normally means that the business unit leaders within these incentivizing style-led groups should implement the visioning activity-focused, inspiring leader style.

Delivering-focused leaders need to remove any paradox from their followers, so that they are clearly focused on achieving the targets agreed with them. In terms of our key leadership capabilities, incentivizing style leaders themselves need excellent skills in the capability of handling paradox so that they can provide to their followers complete clarity of what is wanted. The common strong linkage of business performance to management incentive payments means that, for this style of leadership, 'what you measure is definitely what you get'. The measures used therefore must avoid contradiction and concentrate the efforts of the managers running the business units; the value created by the incentivizing style leaders comes from refocusing existing energy inputs of their followers. These followers, if they then take on visioning-focused leadership of their own business units, may be able to increase the energy inputs of *their* employees as they become positively committed followers.

If they are to be capable of doing this, they must be given freedom to act. This means that the incentivizing style leader sets specific, measurable goals but does not need to get involved in the detail of how these goals are achieved. As shown in Figure 5.2, this tightly focuses the communicating for success capability. The corporate leader delegates almost total

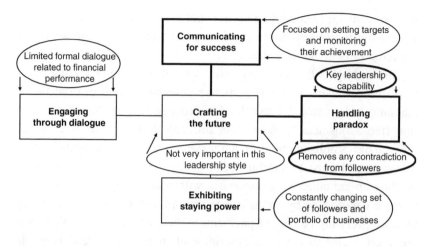

Figure 5.2 Critical leadership capabilities: the incentivizing leader

discretion as to the actions that can be taken by lower-level leaders but then accepts no excuses for any failure to deliver the expected results. Communication is almost exclusively about either setting the clear stretching targets or monitoring the actual results compared to these goals. Incentivizing style leaders are often highly judgemental on the actual results and many operate a 'no surprises' or even a 'no changes' culture.

The 'philosophy of making money' is almost the only thing that binds many of these groups together and this makes the crafting the future capability much less important in such circumstances. The group's future composition is often opportunistic as it depends on the next acquisition opportunity. Quite frequently, divestments may be made to provide either funding or senior executive capacity (i.e. time) to take on such an acquisition. The consequence of this external focus by the leaders at the very top of the business is that many more internally focused leaders are needed at lower levels in these organizations.

There is often minimal engagement through dialogue between incentivizing style leaders and their followers in the businesses. Whereas the inspirational leadership style needs the ability to surface the real underlying sentiments behind the behaviour and statements of their followers, delivering activity-focused leaders tend to be insensitive to such sentiments. They can also be low on personal loyalty to followers and accept that those who fail to achieve their stretching targets are likely to leave;

they may even encourage them to do so. They are confident that the high potential rewards for success will produce a more than sufficient supply of followers who want to take up the challenge of trying to achieve the next stretching target.

This means that the exhibiting staying power capability is really only for the next target and its associated incentive plan as far as these followers are concerned. However, incentivizing style leaders are often in place for quite long periods and they need the capability to cope with a constantly changing set of followers.

The consequence of this specific combination of capabilities together with the focus of this leadership style is that only a relatively low level of buy-in from followers is normally achieved. This does not stop these leaders from creating value, and they can do this while they have only a few of these not totally committed followers. As shown in Figure 5.3, their source of value creation comes from refocusing the existing energy of their direct followers. This is done through the complete clarity that is needed in the measurable, normally financial, targets that are agreed with these followers. If what is important to their leader at the corporate centre is made absolutely clear to them, most followers in the business units will not waste energy on other activities, particularly when their personal income is directly linked to their performance in these areas.

This places a significant emphasis on the incentivizing style leader's ability to identify the right measures for all the businesses in their portfolio. As illustrated later in the chapter, this can create some problems, but it also explains why many groups led in this way comprise similar

Number of followers needed	Few
Level of buy-in required	Low to medium
Source of improved performance	Refocusing existing energy
Type of leadership	Medium strategic and transactional leadership

Figure 5.3 Overview of incentivizing style

types of business units. The most obvious problem is caused if the measures used in the stretching targets exclusively reflect short-term improvements in financial performance. It is well accepted that many short-term performance improvements can be achieved at the expense of the longer-term performance of the business. This may be of limited concern to the extreme incentivizing style leader who intends to divest most businesses after a few years as part of the group, preferably before this deteriorating future performance becomes visible to any prospective purchaser.

For the vast majority of delivering activity-focused leaders this puts the emphasis on their strategic leadership ability so that they can set targets that enhance financial performance in a sustainable way. Also they want to make their underlying businesses operate more efficiently. They are less interested in high-risk strategies that involve developing completely new products for as yet unproven market segments that may produce very high financial returns at some time well into the future. These leaders consequently focus on transactional, rather than transformational, leadership and place less importance on the people leadership skills that were so critical to the inspirational leadership style.

Ideal Follower Profile

These leadership attributes and capabilities enable us to identify an ideal profile for followers of incentivizing style leaders. The only group-wide culture in many such groups is the total results orientation of senior executives at group level and in the underlying businesses. There is often an almost obsessive focus on the latest actual or forecast results, with many rolling forecasts of the possible and probable out-turns against the target both being produced within the business unit and being sent to the corporate centre.

Beyond this results orientation, organizational culture is developed at the underlying business unit level and is heavily influenced by any leadership style that is implemented at this level. As indicated in Figure 5.4, this means that the primary identification of most followers, and indeed most employees, is with the particular part of the group in which they work or are physically located. This absence of a strong common culture across the group is often reinforced by the top incentivizing style leaders as they actively discourage cross-fertilization activities among the separate business units. As already mentioned, it is not unusual for many

Culture within group	Results-oriented
Primary identification of followers	Specific business unit, function, department in which follower located
Minimum level of trust needed	Low
Minimum level of respect required	Grudging
Source of respect	Governance/ planning and control expertise
Communication style	Limited, formal around budgets and financial results

Figure 5.4 Cultural implications of incentivizing leadership style

employees located in such a business unit to be completely unaware that they are actually part of a much larger organization.

The remoteness between these group leaders and their underlying businesses that frequently results can obviously make it easier, and much less disruptive, to sell off a particular business unit as and when this becomes economically attractive. This potential future disposal puts a further limit on the level of trust that is built between an incentivizing style leader at the top of this type of group and their direct followers who are running individual business units. There is also quite often an almost grudging level of respect from these followers to their leaders. They acknowledge that the leaders are absolutely excellent at what they do in terms of setting 'just about' credible stretching targets and actively managing the group's portfolio. This does not necessarily go as far as admiration and friendship, but this is not essential to the success of such a leader-to-follower relationship.

Indeed, there is commonly only limited communication and physical contact between such leaders and their followers. This is normally through the planning and control process so that it is focused on the agreement of the business unit's budget and financial targets, and the consequent tracking of the actual delivery against these targets.

So, who wants to be a follower of this leadership style? As shown in Figure 5.5, such a follower ideally needs to have relatively low needs for affiliation and recognition as they are unlikely to get much of either

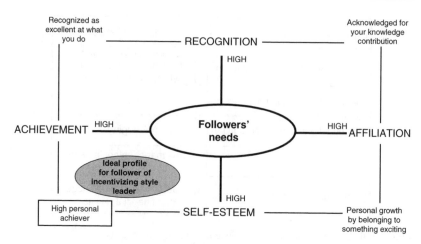

Figure 5.5 Implications of incentivizing leader style for followers

from this type of leader. They should be high personal achievers who thrive on being set challenges that they rise to meet and even surpass. Such people will be highly motivated by the stretching targets set by their leader and will gain a great sense of personal achievement from exceeding them. They do not need the celebratory group awards dinners held to recognize significant contributions to the business; they can have their own celebrations using their significant incentive-related rewards for achieving their targets.

One of the very interesting outcomes of our research is the relationship between the needs of people as followers and their own styles if they themselves also operate as leaders at a different level in the organization. Figure 5.5 helps to illustrate this for such direct followers of incentivizing style leaders at the top of a group who are themselves leaders of their own business units within the group. As we have just argued, the most successful followers are quite likely to be 'high personal achievers' but they also really need to be visioning leaders themselves. This means that they need to motivate followers who, like them, have high needs for self-esteem but who also, unlike them, require a strong sense of affiliation, which is not generated at the overall group level.

This 'high personal achiever' follower therefore needs to create, for their own followers, a real sense of excitement from belonging to, and identifying with, their specific business unit with its own tailored aspirational vision. This can be achievable as it requires the 'follower-to-leader' transition to change only one dimension on our followers' needs analysis. More generally we have found significant problems where transitions involve changes in two dimensions simultaneously, i.e. diagonally right across Figure 5.5. For example, an ideal follower of a directing style leader would need to be recognized as being excellent at what they do: a combination of high achievement and high recognition needs. If such a follower was required to act in an inspirational leadership style, they might struggle to understand the completely differing needs of their ideal followers as they have high needs for self-esteem and affiliation, neither of which are so important to their leader. This idea is developed in Chapter 8 where these aspects are examined in depth.

Connecting and Aligning Activities

This type of analysis highlights another issue for our incentivizing style leader. We have illustrated where and how the visioning activity often takes place in individual business units in addition to the delivering activity focus right at the top of the organization. The only issue resulting from the visioning activity at this business unit level is that it is effectively being done after at least the initial set of targets has been set. These primarily financially focused, and often short-term, targets can act as a constraint on the scope of the vision that is established for the business unit.

However, the main issue for this leadership style when implemented at the top of a company is how and where the organization undertakes the two remaining value-creating leadership activities, connecting and aligning. The connecting leadership activity potentially creates value by leveraging knowledge right across the organization, often cutting across the formal organizational structure to do this. This can be difficult in incentivizing style-led companies as the primary identification is with the individual business units rather than with the overall group. Followers at this level know that their leader's focus is on the performance of the business unit for which they are held responsible and that any more general contribution to the group will not offset a failure to deliver their individual stretch target. Accordingly there is little motivation for sharing knowledge with colleagues who they hardly know. It is also quite difficult for these followers, who are likely themselves to be high personal achievers, to act as enabling style leaders and have strong empathy for the high recognition and affiliation needs of their ideal followers.

The aligning leadership activity can be similarly problematic even though it can be implemented through a change in the organizational structure, which may be mandated by the top leader. Such structural changes are long-term strategic moves, often requiring sizeable investments with reasonably long financial payback periods. If it is quite possible for the composition of the group's portfolio of businesses to change during this time-frame, there will be no clear financial motivation to make such a change. This type of group is very keen on clear financial motivation. As mentioned in Part 1, some incentivizing style groups have found ways to overcome these problems and implement the connecting and aligning activities within their businesses, but these are more the exception than the rule. In most cases, these potentially value-creating activities happen only within individual business units or geographically discrete parts of the group.

Shareholder Style Leadership at Lower Levels of the Business

As usual, we have quite deliberately concentrated on leadership at the top of the company as this normally creates the greatest value. However, it is important that all companies implement the delivering leadership activity at the most relevant levels. From Chapter 4, it should be clear that a company led by a visioning activity-focused leader needs a number of incentivizing style leaders at lower levels if the full potential of the organization is to be delivered. These leaders may be at the top of the individual business units within a group or, in a single business company, may be responsible for separate areas of the business.

Similarly, as is shown in Figure 5.6, the delivering leadership activity is also important in companies with enabling or directing style leaders at their top. Given the earlier analysis based on Figure 5.5, it is easier to have incentivizing style leaders at lower levels in an organization led by aligning activity-focused leaders. The ideal follower profile of this directing style is a combination of high achievement and high recognition. This only requires a change in one dimension, from high recognition to high self-esteem, when this follower becomes an incentivizing style leader seeking to motivate their own followers. As already mentioned, the transition directly from an ideal follower of an enabling style leader, with the follower requirements of high recognition and

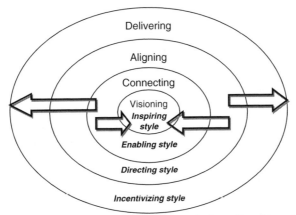

Enabling or directing style leaders at the top of organizations still need incentivizing style leadership at lower levels to deliver extraordinary performance

Figure 5.6 Variant of in-and-out framework

high affiliation, while also being an incentivizing style leader is more challenging.

The Classic Examples

An excellent early exponent of this idea of decentralized responsibility within a framework of tough financial controls and appropriate managerial performance incentives was the Hanson group (known as Hanson Industries in the USA). The group primarily focused on businesses at the maturity stage of a relatively low-technology, and hence long, industry life cycle. Through a succession of increasingly large acquisitions Hanson built up a wide-ranging portfolio of mainly UK and US-based businesses.

Many of its best acquisitions were of groups that had themselves tried to diversify into growth areas, using the cash generation of the original, but now mature, business to fund such diversification. Many of these moves were proving unsuccessful as the existing leaders located in these corporate centres did not possess the leadership skills necessary for adding value to the new growth industries that their groups were entering. Neither did Hanson, but the lack of performance of these acquisition targets enabled it to buy these groups at what it deemed a 'good price'. The genuine growth parts of the acquired groups were then normally rapidly sold on (or floated off as independent companies), often recouping for Hanson the bulk of its original total purchase cost. This was possible as stock markets can find it very difficult to value complex diversified groups that are comprised of high-growth elements as well as mature and declining businesses. Not only is it complicated to assess the overall price earnings (P/E) multiple that should be applied to the earnings of such a group, but also the most appropriate financial strategy, in terms of the dividend pay-out ratio and the debt to equity ratio, can be unclear.

Hanson avoided any such ambiguity and associated potential paradox by ensuring that all its retained businesses were relatively mature operations that would benefit from the financial disciplines that would be imposed by its corporate centre. This meant that the key skills of acquisitions and subsequent financial control were critical to the success of Hanson and these were the focus of the top management team. The group was built up by a small corporate centre headed by Lord Hanson and Lord White. Lord White looked after the new acquisitions, while Lord Hanson oversaw the management of the current portfolio.

The ideal target businesses would operate in comprehensible technologies (like Warren Buffett, Lords Hanson and White did not believe in buying into industries that they did not understand) and be based in markets where the published financial statements, legal frameworks and capital markets made the pursuit of hostile takeovers an economic practicality; hence the US and UK focus of the group. Further, they preferred businesses that were not facing very tough competition and hence had not already had to become lean and mean to survive, let alone flourish. This meant that the group did a vast amount of financial analysis on potential acquisition targets and could track companies for a number of years before, if ever, it decided to attempt an acquisition. Indeed, these deals were tremendously driven by the existing financial numbers and what Hanson considered that the business could achieve when under its guidance. One of Lord White's famous quotes was that he had never physically visited any business that Hanson was acquiring.

As part of its pre-acquisition screening, Hanson would have already decided on which, if any, divisions of a target company would be rapidly sold off after completion, so that it could then focus on improving the performance of the remaining business units. This performance improvement was first generated by the rapid imposition of tight financial controls over expenditure (if it is not essential, then do not spend it, being the basic maxim). This was followed by the imposition of a strong results-oriented focus, reinforced by very high levels of incentivization for the senior managers at each business unit. There were also severe sanctions for non-performance.

The emphasis was on short-term improvements in key financial ratios so that year-on-year profitability ratio increases were key; improving the bottom (profit) line was considered much more important than growing the top (sales revenue) line. This highlights why the orientation towards mature, long-life businesses can be so important to this type of strategy. High-growth strategies in mature or slowly declining markets can desta-bilize the whole industry by reducing the total profit pool available to all the companies in the industry. One player's volume growth must come at the expense of another competitor and this may well force an aggres-sive competitive reaction, the most common being the start of a price war that can destroy value for everyone in the industry.

Also in mature industries the short-term focus of annual profit improvements should have a smaller negative impact on the long-term profit potential of the business, compared with a high-growth industry where the impact can be disastrous. Indeed, in many such industries, the sustainable cash-generation capability is actually greater than the profit level due to the non-reinvestment of all the depreciation expense and potential reductions in the working capital tied up in the business. Hanson not only completely understood these issues but the leaders at its corporate centre could provide the expertise to show the new business units how to achieve considerable savings in net assets employed as well as operating costs.

This targeting process was not exclusively top-down as there does need to be buy-in from the senior divisional managers in order to believe that, although stretching, the key performance measures they are being given are possible. This delivering activity-focused leadership style does need a degree of buy-in from those few key followers who will actually achieve the improved performance levels. Thus a sense of realism has to pervade the planning process, otherwise the business unit management teams can become totally demotivated very early in the financial year, as significant potential bonuses move increasingly out of reach no matter how much effort they put in. However, the planning process can concentrate on agreeing these stretching targets without having to get involved in the detail of the competitive strategy that is needed to produce this required level of performance. This is left to the management team in each individual business and the group may therefore be implementing a number of specifically tailored competitive strategies. After all, Hanson was involved in a wide range of industries (cigarettes, bricks, energy, electrical consumer products, zips and fasteners, etc.) that all had their own distinct competitive environments and bases of competition. The incentivizing style leaders in the small corporate centre could not, and did not need to, be experts in the specifics of each of these industries.

The major problem with this very successful corporate strategy is the relatively short period during which these specific leadership skills add significant value to the business units. This can be sustained through the dynamic acquisitions and disposals strategy that was an integral part of Hanson. However, as the group increased in size the corporate centre had to identify larger and larger acquisitions in order to have the same proportionate impact on the overall group's profit and cash flows. Further, the presence of such aggressive players in the market forced a number of potential targets to review their own corporate strategies, before it was done to them by Hanson or someone like it.

Subsequently several large groups were created on the same principles and, indeed, some had learned the concepts while at Hanson. Thus Greg Hutchings, who with Ian Duncan built Tomkins into a similarly widely diversified group (from cakes to guns), had been an acquisitions manager with Hanson. It is interesting that he had been involved at the centre of the group before setting out to build his own group using the same leadership style as the one that he had already seen implemented so successfully. In the previous chapter, we saw the example of Jack Welch continuing with his inspirational leadership style when he rose to the top of an existing, and at least equally successful, incentivizing style-led group. Most of these groups have now themselves been split up which indicates the problem of long-term sustainability of value creation by this style of leadership in such mature industries. In Hanson's own case, this was done by Lord Hanson after the death of Lord White. It is testimony to the lack of excessive cost at the corporate centre that this eventual self-imposed demerger of the group into four separate companies created no real shareholder value, even though there had been no large acquisitions in the preceding few years.

The Planning and Control Process

The discussion of the Hanson group's success has highlighted the fact that the planning and control process designed and implemented by an incentivizing style of leadership is critical to its value-creating role. Although leaders in such a corporate centre have only an indirect involvement in the underlying businesses, an appropriately developed planning and control process across the group can still give them a very effective level of control over these businesses.

This level of control is achieved through a focus on measuring the individual achievements of each business, with the result that there is normally virtually no cross-fertilization of new ideas or current practices among the business units within such a group. The perceived importance of these measurements is normally increased by tightly linking the overall remuneration of the senior business unit managers to their relative levels of performance. Thus a large proportion of their total potential income consists of incentives, but these incentives are based almost exclusively on their own business unit's performance, whereas in many large groups a significant proportion of such incentivization schemes for top business unit managers would be based on the performance of the total group, such as by granting stock options over shares in the ultimate parent company.

Consequently, the leaders need to identify appropriate measurable outputs that can be objectively assessed at the divisional level, but that also motivate the business unit managers to act in accordance with the aims of the overall corporate strategy. Not surprisingly, these incentivizing style leaders utilize almost exclusively financial performance measures, and then normally establish group-wide accounting procedures so as to ensure that all business units are playing by the same rules.

The use of such financial performance measures is, however, only the first element in the required planning and control process. The performance of each business unit has to be placed into its appropriate context and this is achieved through the targets that are issued by the centre to each business unit. It is now well accepted that managerial performance measures should only include areas over which the specific managers can exercise some degree of control. Thus, as more constraints are placed on managerial discretion by higher levels of management, the relevant performance measures that should be used become more and more limited. If incentivizing style leaders want to hold their business unit managers fully accountable for the actual profits and cash flows generated by their businesses, they need to give them a high level of freedom in how they actually run these businesses.

This is, of course, exactly what leaders in these indirectly involved corporate centres want to do, but this can, in some groups, be subject to a number of caveats. It is very common for such leaders to allow only a very low level of business unit discretion in terms of capital expenditure. This means that the business units have to request permission from the corporate centre before they are able to commit to any sizeable investment expenditure. In some cases, as was mentioned for Hanson, this is done quite deliberately when the business unit is new to the group in order to create a frugal, cost-conscious culture within the business unit itself that will rigorously challenge the justification of all expenditures. This is normally fine as the final decision is in reality left to the business unit managers but, in other cases, it can impose an unnecessary restriction on the ability of the business unit to achieve the targets that are set for it.

An alternative is to introduce a set of investment approval procedures across the group that allow business unit managers a much higher authorization level as long as the return from the proposed expenditure is expected to beat the group's financial requirements. After all, the key measures that are used to assess the performance of the business unit management team are the profits, cash flows and return on investment of the business unit. If these business unit leaders believe that making additional investments in their business is likely to enable them to achieve their targets then, as long as these targets take into account the additional return required on the new investment, the leaders at the corporate centre should be willing to let them have the funds to make the investment. In most such groups, any substantial shortfall against expected performance has a dramatic effect on a managerial career. This downside can have a significant impact on the risk-taking appetite of business unit managers.

The emphasis on the achievement of objectively measurable outputs as the basis for the high managerial incentive payments means that the centre-established targets are usually focused on short-term performance: normally one to three years ahead, with the greatest focus on the first year. This has resulted in the widespread use of the payback technique (whether discounted payback or simple payback), rather than the more sophisticated full discounted cash-flow computations. Investment proposals that immediately start to generate high levels of return are very highly rated by the payback technique while slower-starting, but ultimately more value-creating, projects would be more highly ranked by a full discounted cash-flow appraisal. The unsurprising consequence of this short-term focus in most incentivizing style-led groups is that the underlying business units are unwilling to undertake long-term strategic investment projects that do not generate high short-term returns, such as developing new technologies, new brand-building expenditures, entering new markets or some very new segments, and launching completely new products. Business units within such groups tend to concentrate on doing better what they already do quite well, rather than trying to do something different. As already discussed, this is in line with the transactional leadership focus of the incentivizing leadership style; the leaders at the centre are focused on trying to make these underlying businesses more efficient at what they already do. If new businesses are needed to generate growth for the group, these businesses can be acquired by the leaders at the corporate centre.

Although the short-term financial targets are issued by the corporate centre leaders, they should not simply be arbitrarily imposed on the business units. As already stated, there needs to be a level of agreement with or, at least, acceptance of the targets by the top managers of the business unit as being 'just about achievable'. If these targets are seen as completely unrealistic by these managers then their incentive plans, which are based on achieving these targets, will cease to offer any incentive at all. Different incentivizing style-led groups obviously have their own ways of actually implementing their incentive plans depending upon how stretching their targets are. Thus bonus payments can start to be paid even though the business unit performance only reaches 90 per cent, or even 80 per cent, of the very stretching target. In another group with more realistic targets, the incentive plan may only start when the target is reached, but increasing payments may be earned for outperformance, although often up to a maximum level.

The details of these incentive plans and their interrelationship with the target-setting process can have a major impact on the behaviour of business unit managers. The corporate leadership is normally showing an exclusively financial interest in these business units, particularly where it is well known that it is willing to sell them to any sufficiently high bidder. Not surprisingly, this tends to be reflected in the relationship that business unit managers have with their leaders at the corporate centre. They are motivated almost totally by their remuneration package and this is largely controlled by the high incentive plans and their targets.

This can lead to very sophisticated 'game playing' by the business units both in the target-setting process and in their financial reporting of actual results against this target. During the planning process, the business unit will try to get its target for next year set at the lowest possible level as this will obviously make it easier to achieve. This tends to make planning an iterative round of negotiations between the centre and the business units before a final target is agreed, but this means that corporate leaders need both good negotiating skills and the knowledge of what is actually achievable by the business unit. As many such targets are set by reference to the actual current performance, e.g. year-on-year profit improvement or cost decreases, etc., the business unit has an incentive to be ultra-conservative on its current performance until the target for next year has been agreed.

Also the business unit may not want to outperform in total this year if this will lead to a tougher target for next year or the year after. This is particularly the case where the incentive scheme has no increased payments for outperformance. Once the current target is reached the business unit managers may seek to hide away (in the form of conservative accrued expenses and provisions) any excess profits, so that these provisions and accruals can be released in the following year when they can help to achieve that year's bonus. Clearly if this game playing becomes excessive it can significantly reduce the value created by this leadership style. Either the corporate centre's leaders have to incur additional governance costs to check the business units' plans or the actual performance of the business units, after incentive payments, is less than it should be. This reinforces the lack of total buy-in by even the key followers at the head of the subordinate business units.

The performance of the overall group is assessed from the consolidated results of all the business units minus the costs incurred by the corporate centre. One of the strengths of many incentivizing style-led groups is that the diversified nature of their business units makes them relatively unaffected by industrial downturns and even quite substantial economic cycles. If one or more of their businesses is suffering an adverse economic environment, the corporate leader can increase the required target slightly from the other business units so that the overall financial performance of the group is still in line with their shareholders' expectations. This ability to maintain short-term overall financial performance in terms of profits and dividend payments is a major attraction to investors in this type of group. Of course, this is much easier to achieve if the performance problem is identified during the planning process, i.e. before the targets for the other businesses are agreed. In order to emphasize this need for early warnings of potential problems, many such shareholder style-led groups implement a very strong 'no surprises' or even 'no changes' culture across the group, whereby the delivery of the planned profit level is regarded as a firm commitment by the business unit to the centre. Some incentivizing style corporate centres in larger groups even allow for the under-performance of some business units by ensuring that the sum of the expected profits from the businesses exceeds the total group profit requirement. In other words, they build a central contingency into the planning process.

Developing a portfolio of businesses to which these incentivizing style corporate leaders can apply their tight formal planning and control processes is very important to their value-creation capability. This centrally controlled targeting and monitoring process, through which the leaders at the centre standardize the financial measures used by the businesses within the group, removes the need for each of these businesses to develop its own process. Thus these businesses, hopefully, gain access to an excellent process and the group generates a governance-based economy of scale by applying its process across a large number of businesses. It is important to remember that the key value-creating element is the focus on relevant measurable outputs in order to improve financial performance. It is not necessary, and can be very counter-productive, for the incentivizing style corporate leader in a highly diversified group to force all the business units to go through exactly the same detailed planning process. The leaders in the corporate centre impose the targets on the business units and dictate the way in which the actual performance against those targets will be reported. They should not get involved in the details of the competitive strategy that will be implemented to deliver the required performance, and the detailed planning process in each business unit should be tailored to this competitive strategy.

A more Sustainable Role Model?

Incentivizing style leadership is not only relevant to mature, cash-generating businesses. This style can add value wherever excellent governance processes can improve the financial performance of the group's businesses. This has been demonstrated in many service industries but probably the best example comes from the advertising industry through the development of both Saatchi & Saatchi and WPP.

The traditional structure of the advertising services industry was based around a small creative team, who set up their own agency on the back of a limited number of client accounts. If this initial start-up was successful, a constraint on the ultimate size of the business seemed to be the tendency for a few of this now expanded team to leave and set up *their* own advertising agency. This created an impression to any outside potential investors (such as public stock markets) that clients were primarily loyal to the account team handling their advertising and promotions, rather than to the advertising agency employing this creative team. It was also largely true that the main strategic thrust of these businesses was based on delivering a high quality service to the customer; thus there was a low emphasis, within most of these small agencies, on financial management and control. During this period of development, a relatively small number of large, international agencies did develop, but even these tended to be built around either a limited number of very large international clients or a leading industry creative figure. Thus there were independent US-based names such as J. Walter Thompson (JWT), Ogilvy & Mather (O & M) and Ted Bates, but all this was to change.

In August 1970, Charles and Maurice Saatchi launched their own advertising agency. Charles Saatchi, at 26, had already established a reputation as a brilliantly creative advertising copywriter, but the innovative element in this equation was Maurice. Aged 23, Maurice Saatchi had been working in the publishing industry and his expertise was much more on the finance and administration side of the business than in developing creative advertising. Their new business was quickly successful and growth was rapid. The brothers were able to attract other small agencies to join them and so the initial growth was both organic and dynamic.

In 1975 they made their first major takeover of the larger and publicly quoted agency Garland-Compton (this brought them the prestigious Procter & Gamble account). It was also the stimulus for the company to become publicly quoted itself in 1976. This led to the recruitment of Martin Sorrell as financial director to help Maurice in controlling the embryonic empire.

The pace of acquisitions was intense and the acquisition strategy had two main themes. First, acquired businesses were usually left alone from a creative standpoint but the original principals behind these agencies were incentivized to maximize their medium-term growth in profits by making the final acquisition price dependent upon the profits achieved over an earn-out period. These earn-out periods were normally three to five years, but could be as long as seven years. Second, Saatchi & Saatchi developed a very strong central financial control system that concentrated on tight cash management, so as to maximize the benefit of potential cash-flow timings from the client through the agency and on to the media supplier. Thus, if successfully implemented, these acquisitions could almost guarantee to generate growth in profit yet not to use excessive amounts of cash in funding this growth in the early years after purchase.

This 'shareholder' style of leadership also had an external focus as Maurice Saatchi put considerable effort into demonstrating to financial analysts and investment institutions that there was actually a low rate of change by clients in the advertising agencies that they used, thus improving the perceived value of current profit streams and raising the earnings multiples that were applied by the stock market to the advertising industry.

The resulting twenty-fold growth in earnings per share over its first ten years as a publicly quoted group gained Saatchi's a premium stock market rating over its re-rated sector, and a share price that outperformed the FT All Shares index by around 2,000 per cent. The acquisition of Ted Bates in 1986 made Saatchi & Saatchi the world's largest advertising agency group, with over half the world's top 500 corporations as clients.

However, in 1985 Martin Sorrell had left to set up his own marketing services business, using an existing small quoted company called Wire and Plastic Products plc that he and an original partner bought into. The originally stated strategy was not to compete directly with Saatchi's, but to focus on promotional activities (referred to as 'below the line', while media advertising is termed 'above the line' activity, although nobody really seems to know where this 'line' should be drawn nowadays) and other value-adding marketing services (such as marketing research, design and public relations). Rapid growth through acquisitions followed, mainly using the earn-out formula, and these businesses were then also subjected to a much more rigorous financial planning and control process that was driven from the small corporate centre. WPP Group plc (as it had been renamed) also delivered spectacular shareholder value with its share price growing from below 40p in 1985 to over £10 by May 1987, which gave the group a market capitalization of £125 million.

In its first-quarter results for 1987 JWT surprised the stock market when it reported a loss and there were clearly senior management conflicts as some key personnel had left the organization; the share price fell to around half its level at the end of 1986. WPP launched a $560 million (£375 million, i.e. three times its own market capitalization) bid for JWT, financed by a very large (2 for 1) rights issue together with a substantial level of new borrowing. Martin Sorrell's leadership and the excellent governance skills of WPP's corporate centre rapidly restored JWT's previous operating margins *and* released around $150 million of cash by implementing a much tighter working capital management process. As a result WPP announced a 71 per cent increase in its earnings per share for 1988 over 1987.

Despite the stock market crash in October 1987, both Saatchi & Saatchi and WPP were actively looking for acquisitions but, as with Hanson, these were getting more difficult to find. Saatchi's was starting to talk about 'globalization' and 'cross-fertilization' between its communications businesses as being key to its future. This took the public form of abortive approaches to both Midland Bank and Hill Samuel, the merchant bank. It then made a shock 'profits warning' announcement, which resulted in a dramatic fall in its share price.

This did not stop WPP from launching, early the following year, an originally hostile bid for Ogilvy & Mather that, if successful, would make it the largest advertising group in the world. Eventually, after a very public and highly volatile series of negotiations, WPP announced an agreed bid of $864 million (around £550 million) for O & M. This bid value was over twice the market capitalization of WPP at the time, but the reputation of WPP's leadership team made it possible to raise the required financing. However, O & M was a very different acquisition from the JWT turnaround deal, as it was already achieving industry-average profit margins and did not demonstrate the same level of potential for freeing up excess working capital. Despite this apparent lack of dramatic growth potential, the enlarged group achieved earnings per share growth of 34 per cent and 77 per cent in the two years following the deal.

Then WPP announced its own profits warning, since which both groups have required fundamental changes to their capital structures. These have included significant modifications to their shareholders, as much of the financing originally raised as redeemable debt had to be converted into permanent equity capital. The Saatchi brothers left their group to restart on their own, but Martin Sorrell is still at the helm of WPP.

The incentivizing leadership style has been applied by businesses in other people-based, fast growing, owner-managed industries such as employment bureaux, consultancies, software companies, and even contract catering. Obviously the specific issues of each industry make the detailed implementation slightly different but, in each case, the leaders at the top of the business could create value through their ability to change the group's portfolio of businesses significantly through acquisition and, where necessary, subsequent divestment. This element of value creation comes in two parts. The first part is generated if the leaders at the centre have very high acquisition skills, so that they can buy businesses at good prices (i.e. below their full economic value). Such leaders can, however, create much more value through the second part by improving the financial performance of the acquired business once it has been incorporated within the group.

Sustainability Issues

As just discussed, there is no reason for the incentivizing leadership style to restrict itself to only one type of business unit (e.g. the mature businesses of Hanson and Tomkins). As long as the leaders can develop appropriately tailored performance measures for all of the different businesses in the group, they can still create value. However, the emphasis on improving performance makes the use of objective measures very important. It can be very difficult to continue to motivate business unit managers through the commonly used high incentive payments based on performance if the assessment of that performance is felt to be extremely subjective and judgemental, particularly if that judgement is being exercised by leaders in a corporate centre that is perceived to be quite remote from, and uninformed about, the underlying businesses. Hence there is the already discussed strong tendency for incentivizing style leaders to emphasize financial performance measures and to specify throughout the group how this financial performance is to be calculated. This has often resulted in the use of standardized financial measures (such as profit, cash flow, return on capital employed) across *all* the businesses in the group, sometimes with very detrimental results.

GEC during Lord Weinstock's period as Chief Executive was a good example of an incentivizing style-led group. In the 1960s and 1970s Weinstock had restructured the UK's electronics and defence contracting industries through a series of takeovers and mergers. He then, across this group of businesses, established rigorous financial control processes that included very tight cash management. The decentralized business units were set annual profit improvement and cash-generation targets that eventually generated a £2 billion cash mountain that was held at the corporate centre. Part of this cash was used to repurchase the group's own shares as organic reinvestment opportunities seemed limited. Unfortunately, even at this stage in their business life cycles, not all of the businesses in the group were completely mature and could probably have benefited from greater levels of reinvestment. This was reflected in the stock market rating of the group towards the end of Lord Weinstock's tenure as its leader. The group's leadership would argue that investment funds were always available provided a good financial case was put forward. However, if, as a divisional manager, you are going to be expected to generate a higher rate of return on the capital employed in your business next year than you achieved this year, you may think twice before you put in a request for substantial new investments.

Thus the incentivizing leadership style can be a constraint on the organic rate of growth that is generated within a given set of businesses. However, a bigger negative impact can be generated from running a mixed portfolio, particularly when the whole portfolio is built around one large, mature, cash-generating business. BAT Industries, as already mentioned, was a good example of this. For most of its 100-year history in tobacco, the tobacco business was run from the corporate centre as four completely separate groups that actually competed against each other in certain parts of the world. These groups were each set profit, return on assets and cash-generation targets and the free cash flow was basically remitted to the centre. Using this very strong cash flow, BAT's corporate leaders acquired a sizeable portfolio of diversified businesses (financial services, retailing, and paper businesses in both the UK and the USA). All of these acquired businesses reported into the corporate centre separately and were initially run as stand-alone businesses by the incentivizing style leaders at the centre.

It was during this period of rapid diversification, with the consequent pressure on them to generate increased profits and dividends, that the combined tobacco businesses lost their overall leadership of the international cigarette market to Philip Morris. During this period the profitability of this international cigarette market increased substantially. The much changed BAT plc is still, nearly 20 years later, trying to regain this leadership.

Not too surprisingly, the stock market was not wildly impressed by BAT's diversification strategy with the result that the share price was based on a very low earnings multiple of the group's current profits. At the end of the 1980s BAT was attacked by a special purpose vehicle called Hoylake, with a view to splitting up the group and closing down what was perceived as a value-destroying corporate centre. It is interesting that one of Hanson's most successful acquisitions was of Imperial Group, following which the more highly rated businesses such as Courage Breweries, Golden Wonder and KP Nuts were sold off recovering over £1.5 billion of the £2.1 billion total acquisition cost, and the mature, cash-producing Imperial Tobacco was retained. Also RJR Nabisco in the USA, which included the RJ Reynolds tobacco group, was subjected to a very famous leveraged buyout by KKR at the same time. That Philip Morris did not suffer the same fate is due, in part at least, to the different leadership style at its corporate centre, as is discussed in Chapter 6.

BAT Industries rapidly implemented a change in its corporate strategy. The paper businesses were merged together and floated off onto the stock market, as was the UK retailing business. The US-based retailing business was sold and the group's substantial cash mountain was used to finance a share repurchase programme in the stock market. There was also an announcement that the future dividend pay-out ratio would increase from below 25 per cent to around 50 per cent of normalized post-tax earnings. This left two types of businesses, tobacco and financial services; a cynic might regard cigarettes and life insurance as an interesting form of diversification. What is interesting from our perspective is that this response to the external threat is totally in keeping with 'shareholder' style leadership. The leadership at the corporate centre changes the portfolio of businesses that it owns rather than becoming more involved in managing them through direct intervention. The main changes that such leaders implement are externally focused; the share buy-back and change in dividend policy were reinforced by the adoption of a more aggressive debt-based funding strategy. This strategy change became more fundamental following the retirement of Sir Patrick Sheehy. The new group board, led by Martin Broughton, brought together the four tobacco companies into one global group and then exited from financial services by merging all its interests with the Zurich group. This left a totally focused tobacco group and this group has since then made a number of significant acquisitions and new market entries. The new leadership team in the corporate centre has now established a clear vision and set of guiding principles for the group.

We have already stated that incentivizing style leaders should be willing to divest business units where their leadership is no longer value creating. However, for some groups this is much easier to say than to do in practice. This can be illustrated with the previously discussed acquisition and long-term retention of JWT by WPP. Within two or three years, Martin Sorrell's leadership and associated governance skills had restored JWT's profit margins and dramatically improved its working capital management. (Incidentally, after the acquisition, it also found that JWT *owned* the office block that it occupied in Tokyo, the rapid sale of which provided a further significant cash inflow to offset another large part of WPP's initial purchase cost.) These changes had in a short time created most of the potential shareholder value that could be expected to be generated from WPP's incentivizing style corporate centre. Hence the most focused and objective decision could be to resell the now more valuable business, whether in parts to trade buyers or refloated as a single entity. One possible counter-argument is that such a sale would not have realized any surplus over the ongoing value if retained or the original purchase price, but this would simply mean that the group had originally paid too much to gain control over a business that was self-evidently in trouble. This should not be the case for any business that has acquisitions as one of its core competences. However, WPP did pay a significant premium over the sharply discounted JWT share price in order to guarantee that it would succeed with its pre-emptive bid.

A further argument for a subsequent sale is that any move, let alone such a large move, into advertising agency ownership was not part of the group's original corporate strategy; it had intended to focus on 'below the line' marketing services businesses. However, having bought one large advertising agency, the subsequent opportunity to overtake Saatchi & Saatchi (which, by then, was in trouble) as the world's largest advertising group through the acquisition of Ogilvy & Mather may have been too good for WPP's corporate leadership team to turn down. Unfortunately, there is normally a distinctly negative correlation between satisfying an ego and creating shareholder value.

Our detailed examples of success from implementing the incentivizing style of leadership show that it can create significant value through its well-developed, highly tailored competences. However, for such acquisition-created groups, achieving a rapid change in the financial performance of a new addition to the group normally requires a significant level of corporate centre involvement for the first year or so. This initial stage of ownership by this 'interested, focused shareholder' often results in a step change in the financial performance, as many non-essential and non-value-adding cost items are cut. Once the business unit understands the rigorous results-oriented culture of this leadership style and has been through the whole planning and control cycle at least once, the level of corporate leadership involvement can be substantially reduced. The financial performance of the new business unit may still be improving significantly as the benefits of the corporate leader's governance processes feed through into increased financial returns. The reduced involvement of the corporate leader (and hence attributable cost levels incurred by the corporate centre) in this business unit can mean that the 'net' value created for the group during this second stage of ownership is still very high.

Even for these world-class examples of this leadership style, there is a relatively short period of high value generation from any specific business, unless the corporate leaders can continually improve their targeting and control processes. Thus, for any fixed set of businesses, there will be an automatic tendency for the value created by the centre's indirect involvement to decline. As long as the group actively manages this portfolio of businesses, this natural movement can be resisted by a regular influx of new challenges for the corporate leaders to work on.

The divestment of more established business units in order to realize the bulk of the value created is not essential, as long as the corporate centre can maintain this now improved level of performance with only a very minimal level of involvement. This avoids the need for the corporate centre to grow significantly in size as the portfolio of businesses grows; indeed, the corporate centre should be realizing its own economies of scale as the total group expands. The challenge for such groups is to continue to identify suitable acquisitions and to complete the purchase at prices that subsequently allow them to create added value. As their reputation and appetite for acquisitions spread this can become more and more difficult, as prospective vendors seek to gain a greater share of the total potential value of the targeted business. In other words, prices start to rise, even though the value is created by the post-acquisition actions of the incentivizing style-led group. Alternatively, these potential acquisition targets start to 'do it to themselves before it gets done to them' by the predator, as was the case of BAT Industries when attacked by Hoylake.

Conclusion

It should by now be clear that it is quite difficult for incentivizing style leadership at the corporate centre to sustain a high value-adding role over time with a stable portfolio of businesses comprising the group. Any initially high level of performance improvement is likely to decline over time as each business unit fully adopts the best governance practices from these corporate leaders. Thus to continue to add substantial value the delivering activity-focused leader must either develop their own skills to an even higher level of expertise or change some of the businesses to which their existing skills are applied. This does not mean it is inevitable that a static incentivizing style-led group will become value destroying over time. If the corporate leaders adopt a highly indirect level of involvement in their business units, they can keep the costs of the corporate centre very low. These leaders have to be more involved in the acquired businesses immediately after acquisition. Over time they can reduce the level of their involvement as the disciplines of financial control become embedded within the business unit. In this sense the business unit managers may develop self-control, reducing the requirement for the involvement of the leaders at the corporate centre. Also they can maintain the pressure on performance through their planning and control process, so that the existing high levels of financial return do improve, albeit more slowly than in the earlier years.

However, the incentivizing style is not the most sustainable value-creating style of leadership in terms of creating high value from a constant mix of businesses. The counterbalance is that it is the best in terms of the ease with which the portfolio of businesses comprising a group can be significantly changed. In a volatile external business environment, the associated governance expertise can suddenly become highly relevant to a new range of businesses and, if the leaders also have acquisition expertise at the corporate centre, the group may be very willing and able to apply its skills in these new areas.

Thus, although several of the original acquisition-led, highly diversified incentivizing style-led groups have themselves been unbundled, they are being replaced by a whole new set of incentivizing style-led corporate centres. These are the private equity businesses, many of which are investing on behalf of major financial institutions that are now building up very sizeable and increasingly diversified groups. These groups are being developed by acquisitions, often of already mature, cash-generating businesses, and the leaders at their corporate centres are experts in deal structuring and execution. It will be very interesting to see, over the next few years, whether these leaders already possess, or can develop, the planning and control expertise that is so essential to continue to add value to their acquisitions.

6

Connecting the parts of the business

In order to create shareholder value, the enabling style of leadership requires at least a moderate level of buy-in from a significant proportion of the total workforce within the business. Thus, by comparison to the extreme needs of the inspiring leader style that were considered in Chapter 4, this leadership style can be viewed as somewhat less demanding. Not surprisingly, it is also normally correspondingly less value generating, as well as still being difficult to sustain over time when it is implemented right at the top of an organization. However, enabling style leaders at several levels in the business are essential to any company that aims to sustain the delivery of extraordinary financial performance.

As shown in Figure 6.1, this leadership style creates value by releasing psychological energy and this is achieved through sharing existing knowledge and best practice across the business. This stops potentially valuable but already expensive employees from regularly having to reinvent the wheel simply because they are not aware of what has already been done elsewhere in the organization. In most businesses, this released psychological energy is reinvested in the business in order to enhance the level of differentiation that can be achieved against competitive offerings. This is in marked contrast to the value-creation potential of directing style leaders which comes from the release of

Number of followers required	Many
Level of buy-in needed	Medium
Source of improved performance	Releases psychological energy
Type of leadership	Medium people and transformational
Key value-creating activity	Connecting

Figure 6.1 Overview of enabling style

physical energy, as this is often taken as a direct cost saving through reducing the number of workers employed.

The key value-creating leadership activity of the enabling style is therefore connecting together what could otherwise be totally disparate parts of the organization. This is done by spreading existing knowledge as widely as is relevant across the business. The value is consequently created by changing what is done elsewhere in the business so that all areas can conform to the best existing practice within the group. This requires a transformational type of leadership to change what is done, together with good people leadership ability. People leadership is needed to gain the confidence of both sides of the required knowledge transfer.

Enabling style leaders do not need personally to create the knowledge that is to be shared. However, as shown in Figure 6.2, they do need very strong process skills to make this knowledge readily transferable across the organization. This can often involve codifying what is currently tacit know-how that is somehow being intuitively applied to great effect in one specific area, so that it becomes more generally usable knowledge for the rest of the business. In addition, these leaders also need sufficient understanding of the differing needs of various parts of their companies so that they can identify where this codified knowledge will create value. As discussed later, this results in enabling style leaders often having very strong functionally-based expertise as well as the essential process and systems skills needed to codify this existing knowledge.

A significant challenge for the enabling leadership style is to achieve sufficient buy-in to the necessary corporate culture of willingly sharing.

Focus of leader	Leveraging existing knowledge
Key skills required	Process expertise/business knowledge
Key leadership challenges	1) Achieving buy-in to sharing philosophy 2) Identifying new knowledge to share

Figure 6.2 Focus of enabling style leaders

This means getting rid of any 'not invented here' negative mindsets that can make employees unwilling to accept and apply knowledge that they did not think of themselves. Many companies are trying to achieve this with slogans such as 'borrow with pride', but this leadership style seeks to go much further. It aims to get employees to give willingly, or 'lend with pride', for the overall good of the organization, so that those who have developed new ideas, processes or knowledge really want them to be spread to their colleagues. There needs to be sufficient trust between enabling style leaders and their followers that such new knowledge is both readily offered to the leader and also readily accepted by those with whom the leader then shares it.

Ideally, this knowledge should be improved upon as it is applied in new contexts across the group and the originator can thus benefit by subsequently getting back an improved version of what they had 'lent with pride'. However, these subsequent improvements normally represent the law of diminishing returns and this highlights the greatest challenge to the sustainability of the value-creating role of this leadership style. Once all the existing knowledge has been codified and spread across the group to wherever it has relevance, the continuing value creation from the connecting activity depends upon identifying new knowledge that can also be shared.

The role of enabling style leaders should be transformational but, over time as existing knowledge is disseminated across the company, it is quite common to see the role becoming increasingly transactional.

These originally transforming leaders get more and more involved in the actual day-to-day operations of their underlying businesses. The connecting leadership activity should affect what is done across the organization and this is achieved through standardizing processes. If the leaders become involved in the detail of *where* the process is carried out or exactly *how* it is carried out, they have moved into the more transactionally-oriented, directing style. As is discussed in Chapter 7, this requires a higher level of buy-in from a different group of followers. As already stated, the enabling style leader needs reasonable buy-in from a very broad range of potential followers, that includes all those who may either possess or benefit from knowledge that has potential relevance elsewhere within the business.

Focusing on the Connecting Activity

This requirement for buy-in from a wide range of followers potentially spread right across the company highlights that an enabling style leader often needs to have impact unrestricted by any formal organizational structure. Leaders can, and frequently do, have followers who are not formally their subordinates or even below them in hierarchical terms, but such a requirement places great emphasis on their communications leadership capabilities. We have already stated that all our leadership styles require a high level of the communicating for success capability, and in the enabling style this is reinforced by the need for a very strong engaging through dialogue capability.

As shown in Figure 6.3, this style needs to create an environment where genuine dialogue is both encouraged and expected. Communication should take place in all directions within the organization so that knowledge sharing is maximized. The corporate leaders must hear as soon as possible about new ideas and processes if they are to be able to spread them as widely and quickly as is value maximizing. They also need to know of particular problem areas so that they can actively seek out any better processes that already exist within the group.

Engaging through dialogue should also be used with the exhibiting staying power capability to create a company-wide culture that is 'willing to share'. This means that the culture rewards loyalty to the internal organization in preference to creating external personal networks that individuals can use to further their own careers. Such a loyalty-focused

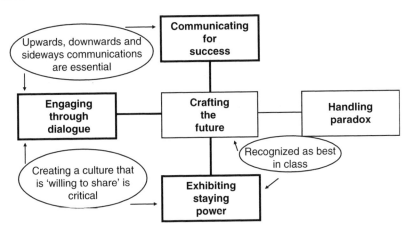

Figure 6.3 Critical leadership capabilities: the enabling style leader

culture, together with the crafting the future emphasis on each area of
the business being recognized as the 'best in class', means that the ideal
follower profile has high needs for both recognition and affiliation.
As shown in Figure 6.4, such a follower can be described as an acknowledged contributor, to whom a sense of belonging to something greater
than themselves and to which they have contributed through their own
knowledge is very important. The enabling style leader can respond to
these needs through the sense of community that they create among their

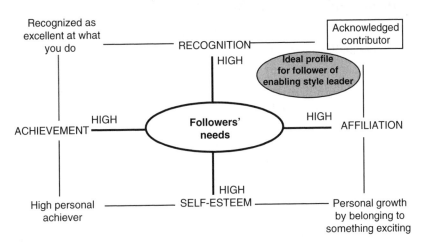

Figure 6.4 Implications of enabling leader style for followers

frequently physically dispersed followers and by openly recognizing the sources of the knowledge that they share across the business. With this ideal type of follower, the recognition given to the first knowledge contributors will make the rest very keen to be seen to share their own knowledge with their leaders and their fellow followers.

This style of leadership also highlights one of the common paradoxes that must be handled by a leader. The benefits of spreading knowledge are clearly realized in the area of the business where the new knowledge is applied. Yet most of the costs of generating these benefits are incurred in the area where the knowledge was originally developed and by the leader, particularly if tacit know-how had to be codified before being shared. The leader needs to ensure that originating followers are willing to put in the discretionary effort required to make their personal knowledge more readily applicable across the whole organization. Management-dominated companies, without leaders, often need to resort to issuing commands or to implementing sophisticated financial schemes, such as royalty or licence fees, in attempts to get their subordinates to share their knowledge with others. The potential impact of leadership is that, if leaders can gain sufficient positive commitment from their followers, previously unwilling subordinates can become willing to input extra, discretionary personal effort for the direct benefit of others in the organization.

Enabling Style Leaders at Other Levels

As we have stated, enabling style leaders at the top of organizations face a serious challenge to sustain their value-creating roles over time. In some of the case studies considered in this chapter, this has been achieved by changing the composition of the group. Bringing in new businesses can provide additional opportunities to spread existing group knowledge to these newcomers, but these businesses may also be a source of new value-creating processes that can be spread across the original business units. However, over time, the value-creating potential of enabling style leaders normally reduces and the leadership style at the top of the company may need to change, as is discussed in Chapter 8.

This in no way means that enabling style leadership itself is no longer relevant or value creating for such a company. As we have argued throughout the book, sustained extraordinary levels of performance are only achieved by the implementation of all four leadership styles within any particular company. However, these styles do not all need to be, and indeed should not be, implemented at the same level in the organization. The connecting leadership activity is a key enabler in getting separated parts of the business to work together in support of the overall vision and mission. This can be especially beneficial for the value-creating functions within a multi-business group, particularly if these functions are physically spread apart as they are when some elements are located in individual business units with other parts being based at the corporate centre.

As a result, it is quite common to find functional heads of critical knowledge-based, value-creating areas of a business operating in the enabling leadership style. A leader of the marketing, research and development, or IT function should see their value-creating role as involving connecting together the highly skilled professionals working in their functions rather than merely line managing these people as subordinates. Not surprisingly, this can have significant implications for the skills and personality required by the individual aspiring to a role as an enabling style leader of such a critical knowledge-based function.

In most large groups, the business unit-based functional heads have, in organizational terms, a 'hard' line to the general manager, or managing director, of their specific business unit with a 'dotted' line to their own group functional head. If the company is controlled by managers without leadership ability, or led by leaders who are implementing contradictory or conflicting styles, these dual matrix style reporting relationships can cause significant problems. The logical career path for professionals in these fields such as marketing, R&D and IT is to move through a series of increasingly challenging and responsible roles in various business units within the group. Hence they will want to be recognized by their functional colleagues as having something to offer as a value-creating professional in their field of expertise. This can obviously be achieved by the sharing of their personal knowledge across the group that is facilitated by 'consultant' style leadership. They will also want to be seen as making a strong positive contribution to the specific business unit in which they are currently working. Such an immediate business contribution can be significantly assisted through the adoption and implementation of knowledge or processes developed elsewhere in the group. Being willing to 'borrow with pride' when appropriate, and then to improve the borrowed process, highlights the individual's team-playing ability and their focus on achieving the vision and objectives of the business. This type of behaviour is clearly rewarded by an enabling style leader and does not necessarily conflict with the requirements of the leadership style being implemented at the top of the business unit in which this particular professional is currently located.

This style will depend upon the leadership framework that is being implemented within the company, as was outlined in Chapter 3. If an 'in-to-out' framework is in use, with visioning activity-focused leadership at the top of the organization, the business unit leader is likely to be focused on the delivering leadership activity and to be consequently operating in the incentivizing style. This style of leader is almost exclusively interested in results and therefore will not mind at all if their marketing department has implemented great ideas that were developed elsewhere. They just want to know whether they will work in their business unit or not.

In the 'out-to-in' framework, the business unit leader will normally be acting as an inspirational visioning leader as this role has been delegated to them by the incentivizing style leader at the top of the organization. As already discussed in Chapters 3 and 5, there is often a problem with the 'out-to-in' framework in terms of where and how such businesses can implement the connecting and aligning leadership activities. This is caused by the absence of any group-wide vision or mission that goes beyond 'making money' and the rapid changes to the composition of the group that are common. However, several such incentivizing style-led groups have found it value creating to enable functional professionals to share their knowledge across the group so that better practices and processes are implemented wherever relevant. This requires enabling style leadership at the top of the selected functions to create and motivate the willing followers who will actually improve these processes. Once again there is no conflict with the desires of the inspirational leadership style of the people leading each business unit. They and their team are totally focused on achieving their tailored vision. If they can get access to a much broader talent pool of ideas and knowledge, their chances of success can only be increased.

In this discussion, we have deliberately emphasized the relevance of the enabling leadership style to functions such as marketing, R&D and IT. There is no conceptual reason why other knowledge-based functions such as finance, operations and human resources should not also be led by this style. However, as discussed in Chapter 7, these functions are most commonly found to be led in the directing style with its focus on the aligning leadership activity. Before considering the reasons for this, we need to consider several examples of the enabling style being implemented at the top of the organization. We start with a company that has very successfully maintained this style for 50 years, but at the time of writing there are active discussions about the possibility of splitting the group back into its component parts. Possibly even this great example of enabling style leadership has come to the end of its value-creating life.

Leveraging Brand-building Expertise

Altria Inc. has a publicly stated mission of being 'the most successful consumer packaged goods company in the world'. Its main strategy to achieve this is through 'building and protecting' very strong consumer brands that are product based, with the first and still leading example being Marlboro.

Unlike the Coca-Cola brand, which is discussed at the end of this chapter, Marlboro has not always dominated its market in the USA. Philip Morris, as the group was then known, only entered the US cigarette market in 1934 when volumes were already over 100 billion units per year. Marlboro itself was launched in 1937 and peaked at sales volumes of 2.3 billion cigarettes in 1945. By 1953 Marlboro had a negligible share of the market and was targeted specifically at female smokers. It was relaunched in 1955 as a filter-tipped cigarette aimed primarily at male smokers. Then, in the late 1950s an advertising campaign featuring a cowboy and wide-open spaces was introduced. At this time the leading US brands, Lucky Strike, Camel and Chesterfield, were all non-filtered, plain cigarettes. These brands did not launch filtered versions until the 1960s, by which time Marlboro was well established.

Marlboro's growth was steady rather than spectacular and was fuelled by very high marketing support (i.e. brand development investment) so that in 1975 Marlboro became the largest cigarette brand in the US market. In 1983 Philip Morris (PM) became the largest US-based cigarette company, selling 205 billion cigarettes out of 597.5 billion, of which 120 billion were Marlboro. This was interesting because the US market volume peaked in 1981 at 638 billion cigarettes, and then went into a slow but continual decline. This meant that PM had followed the well-established shareholder value-enhancing strategy of gaining market share while the market was itself growing.

Once it had the leading position in this now mature market, its strategy changed and it looked to increase both its own profitability and that of the total market. Accordingly, as the price leader with the dominant brand, PM took retail selling prices up significantly faster than inflation: through the 1980s, price rises averaged 7 per cent per annum in real terms. Consequently, although total industry volumes were declining at 3 per cent per annum, the total profit pool was still increasing. This meant that the profits of all the other cigarette companies could increase, even though PM was taking an increasing share of this profit pool.

Moving international

The initial success of Marlboro in the USA led the group to make a major corporate leadership move. In the 1960s the group CEO, Joe Cullman, identified international cigarette markets as the best opportunity for long-term growth. Thus, well before Marlboro had actually achieved leadership of the US industry, he reassigned George Weissman, who had been leading the US domestic business (then 99 per cent of total group sales volumes), and put him in charge of the embryonic international operations.

He very rapidly refocused the business on Europe and Australasia and based the long-term strategy around Marlboro. This meant that Marlboro also became the best-selling cigarette brand outside the USA, mainly by taking large market shares in similarly mature markets. This is important because the group's marketing competences are most suited to particular types of competitive environment.

Marlboro has been able to build very high brand recognition globally through consistent marketing investment, such as through sponsorship of Formula One motor racing. The actual product has been modified where necessary to meet either specific market requirements (such as using Virginia tobacco rather than the normal US blends) or changing consumer requirements. Thus, as the age profile of full flavour Marlboro 'Red' cigarettes increased, the company introduced Marlboro Lights to appeal to a younger age group. However, the brand imagery has always been maintained and other cigarette brands sold by PM are carefully positioned to be compatible with Marlboro. For example, in many markets PM has brands called Philip Morris and L & M, with L & M often being referred to as 'Little Marlboro'.

The very high brand awareness generated for Marlboro should make it easier for the group to gain distribution through wholesalers and retailers in any market. However, the company is most successful in markets where the distribution channels are well organized so that it can negotiate national or regional deals with distributors, wholesalers or multi-outlet retailers. Marlboro has only small market shares in several less developed countries where many cigarettes are still sold to smokers as individual 'sticks' by street vendors.

Also Marlboro is a premium-priced cigarette in most markets around the world. This means that the issue of affordability is critical to gaining a dominant market share and explains why well-off countries such as Germany, France, the UK and Italy have been such successful competitive environments for Marlboro. In fact, the group has also learnt how to identify when Marlboro becomes very attractive in a specific market, so that it can launch its aggressive marketing campaign at the most opportune time. This can be illustrated by looking at its development in Argentina.

An appropriately tailored strategy

The Argentine economy had been ravaged by hyperinflation and the 1980s debt crisis. Early in the twentieth century, Argentina had been in the world's top ten countries in terms of trading and GDP per head. However, following the election of Juan Perón as president in 1946 the country went into a long period of economic decline. This resulted in a series of military coups until democracy was restored in 1983 following the Falklands/Malvinas war with Great Britain. Democracy was restored but the economy was not, as rampant inflation took over. Annual inflation for 1989 was 4,923 per cent and for 1990 over 2,000 per cent; it actually peaked during 1990 at an annualized rate of 20,266 per cent.

In 1989 Carlos Menem was elected president as leader of the Peronist party. However Menem, with Domingo Cavallo as his finance minister, used free market policies to try to turn the economy around. The government ran a fiscal surplus by increasing the tax base and reducing expenditure, and privatization of inefficient state-owned industries was rapidly introduced. The economy, previously protected by tariffs, was opened up through the development of Mercosur as well as the establishment of closer trading links with the USA and the rest of Latin America.

In 1991, the government launched the convertibility plan that fixed the local currency against the US dollar. However, the critical point of the plan was that the internal monetary base of the country had to be backed by foreign currency reserves. Thus if foreign currency reserves fell, the government had to reduce the domestic money supply. Government deficits could no longer be financed by printing money. No more printing money should, in theory, lead to no more inflation, or at least only the same low rate of inflation as the USA to which the currency was tied. Also the government did not have to increase the domestic money supply if foreign currency reserves increased.

Inflation fell dramatically to 4.1 per cent in 1994 and 1.9 per cent in 1995 (below the rate in the USA) but GDP growth in this period was substantial (1991, 8.9 per cent; 1992, 8.7 per cent; 1993, 6.0 per cent; 1994, 6.5 per cent). This phenomenal run was obviously too good to continue and the economy moved into recession towards the end of 1995 and Argentina faced another currency and political crisis at the end of the century.

Before the hyperinflation period, Philip Morris already had, through a local company, a presence in Argentina with Marlboro. However, its market share was small and the market was dominated by local brands. The leading cigarette company was the BAT Industries local subsidiary that had the largest local brand, Jockey Club, with around 30 per cent market share. Although Marlboro's actual market share was low, the company was aware through its consumer research that it had a much higher penetration of adult smokers, with around 25 per cent smoking Marlboro at some time. This indicated the minimum potential market share for the brand if smokers could afford to buy it on a regular basis.

During the previous economic plan, PM had launched a very low price brand into the market that, not surprisingly, had started to gain market share. This prompted a rapid response by the leading competitor that launched its own equally low price brand. This brand not only recaptured the share that had been lost but took a sizeable proportion of the total market. By 1990 its share was over 20 per cent but most of this volume had been gained at the expense of its own higher priced Jockey Club brand. While its total market share had been protected, the profitability of BAT's Argentine company had been decimated.

As inflation started to fall and GDP per head to grow, PM supported Marlboro even more aggressively with much higher levels of marketing expenditure. The company's market support for Marlboro had, for some years, been excessive by reference to its current low market share. As consumers' purchasing power increased, the industry looked to recover some of its former profitability by increasing selling prices in real terms, particularly of the marginally profitable, but dominant, very low priced products. This gave Marlboro a significant competitive opportunity as it had always been established in the higher priced category and its pricing had not been discounted in the earlier price wars.

PM was able to close the *relative* price gap between the very low price brands and Marlboro by maintaining the *absolute* price differential through 1991 to 1995. This made Marlboro much more affordable in the eyes of the target consumers and its market share grew very rapidly to over 35 per cent by the end of 1995. This gave PM's Argentine company a total market share of over 50 per cent, which it has maintained since.

Not surprisingly the group has sought to implement very similar competitive strategies in other countries that face equivalent economic challenges. Argentina's much larger neighbour, Brazil, with its five times larger population and comparable government-driven economic plans was an obvious target. To date, BAT's local subsidiary has retained its market leadership but PM has been more successful with a very similar strategy in several Central and East European markets.

Another very good, recent example has been in Turkey where, since its entry in 1992, the company has already become value and volume market leader with its market share being largely gained from Tekel, the previous monopoly supplier that is still state-owned.

Moving away from cigarettes
The very strong cash generation of its highly successful Marlboro brand-led cigarettes business enabled the group to acquire other branded product companies. At the same time, all the other major cigarette companies were also diversifying out of tobacco as a defensive measure against the increasing threats to their existing earnings streams. However, Altria has had by far the most successful acquisition-led growth strategy as it deliberately set out to leverage the key existing knowledge held by the group. Altria had already demonstrated its

ability to build a domestic market-leading brand that could then be translated into equally leading positions in many international markets.

Its acquisitions of non-cigarette businesses were of brands in 'not-so-healthy' consumer products where the group felt that its marketing expertise could add value. All of these had quite good positions in their domestic markets but had not established similarly strong brand values internationally. Thus these acquisitions were in brewing (Miller), soft drinks (Seven-Up), coffee (Maxwell House from the purchase of General Foods), processed cheese (Kraft), and chocolate (Jacob Suchard). Not all of these were successful but the group did try to ensure that it learnt from its mistakes.

The best example of this was its purchase of Seven-Up in 1978 that never worked out and ended when it was sold in 1986 at a loss. In several subsequent publications senior executives have openly discussed the thousands of hours of management time that were spent in trying both to make the acquisition successful and then to learn why it did not work as part of the group. Miller brewing would be classified as a successful beer company by most of its competitors. However, it could not achieve the relative brand strength, compared to its global rival Budweiser, that Altria expects of its leading brands. As a result Altria merged Miller into SAB (South African Breweries) to give it a significant minority stake in the greatly enlarged SAB Miller business.

The group's main US-based competitor, RJ Reynolds, from which PM took leadership of the US cigarette industry, also made a large number of acquisitions. Some of these were of fast-moving consumer goods (FMCG) businesses (e.g. Nabisco) but Reynolds also bought a large shipping container company (Sea-Land) and an oil company (Aminoil). These true diversification moves actually destroyed a lot of shareholder value, for example Sea-Land was sold five years later at a significant loss. Even the more related food acquisition did not create value as the group had no really relevant knowledge that could be leveraged across these acquisitions. At the time of its acquisition Nabisco had brands that still had leadership in their domestic market; spreading the knowledge of how to lose this leadership is not value creating. Subsequent to RJR Nabisco's highly leveraged buyout by KKR in 1989 and the disposal of its international tobacco business to Japan Tobacco in 1998, RJ Reynolds sold its Nabisco food businesses to Altria. This left

Reynolds as a focused US-based cigarette company and in 2004 it merged with BAT's US-based subsidiary, Brown & Williamson.

BAT Industries' own value-destroying diversification strategy was discussed earlier in the book but BAT plc is now totally focused on the global tobacco industry. However, as it does not possess the leading global brand, it cannot apply exactly the same knowledge leverage as Altria. Indeed, the challenge facing BAT is that its success in the many markets around the world where it is the leading cigarette company (e.g. Canada, Brazil, South Africa and Malaysia) seems to be based on significantly different factors. Identifying any key knowledge that can be leveraged across the group is not therefore as straightforward for BAT as it is for PM, should BAT decide that it wants to focus on the connecting leadership activity.

This need not be of itself a bad thing as long as the corporate leadership focuses its attention on identifying this key knowledge. Altria has really been applying a 'one-size fits all' branding strategy that works very successfully as long as the marketplace is not highly segmented. If different groups of consumers really want different things, it should be possible for a competitor to develop an appropriately tailored brand portfolio where each brand is targeted at a different segment of the total market. Such a segmentation strategy may restrict the total market share of any single brand as it cannot be the *most* relevant brand to several different groups of consumers. Indeed, its previous broad-based general appeal may mean that it is not the most relevant to *any* single segment.

In this kind of focused marketing-led strategy, the critical knowledge for the businesses becomes how to understand the specific requirements of individual consumers and how to group these consumers together into meaningful market segmentations. Thus, although the brands used in individual markets where BAT is market leader may be different and even the consumer segments may be unique to that market, the marketing research *processes* that were used to understand the particular needs of these markets may be very relevant to many other markets. This means that the role of the corporate leaders would be to identify and codify these key marketing processes through which each separate market will develop its own specifically tailored brand portfolio.

A company like Altria can be much more prescriptive and almost formulaic in the knowledge that it spreads across the group. Its direct competitor may need to be less directly interventionist but could still add a lot of value by identifying the real value-adding knowledge that has general application across the group.

Cultural Implications and Leadership Challenges

Clearly these differences impact on the organizational culture within the group. Where the competitive strategies being implemented by the individual business units within a group are very similar, the corporate leader may be able to identify a number of highly significant developments in the external competitive environment that should enable the business unit to implement the next stage of the strategy. For example, it is now well established that the demand for various categories of consumer products increases dramatically when GDP per head passes through certain critical levels (such as consumer durables at $1,000 GDP per head). This group knowledge can clearly be leveraged to optimize the timing of marketing expenditure in markets approaching such critical points. If this knowledge has already been validated in many markets, the resulting high level of confidence means that its implementation may be mandated by the enabling style corporate leader. The upwards communication that is needed from the business unit is the prediction of when the triggering event will occur: e.g. when will Marlboro become generally affordable in a particular market?

Of course, the knowledge that is to be leveraged may be less precise and require much more interpretation or modification before being applied successfully in other parts of the group. In these cases it may be sensible for the leaders to be less prescriptive in the way they spread the knowledge across the group. The knowledge may be expressed as best practice or described as a 'successful case study' of what was done by a specific business unit. The danger of this approach is, of course, that there will be much less take-up by other business units with a correspondingly lower level of conformance achieved across the group. Achieving conformance across the group in the application of leveragable knowledge is important to the success of the enabling style corporate leader.

A very interesting result of our research is the identification of a common difference on this dimension between US-led groups and European-based ones. Altria and BAT have already been mentioned but the same differences can be highlighted between Procter & Gamble and

Unilever, or by comparing Shell to its US-based competitors such as Exxon-Mobil.

Procter & Gamble (P & G) was founded in 1837 by two brothers-in-law who found that their businesses used the same raw materials. William Procter was a candle-maker while James Gamble manufactured soap. Although the early business grew quite slowly from its base in Cincinnati, the founders established the very strong culture that still pervades the group today. There is a P & G 'way of doing things' that new entrants to the group learn by a process that has been described as indoctrination. Successful employees have to be totally comfortable with this 'tightness of fit' that is applied in all the countries where the group operates. The P & G culture is therefore seen as coming before the specific national culture of the employees. This is strongly reinforced by a policy of promotion from within, so that senior managers will all have developed within this cultural environment.

However, the group avoids becoming outdated through its internal processes and fundamental beliefs in product excellence and continuous improvement. Sales and marketing are absolutely core business processes of P & G and it was the first major group to introduce the idea of self-competing brands in 1931. Also, even further back in 1919, it revolutionized the industry's distribution system in the USA by going straight to retailers rather than selling through wholesalers. Since then it has continually leveraged its brand-building expertise and sales management knowledge across the group. Attaining the essential buy-in to this philosophy of sharing in order to achieve economies of scope by leveraging existing knowledge is quite easy in a group that has such a strong culture and a willing acceptance of a P & G way to do things.

It also enables the corporate centre to take a quite strong leadership role within the group without creating resentment at the business unit level that the centre is interfering too much. This is much more difficult in a less centralized group such as Unilever.

Unilever was formed in 1930 by the merger of two already well-established businesses, Margarine Unie and Lever Bros. The group developed into four global business groups based on food, detergents, personal products and speciality chemicals; the speciality chemicals business group has now been sold to ICI. Unilever has a relatively decentralized management style but the corporate centre has a connecting leadership role that ensures best practices are shared across the relevant business units. The group has also developed very strong skills in concept marketing to mass-market consumers, with the corporate leadership focusing on marketing research, trade marketing, promotions and advertising, and fostering a company-wide marketing culture. However, the central marketing function is seen as a service organization, working for the business groups and having to gain buy-in from each business group for any major new initiative.

This has resulted in some excellent processes being implemented across the group as marketing knowledge is leveraged by the leaders at the centre, but the 'independent' business units have used these common processes to develop their own tailored brand portfolios. Unilever therefore found itself with a worldwide portfolio totalling 1,600 brands and implemented a global 'Path to Growth' programme to rationalize this to a total of 400 brands. This is being achieved by more direct intervention from the corporate leaders.

Conversely P & G never developed such a localized array of brands but it is also having to reconsider the role of its corporate centre, following its current failure to achieve its aggressive sales growth targets. It is actually moving to slightly more of a Unilever structure with seven global product category businesses replacing its previously geographically-based businesses. The logic is that this is required to serve increasingly global retailers such as Wal-Mart, Carrefour and Tesco, but it will mean even less autonomy for the individual country-based business unit managers. This increased centralization increases the risk that the leaders at the corporate centre actually identify inappropriate knowledge to leverage across the group.

Leveraging the Product Development Process

Of course, the ideal, sustainable, enabling style corporate leader will identify and exploit a progressive series of competitive advantages that enable the group to establish a very strong corporate advantage. This may involve managing the group's exit from some businesses where the corporate advantage is no longer relevant. The Intel group is a good example of this.

Intel was founded in the 1960s to make memory chips and based on this chip expertise it launched the 4004 microprocessor in 1971. The group implemented an innovative strategy for its microprocessors in that it deliberately targeted the end-user as its customer, rather than the original equipment manufacturers (OEMs) that most competitors were selling to. This strategy obviously took time to come to full fruition but the group emphasized new design wins (i.e. new customers) rather than sales volumes or even new products. In 1980, Intel had 2,500 new design wins and then in 1981 it got Ford Motor Company as a customer. By 1983 150,000 Ford cars per month were being fitted with Intel microprocessors. Then, in 1984, Intel beat Motorola to win the IBM personal computer contract with its 8088 microprocessor.

During this period Intel had licensed its microprocessor designs to several other manufacturers for a number of reasons. It stopped these manufacturers investing in R&D directly and it gave Intel a more guaranteed demand for each new product innovation. These competitors were primarily selling to OEMs, which were not Intel's main targets, and this helped to make Intel's product architecture the industry standard. IBM also required a second source for its PC microprocessors.

However, Intel then stopped this licensing strategy and this forced previous licensees to reverse-engineer all of Intel's new products. This gave Intel about a one-year time advantage on its new products and therefore refocused the corporate advantage to its product development process timescales. Intel now had to develop and market new generations of technology faster than competitors could copy them; it rapidly halved its product development time to well under one year, and keeps reducing it even though the technology gets more complex. The group moved to parallel generation development in three locations (California, Oregon and Israel) where completely new product ranges are started each year.

Intel's next move was into chip sets and then motherboards, which drastically reduced the entry barriers into the PC manufacturing industry. This gave it much greater competitive strength relative to the existing dominant computer companies, such as IBM, Compaq and Toshiba. Effectively Intel, with very strong help from Microsoft, was commoditizing the actual PC industry. This was reinforced by the 'Intel Inside' marketing campaign aimed directly at consumers. This was launched in 1991, when direct consumer sales of PCs were still not that significant. Intel's market dominance meant that OEMs competed for the exclusive right to use the latest Intel design, because consumers would pay a premium to buy products incorporating these components. Once competitors were able to match this technology, Intel would drop its selling price significantly, but it would already have launched at least one, if not two new products, for which it could charge premium prices.

The development of Intel's microprocessor business had been funded by its early success in memory chips but this success did not continue. During the 1970s the Dynamic Random Access Memory (DRAM) chip market was growing dramatically and Intel was a profitable leading player. However, the dramatic growth attracted many large-scale Japanese competitors and the battle for cost leadership started. Matsushita, Mitsubishi, Toshiba, NEC, Fujitsu and Hitachi all built large-scale production facilities and forced down selling prices to levels at which Intel could not make a profit. In 1985 Intel decided that this had become a commodity business to which its speed of product development and group branding had no relevance. Thus it exited from memory chips and sacked 30 per cent of its workforce.

The key to sustaining such a strategy is clearly focusing on a limited number of things and ensuring that the knowledge gained in one part of the organization can very rapidly be leveraged elsewhere in the group. This applies as much to new process innovations that will reduce the product development cycle as to the actual technology developments on which the group depends. A critical element for any such dominant technology group is avoiding 'shooting itself in the knee-cap' every time it launches a new generation of products that automatically reduces the value of its existing product range. So far, Intel has succeeded in this where other technology-led companies have not to the same extent.

Sustainability Issues

Intel has remained a highly focused group, with well-understood corporate advantages, an appropriately innovative culture and a strong central leadership role. However, enabling style-led groups can comprise quite diverse businesses if they are leveraging more general core competences. The problem is that these more general advantages are less difficult for competitors to copy and this can reduce the group's long-term sustainability. Interestingly, it is possible to have a highly specific corporate advantage that binds together an otherwise wide range of businesses, but this can also limit the long-term value-adding capability of the corporate centre. This can be illustrated by considering the Disney group's development under the leadership of Michael Eisner.

In the early 1980s Disney was in serious financial trouble after it raised a lot of debt to pay 'greenmail' to buy off a hostile corporate raider who had threatened to break up the group. The corporate centre had previously made several poor acquisitions and invested heavily in real estate and this management team was replaced in 1984. When Eisner took over, Disney basically produced movies, operated theme parks and licensed consumer products, but all these were operated as separate businesses. Also these separate businesses each had problems. Attendances at the theme parks were falling and film production had experienced serious cost overruns that had led to a $30 million loss in 1983.

Eisner's initial focus therefore was to improve the core product performance: 14 of the first 15 films produced after he joined were profitable. The group also re-released several of its great animation films from the past and then developed some new blockbusters. However, the key move was to increase the value share that Disney captured from its intellectual content, and Eisner created a central corporate strategy team to focus on that. This started to transform Disney from a 'creator of content' to a 'creator and distributor of content'. The group moved directly into retail to create 'a different shopping experience' and build a more direct link with consumers. This sought to leverage the Disney brand and the specific service culture of the group, where customers are the 'audience' and employees are 'performers'.

Disney dramatically expanded its distribution capability with the acquisition of Buena Vista and then ABC/Capital Cities, which included ESPN and cable channels. This enabled the group to launch its own Disney channel. 1985 was the thirtieth anniversary of Disneyland's opening and the associated advertising campaign increased the number of visitors. However, the problem was that Disney captured too little of the total expenditure of these visitors. Thus Disney quadrupled its on-site hotel rooms and dramatically expanded the range of facilities, adding MGM studios, golf courses, conference facilities, the Disney Institute, etc. It became a complete vacations solutions company, having also expanded its theme parks internationally and moved into cruises as well as Broadway musicals.

Effectively all these businesses not only try to leverage the Disney characters but also comply with the fundamental positioning of the group as a 'family entertainment' company. Thus Disney has brought its specialized knowledge about entertaining kids and adults to a much wider range of businesses. For 15 years this created a large amount of shareholder value but, almost inevitably, there is a limit to the leverage capability of such a specific corporate advantage. If the group tries to spread it too far, it can significantly, and possibly permanently, damage the critically important customer loyalty that has been built up over many years.

Another illustration of this stretch concept is the Virgin group, which relies heavily for its brand positioning on the highly irreverent and exciting lifestyle of its founder, Richard Branson. The group started life as a record label before moving into music retailing. It developed a strong brand image that appealed to young consumers and the group then applied this branding to air travel, financial services, mobile telephones and some consumer products. In each case, its positioning was significantly different from the established products on the market and reinforced the overall brand imagery. Also the Virgin group added value was focused on this brand positioning as the actual product delivery was either completely outsourced or achieved by bringing in a proven top management team with relevant industry expertise. However, the group then tried to apply its branding knowledge to the British railway industry following its privatization. The relevance of the group's branding, with its emphasis on 'fun plus a no-nonsense, easily understood product offering', to this product group is much more difficult to understand.

Leveraging Knowledge through Franchising

The Virgin idea of increasing the potential for leveraging a group's specialist knowledge without losing focus is not new. Many groups have dramatically accelerated their rates of growth by exploiting their knowledge effectively through the efforts of others. As long as the group retains control over the key value-adding knowledge, it should also receive the vast majority of the resulting shareholder value that is created. A common way of implementing this type of corporate strategy is through franchising out the actual localized operations of the group, such as is done by fast-food restaurant chains like McDonald's, and retail chains like Body Shop and Benetton. However, the earliest and best example is Coca-Cola, and it is interesting to see how the group has developed its corporate strategy over time, while always maintaining its leadership focus on leveraging its incredibly strong branding.

Coca-Cola Inc. was able to grow, initially in the USA, very rapidly by focusing on the manufacture of its syrup concentrate and the brand advertising for its soft drink product. The actual production of the finished consumer product was outsourced to over 1,200 franchised bottlers spread across the USA. These bottlers were set up with territorial exclusivity, perpetual contracts and a fixed syrup price. The bottlers did very well during the market's rapid growth but the US market matured in the 1970s with growth rates falling to 3 per cent per year. These franchisees then looked on Coke bottling and distribution as a good profit generator but no longer a high potential business.

Also Coke's bottlers were, by definition, locally based and therefore the group was not structured to do regional and national deals with the rapidly expanding retail chains. Pepsi-Cola could do this as it owned many of its larger bottlers and by 1977 Pepsi had an equal share to Coca-Cola in US supermarkets and the overall gap in total market share was narrowing significantly. Coca-Cola needed to restructure its bottlers but the perpetual contracts and fixed price syrup made this potentially very expensive. Coca-Cola had also started to diversify and in the 1970s was in shrimp farming, plastic straw manufacture, etc.

The new corporate leader and CEO, Robert Goizueta, refocused the group and used a significant product development to achieve a fundamental restructuring of its total value chain in 1981. The company had developed a high fructose corn syrup as an alternative to sugar in the syrup concentrate that reduced the cost by 20 per cent. Goizueta made the lower cost product available to bottlers on the condition of amending the original contracts. Also Coca-Cola altered its relationship with many of its bottlers. In the Philippines, it had lost 70 per cent market share to Pepsi by 1981 when it took a 30 per cent equity stake in its local bottler. It then increased investment in modernization, advertising and placed more emphasis on vending machines and managing key accounts. The resulting improvements were dramatic. During the 1980s Coca-Cola then acquired many of its US-based bottling franchisees and focused on developing the areas of other good bottlers. This significantly increased its asset base and reduced its return on equity, even though these bottlers were themselves highly profitable.

In 1986, therefore, Coca-Cola Enterprises was set up as a holding company for these owned bottlers and a majority stake was floated on the US stock market. This meant that Coca-Cola no longer had to consolidate its remaining minority stake, so its return on equity rose back to its previous very high levels. Also the group generated over $1 billion in cash that could be spent on acquiring more bottlers. This model was replicated around the world as the group grew internationally with its large anchor bottlers that effectively controlled a country or region being partially owned by Coca-Cola Enterprises. During this period, Pepsi-Cola started to move into snack foods and restaurant chains. It acquired Pizza Hut, Taco Bell and KFC, all of which sold Pepsi-Cola exclusively. However, this effectively forced their competitors, Burger King and Wendy's, to switch to Coca-Cola, like McDonald's. Interestingly, in this industry, a key battleground is distribution in restaurants and vending machines, which tend to be exclusive. Consumption and selling prices are both high, with correspondingly much higher profits than in grocery channels. The grocery channel is necessary to promote the brand to consumers.

By the mid-1990s Coca-Cola had a dominant share in the soft drinks market outside the USA and this generated 80 per cent of its $4 billion operating profit. By contrast, Pepsi-Cola generated 90 per cent of its profits in the USA. However, the growth rate in many of these markets is now slowing significantly and the group faces increased competitive pressures in many countries. This is being generated not only by its traditional competitors such as Pepsi-Cola, but also from new entrants such as Virgin Cola and retailer own brand cola products which are sold at much lower prices. Coca-Cola has to date failed to leverage its consumer branding expertise and in-depth knowledge of production and distribution channels across into other product areas. It is therefore, in some senses, a victim of its own success and the limitations of the enabling leadership style at the top of a company. Its stock market rating has inevitably fallen as investors and analysts lower their future growth expectations. The group could deliver continuing short-term growth in profits by reducing marketing support for the brand but obviously this would be at the expense of the company's longer-term future. Alternatively it could alter its corporate leadership style but this also has significant risks, as already discussed.

Conclusion

The enabling leadership style can sustain its value-creating role as long as it can identify areas of knowledge that can be exploited more widely across the group. For many large groups this eventually becomes increasingly difficult. This can result in an excessive level of direct intervention by corporate leadership as it either seeks to leverage inappropriate competences or becomes much too transactionally involved in the operations of the business units.

There are many examples of these corporate centres then changing their focus from leveraging knowledge to directly reducing costs. In other words the transactional leadership emphasis and lack of knowledge advantage has changed the leader's role to the directing style. As discussed in Chapter 7, this is particularly likely as the industry matures and the basis of competition becomes selling price rather than differentiation. Thus, if the latest knowledge that has been leveraged across the group was to do with 'how to reduce costs', it is easy to see how the corporate leaders could decide to implement such cost reductions themselves through centralizing certain core processes or support activities.

Enabling style corporate leaders should focus on transformational leadership roles so that their process expertise changes the way in which the business units themselves compete. However, once the corporate leader has spread any specific knowledge and this is being applied by the business units, they cease to create value until they identify the next source of knowledge able to be leveraged. In some cases this causes the corporate leader to try to stimulate the creation of new knowledge and this effectively means that they are trying to make the transition to the inspiring leader style that was discussed in Chapter 4.

7

Aligning the organization

When we apply our model with corporate leaders in their companies, we sometimes have to overcome some initial confusion between the role and impact of the connecting and aligning leadership activities. It may therefore be helpful to contrast these two value-creating activities before considering the directing leadership style in depth.

As discussed in Chapter 6 and as summarized in Figure 7.1, the connecting leadership activity that is the focus of the enabling leadership style can work right across any organizational structure. Its impact is to change 'what is done' in these structurally unconnected parts of the group, often by spreading existing knowledge more widely. By doing this, the organization avoids the unnecessary duplication of effort that results from employees reinventing what already exists elsewhere in the company. They can immediately implement the existing best practice within the group and then try to improve on that. The source of increased value from the connecting activity is the resulting release of psychological energy, but this energy is normally reinvested by the company. In other words, the same number of people are still employed but they can now work more effectively and so create more shareholder value in total. Indeed, a common impact of this leadership activity can be an increase in the direct costs of the first area to develop and apply any new knowledge, as they make it more readily applicable in other areas of the business. These increased costs should be more than offset by the extra value created as this knowledge is more widely leveraged.

	Connecting	Aligning
Impact on organizational structure	Works across existing structure	Changes structure
Impact on followers	Changes what is done	Changes where and how the same things are done
Source of increased value	Releases psychological energy	Releases physical energy
Impact on cost levels	Increases direct costs but creates value elsewhere	Reduces costs directly Outputs produced more efficiently

Figure 7.1 Contrasting the connecting and aligning leadership activities

By contrast, the aligning leadership activity often changes the formal organization structure by centralizing or outsourcing specific activities so that they are only done in one area, or a few areas, rather than being widely dispersed around the business. The aligning activity therefore changes where activities are done and may also change how these activities are carried out. However, it does not change what is done; it only changes where and how it is done. Centralizing the accounts payable process does not alter the actual activity of paying suppliers; it can change where they are paid from and may alter how they are paid, but they must still get paid. The benefit of this aligning activity is an improvement in the efficiency with which the specific activity is carried out. This achieves a release of physical energy as less total resources will be used following the adoption of the more efficient methods. The aligning activity should therefore directly reduce the costs incurred by the total business. These releases of physical energy are often realized as direct cost savings by the company, rather than being reinvested as is commonly the case with the benefit of the connecting activity.

Overview of the Directing Style

The directing leadership style can be highly effective with only a few followers, as long as these followers include all those most significantly affected by the associated aligning activity. These followers must also

Number of followers required	Few (those most affected by changes)
Level of buy-in needed	Very high
Source of improved performance	Releases physical energy
Type of leadership	Strong strategic and transactional
Key value-creating activity	Aligning

Figure 7.2 Overview of directing style

have a high level of commitment to their directing style leaders and the changes that they propose. This high level of buy-in must come from those areas of the business that are losing current activities that are being centralized, as well as from the areas that are taking them over. This high positive commitment can be achieved if these followers are very confident that these newly outsourced activities will still be performed for them satisfactorily *and* at a lower cost.

This means that the focus of directing style leadership is to standardize common business activities in order to generate economies of scale and reduce total costs. As already stated, the released physical energy is often taken as a cost saving although these resources could be reinvested elsewhere in the organization. There is clearly a risk associated with standardizing business activities and processes across any group. There may have been very good reasons for the specific differences in the ways in which the activity was previously carried out in various parts of the organization. Consequently the standardized process may be cheaper but significantly less appropriate for the needs of some followers. Alternatively, all these various nuances and subtleties can be taken into account so that everyone still gets their originally tailored activity, but the total costs involved are at least as high as they previously were.

This potential conflict highlights the requirement for this style to have strong strategic and transactional leadership capabilities.

Directing style leaders must have a very good understanding of the needs of their business so that their standardization initiatives do not go too far, while genuine cost-saving opportunities are not unnecessarily missed. If these leaders deliver on their early promises of real cost savings from centralization without compromising the valid requirements of the most affected parts of the business, they will build the trust and respect that creates the required high level of buy-in from their followers for future alignment activities.

As these alignment activities frequently involve relatively permanent changes in the structure of the organization, the most critical leadership capability for the directing style is 'exhibiting staying power'. As shown in Figure 7.3, the changes in the organization should obviously make it more clearly aligned to the needs of the corporate vision. In this respect, the leadership capabilities of communicating for success and crafting the future both have roles to play, but the impact of exhibiting staying power is more significant and it is also closely linked to the remaining two capabilities in the directing style.

An aligned organization should have very clear responsibilities and accountabilities that should reduce the potential for confusion and misunderstandings. Thus the leaders are handling the potential paradoxes that can arise from a lack of clarity, but they are also using the engaging through dialogue capability by focusing the dialogue among their followers, many of whom will be lower-level leaders themselves

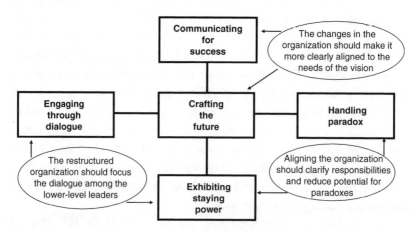

Figure 7.3 Critical leadership capabilities: the directing style leader

in the organization. The restructured and aligned organization, with its clear responsibilities and focused areas of activities, highlights both where dialogue is critically needed and where it is unnecessary and therefore potentially time wasting and cost increasing.

Implications for Followers

This clarity and focus has significant implications for the followers of a directing style leader. The role of these followers is normally clearly defined and they are simply tasked to 'do what you are supposed to do', while being attentive to costs. In other words, they should strive to be as efficient as possible with the emphasis on continuous improvement within their clearly defined area of activity. The ideal follower, therefore, as shown in Figure 7.4, has a high personal need for achievement and values recognition from other people whose opinion they respect. This will obviously include their directing style leader to whom they are highly committed and those other people in the organization that they consider to have related skills and relevant expertise. In some cases, this will include their internal customers but many such followers, who are themselves leading internal group-wide shared service centres, will not rate the opinion of their internal customers too highly. As long as they comply with the requirements of any service-level

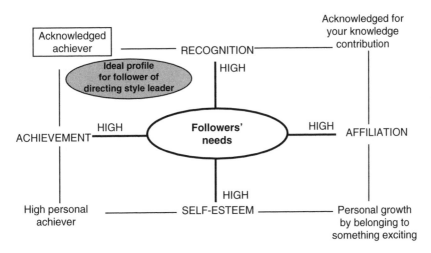

Figure 7.4 Implications of directing leader style for followers

agreement that is established with these customers, they may regard beating their own cost targets as more important than improving the level of service to these customers. This is why it is so important that the specific responsibilities and accountabilities are very clearly defined in such an aligned organization.

It is not surprising, therefore, that directing style leaders tend to create an internally driven set of followers, who are much more concerned with the opinions of their leaders than those of their fellow followers. This results in a culture where the primary identity of these followers is with their own specific activity and/or role rather than with either the group as a whole or even their own overall function. However, there is a need for a medium to high level of trust and respect between leader and follower which is normally based in both directions on technical expertise, although the particular expertise will often be different. As shown in Figure 7.5, the communication style from manager style leaders to their followers can be quite formal and take the form of specific commands, such as 'you will centralize this area of activity and it will be physically relocated'.

This all raises an interesting challenge for the followers of this leadership style when they are themselves looking to act as leaders with their own highly-motivated followers. They need to develop a high level of motivation if they are to achieve the continuing cost-efficiency improvements that will be expected by their own directing style leader. How this can be done depends, not surprisingly, on the particular

Culture within group	Efficiency focused
Primary identification of followers	Identify with activity/role
Minimum level of trust needed	Medium
Minimum level of respect required	Medium
Source of respect	Technical expertise
Communication style	Formal / command style instructions

Figure 7.5 Cultural implications of directing leadership style

business context in which they are trying to act as a leader and the nature of their own prospective followers. In other words, what type of activity are they focusing on and what are the number, calibre and needs of the potential followers who they are seeking to motivate?

Some commonly centralized activities, such as tax, treasury and corporate finance, typically involve only a few highly professional, relatively self-motivating people. Consequently they could be effectively led by an incentivizing style leader who can successfully appeal to their needs for high personal achievement by setting stretching personal targets, as shown in Figure 7.6. Alternatively the activity may still be physically spread around the organization or involve a range of skills, so that getting people to share knowledge across the activity could be very value creating. In this case, the followers of a directing style leader should themselves adopt the enabling leadership style which would appeal to potential followers with high needs for recognition and affiliation. This issue of followers themselves becoming leaders and the relationship between their needs as followers and their style as leaders is discussed more fully in Chapter 8. However, once again, the commonly tried amplifier framework of a follower implementing the same leadership style as their own leader does not work.

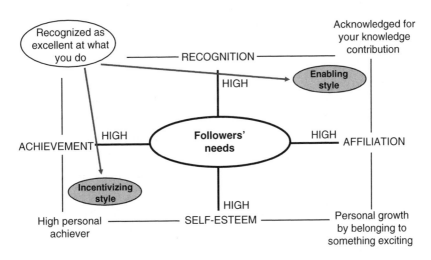

Figure 7.6 From follower to leader

Another Benefit of Alignment

Aligning the organization so that some or all of the common activities across a company are carried out as cost efficiently as possible can clearly create value by reducing the total costs incurred by that company. However, one of the very interesting apparent paradoxes to come out of our research is that it is quite common to find businesses preferring centralization, or some other form of outsourcing, even though it does not save them money. The ability to 'get rid of' essential but non-value-creating activities enables these business leaders to focus on the limited number of key value-creating processes that really matter to the achievement of their vision. Of course, many companies try to achieve this by setting priorities within each function or area of the business, but this cannot create the same very high level of focus within the business.

A real life example may make this clearer. The newly appointed country general manager of a fast-moving consumer goods company was given the challenge of proving the viability of his group's presence in this particular market. He faced a dominant but declining domestic competitor and a few already quite well-established international players also importing products into this market. His company had been trying to gain a viable foothold in the market for over ten years without any significant success and the local business unit was still making losses. Various product ranges and competitive strategies had been tried by a succession of top management teams.

The government had recently announced phased changes in import tariff levels that necessitated an early decision on whether to build a factory on-shore or exit from this market, which was very large and highly profitable. Clearly this decision would be primarily based on the projected sustainable market share that could be achieved. The general manager decided to focus exclusively on developing a new premium brand that had not previously had any profile in this country, although it had had success in other similar markets. This made the strategic focus of the total business unit gaining distribution, trial and consumer acceptance for this single brand. The new leader wanted everyone in his company to be exclusively focused on the success of this brand as, if they could not make it work, the business did not have an economically viable position in the market. Of course, this was also very clear to all their established competitors, who were accordingly determined to make this new strategy fail like all the rest had.

In order to accentuate this focus on getting the single brand established in the marketplace, the leader would have paid a premium cost if it enabled him to outsource, whether to other parts of the group or to an external third party, as much of the general administration activity of the business unit as possible. This creation of very tight focus enabled the top leadership team to develop a highly tailored competitive strategy that increased its chances of success. However, this consumer obsessed, marketing-led strategy required a great deal of flexibility and very rapid responses to changes in the competitive environment. Sales volumes grew very quickly but this made them very difficult to forecast accurately. As new distribution channels were opened, the business needed to expand its sales and distribution capabilities immediately. The strategy was based on a premium-priced brand and hence product quality was vitally important, but the product was still being manufactured in a factory several thousand miles away. The volatility and rapid growth in demand meant that much of the product had to be produced on short runs and air-freighted into the market, rather than using the much more cost-efficient normal operational planning cycle and the cheaper but slower sea-borne shipping channel. Thus the business unit wanted to delegate the provision of even essential activities, so that it could exclusively focus on a few key value-creating activities, but not in a way that robbed it of its essential flexibility. There are clearly short-term cost implications in achieving this but these can be justified by the increase in the probability of success for the selected strategy. Within 18 months this brand became the fastest growing product in the market. Within three years, the general manager was moved to an even larger new market for the group where he rapidly established a stretch mission of becoming market leader within five years!

The key issue in this very strategic use of the aligning leadership activity is that a very high level of understanding and agreement must be obtained from all those most significantly affected by the change. In this example, this means that the providers of all of these outsourced activities, particularly the manufacture and delivery of the product, must be maturely involved followers of the directing style leader. They must fully appreciate the critical importance of meeting the market's seemingly impossible demands with a consistently high quality product, even though this almost certainly runs completely counter to their normal objectives of minimizing total supply chain costs in more stable environments.

From Model T to Today

The issues involved in focusing on the aligning leadership activity could be illustrated by using a number of detailed industry examples, but we have chosen the car industry as it is an industry that was originally built using directing style leadership where aligning the organization resulted in the standardization of many core manufacturing processes.

In 1907 Henry Ford announced that his company would 'democratize the automobile' by producing a car 'that everyone will be able to afford' so that 'everyone will have one'. At this time Ford Motor Company, which had been founded in 1903 as one of over 500 new car manufacturers started in the USA, was by no means the market leader. It had already launched five models (A, B, C, F and K) into the market before the Model T in 1908, but the Model T was the first to utilize the full concept of a mass production-line manufacturing process.

Effectively Ford Motor Company reverse-engineered the Model T Ford because the end-selling price had to be affordable by the average American family. This meant that every car produced was exactly the same, e.g. it was only available in black, in order to gain the maximum economies of scale in the total production process. The new model was such a wonderful success that Ford was able to reduce the selling price by 58 per cent from its launch in 1908 to 1916 during which period 15 million cars were sold. Demand outstripped even this level of supply, so that Ford could in fact have raised prices rather than reducing them; the company was very strongly challenged by some shareholders and much of the business press for not taking advantage of this pricing opportunity. Henry Ford replied that he much preferred to sell large volumes of cars at a reasonable profit as that made more customers happy and enabled the company to employ more workers at reasonable wages.

It also, of course, made Ford Motor Company the US market leader and gave it a sustainable cost advantage that could potentially be transferred to later models in order to maintain this market leadership. General Motors had been formed in 1908 to acquire and reorganize several small car manufacturers; by 1910, it owned Buick Motors, Cadillac, Pontiac and Oldsmobile, with Chevrolet being added in 1918. The new group suffered severely as the Model T gained market dominance and it very nearly went bust. Then in 1921 Alfred Sloan took over as the corporate leader of GM and the group deliberately gave the now car-owning public a choice of replacement models at different pricing levels. General Motors rapidly overtook Ford to become and stay the largest auto manufacturer, as Ford was very reluctant, and hence very slow, to give up its total focus on reducing its cost base through economies of scale.

This very early but classic example highlights one of the major constraints of directing style leadership: maximizing economies of scale requires great standardization in business activities. Such levels of standardization can have opportunity costs that significantly outweigh the benefits of the cost reductions generated by the economies of scale. Of course, the global car companies are now much more sophisticated in their use of centralized activities but there can still be real dangers involved. In these global companies, centralization obviously does not necessarily mean establishing a single physical facility for the worldwide group, but it does entail removing these centralized facilities from the direct control of the end market-focused business units. Thus Ford Motor Company does not have manufacturing facilities in every country in which it sells vehicles and, even where this is the case, the manufacturing plant is unlikely to produce solely for its local market. Thus the centralized sourcing strategy seeks to achieve economies of scale by allowing individual plants to concentrate on a limited range of outputs (e.g. assembling Focus cars, or manufacturing diesel engines), even though this results in a very high level of components and finished vehicles being shipped around the world. Ford was one of the earliest exponents of this more global approach to its industry and set up, for example, its central Ford of Europe organization a long time before most other similar international groups.

Nowadays many of the large automotive groups seek to reduce their total costs by sharing major components across their 'differentiated' range of products. Thus one car group can have similar sized cars that are sold as different brands at very different pricing levels. If these cars were all completely different, this would increase the group's manufacturing complexity enormously and hence reduce its economies of scale equally significantly. However, if the group was able to utilize major elements across all this range, it could be possible to obtain major economies of scale while still positioning the cars in different segments of the market. A good example of this is the VW Group that owns the very distinct brands Audi, Volkswagen, Seat and Skoda. Each of these car brands is positioned in a different market segment but the group seeks to achieve economies of scale in design and manufacturing by sharing some major components across the range, including even some basic body platforms and engines. These economies of scale are gained at the risk that consumers may trade down from a 'top of the range' Audi Quattro to a 'top of its range' Skoda if they realize that under the surface the cars share several features. Thus these car groups are normally very careful to ensure that the marketing and distribution of the individual car brands are kept distinct and separate, even though this reduces any opportunities for generating economies of scale at this level in the group.

This tendency to centralize the production or operations activities but to leave the ultimate externally focused sales and marketing activities under the total control of individual business units can also be seen in many other industries. In the car industry it has also led to a number of significant acquisitions, including some by Ford Motor Company. Although its greatest global rival, General Motors, has consistently used a number of different car brands (particularly in the US market) that are not instantly directly associated by the consumer with the ultimate parent company, Ford has basically used its group name on every vehicle that it has sold. This can be argued to have limited the premium brand positions that its offerings can occupy as Ford is known worldwide as a volume automobile manufacturer. The counter-argument, not surprisingly, is that Ford achieves a significant economy of scale in its marketing expenditure as every communication reinforces the 'Ford' brand. This is true but it may reinforce it as a 'value for money' brand rather than as a premium brand such as BMW or Mercedes Benz. Indeed, consumer research indicated that if Ford Motor Company could put a different 'premium' badge on its largest, 'top of the range' offering it could sell *more* of these cars at a significantly *higher* price. In other words, these cars were viewed as being very well engineered with excellent manufacturing quality, but their generic branding and lack of imagery meant that consumers would not pay a premium price to acquire them.

However, at this time, Jaguar faced the reverse problem. It had a wonderful brand image, particularly in the USA, but a terrible reputation for product quality. Ford's acquisition of Jaguar therefore gave the combined entity the opportunity to apply Ford's expertise in cost-efficient manufacturing and engineering design to Jaguar's styling and brand imagery expertise. A critical element in the success of this acquisition was that the corporate leaders of Ford Motor Company knew exactly where they should directly intervene in the new Jaguar subsidiary and where they should leave well alone. Following its other related acquisitions Ford has now formed a luxury products sub-group where the businesses definitely do not brand their vehicles as Fords; Jaguar, Volvo, Land Rover, Aston Martin probably have more brand appeal to consumers than if they were all called Ford Whatever! Bringing together these business units under one central management team may enable the group to generate some further economies of scale through centralization of additional activities, but trying to achieve still further cost savings through standardizing brand marketing is not likely to be a value-enhancing strategic initiative.

The group has generated significant economies of scale in other areas through directing style leadership but the implementation of any global standardization has to be done very carefully in order to ensure that it does not impact on critical business areas that need to be specifically tailored to the needs of different markets, etc. In other marketing areas it can be quite logical for the corporate centre to centralize media buying and to negotiate a global deal with one advertising agency, as long as the different product groups and end markets are still able to design and deliver appropriately tailored advertising. Global contracting of this type can not only reduce the group's total costs but also free up local management's time to concentrate on their competitive strategies, instead of having to negotiate local deals with a range of suppliers. It also enables the group's internal audit function to validate, in a cost-effective way, that the group is only paying for what it should under the terms of the global agreement.

Another common area for corporate leadership intervention in such global groups is Research and Development as centralization can avoid the wasteful duplication that often arises when several business units each investigate the same areas. However, there are some very common problems that are quite well illustrated by Ford Motor Company. Ford has large R&D functions in North America and in Europe; their European facilities are based in England and Germany but they operate as a centralized entity. As well as more fundamental research projects, these facilities are also responsible for the vitally important development of the group's new automobile models, but the centralization of this process adds significant complexities that have to be considered. Starting at the European level, the development of a new model has to take into account the often conflicting requirements of the different end markets in which the new model will be sold and the centralized manufacturing group that will produce it. Manufacturing clearly wants to minimize the various combinations and permutations of options, fittings, etc. that can drastically reduce any possible economies of scale that would significantly reduce total production costs. (Some years ago, one of us calculated that there were 3 million possible versions of a single Ford model if all the potential derivatives and options were combined. It can be difficult to achieve large economies of scale if you are only producing 2 million units in total of this model each year.) However each individual market needs to offer relevant product attributes and a viable range of choice to its target consumers. Unfortunately, some of these 'relevant' product attributes are not 'as relevant' in other markets. Heated seats and heated wing mirrors and windscreens are highly appropriate in northern European markets, but are less necessary in the warmer southern European countries where air-conditioning and soft-top cabriolet versions are considered more important issues.

The design process has to decide which elements are to be incorporated into the core product, which are to be available as options, and which are to be excluded completely. These decisions can make dramatic differences to the complexity of the manufacturing process and the actual costs involved. To take one specific example: it is much simpler and cheaper to incorporate an opening sunshine roof into every vehicle that goes down an assembly line than it is to try to install the same roof opening into only some cars as they actually go down the line. Clearly if all cars are to have one fitted, the basic body shell will be pressed appropriately while, if it is an optional extra, a hole will have to be cut into an originally solid roof. However, incorporating this feature in all cars will mean an on-cost for everyone, albeit a small one, compared with charging an increased price only to those taking up the option. This extra cost may, of course, have a negative effect on those customers to whom this added feature is completely irrelevant (e.g. those who are having electronic climate control fitted to their car).

This requires that directing style leaders consider very carefully where total standardization can be applied and where the centralized operation must allow for much greater flexibility. In simplified terms for the car industry, its leaders seek to standardize as far as possible on major components (such as body platforms, major body panels, engines, gearboxes, etc.) but allow a great level of flexibility in the final assembly operations. This allows the end consumers to specify in amazing detail what their car will actually look like without causing excessive disruption to the very flexible paint shops and assembly lines that now exist. However, most of these 'very different' vehicles have a common set of key major components and changing any of these does increase the total cost dramatically.

There is an even higher level of commonality that could be applied by Ford's R&D function: developing a worldwide model that would be common to North America, Europe, the Far East and the rest of the world. Although it has been tried, such a project has, to date, proved to be a step too far for the North American-based car manufacturers but has, of course, been a key element in the highly successful strategies of both Japanese and some European producers, which do not have completely different models for the different regions of the world. They have achieved a much higher degree of alignment through their organizations than has been possible for their US-based competitors, some of which are currently struggling due to their very high cost levels.

Using Scale to Mitigate Risk

Centralizing R&D can have other benefits as well as avoiding unnecessary duplication. A corporate leader should have the ability to assess the total potential for a new product or technology across their whole group, whereas any individual business unit will tend to consider only the potential from its own more restricted sphere of influence. Thus, if the R&D is centralized, the initial project can take account of the different requirements of all of the potential markets where a successful outcome can be exploited. Building these issues in at the beginning will normally be much cheaper and more successful than trying subsequently to modify a highly market-specific development.

For several industries, the lack of any significant differences across almost the total global market makes the prospective benefits from a successful research breakthrough incredibly attractive. However, the likelihood of developing a globally successful product is also very low, and the research expenditure required will normally need to be substantial despite these small chances of success. There are therefore considerable benefits in scale as sheer size and financial muscle can enable the company to contemplate taking on this level of expenditure without putting the total business at risk. Of course, the group must have the capability to exploit the full potential of any successful outputs from this significant resource commitment and, for this type of activity, this will require global reach.

This has proved a major issue for many high technology industries including the pharmaceutical industry. There have been several examples of large-scale mergers and acquisitions in order to achieve critical mass in R&D in major therapeutic areas or to gain access to all the main markets for pharmaceuticals, which not too surprisingly are North America, Japan and Europe. The immense size of these global groups enables them to devote very large resources to research into many areas at the same time, but this multi-pronged investment in the future requires the active intervention of their corporate leaders. The key driver for the share price performance of publicly quoted, ethical pharmaceutical companies is the new product pipeline and this is intensely scrutinized by investment analysts. Thus the corporate centre needs to ensure that the group's R&D portfolio is relatively balanced in terms of the timescales and probabilities of bringing any new molecular entities to the market. In the pharmaceutical industry, as with other primarily patent-protected technology industries, outside financial analysts can quite accurately assess the very high profit streams that will be generated from existing patented drugs. Even more importantly, they can precisely identify when these profits will all but disappear; the *sales revenues* of such products tend to fall by over 90 per cent in the year following patent expiry. If the centrally driven R&D activity cannot deliver an adequate replacement stream of profits, the share price is likely to decline dramatically.

Such pressure on new major breakthroughs has led some corporate leaders to change their R&D strategies. This can involve focusing the company's total expenditure on fewer therapeutic areas in an attempt to increase each project's chances of success through greater economies of scale. It can also include effectively outsourcing the new areas of research to a number of smaller, more focused companies, such as biotechnology businesses. If one of these proves successful, the larger group that has financed the research obviously has the exclusive rights to exploit the new technology for a period of time, but normally the smaller company is simply taken over by the mainstream pharmaceutical company.

This is an interesting development of the quite common strategy of a company outsourcing its own centralization of a support activity but now it is being more widely applied to the centralization of core business processes.

Potential Problems of Alignment

There are clearly some very significant implications of the corporate leaders directly intervening so dramatically in such a key value-adding activity for the group, particularly if the justification for the intervention, and the consequent focus of the leaders at the centre, is cost reduction while the emphasis of the business units may be on 'speed to market' or 'effectiveness of the new product' rather than cost. This requires the corporate leaders to be very clear as to their reasons for centralizing any core or support activity; are they really still operating as directing style leaders or should they now be implementing the enabling style of leadership as their focus is on leveraging knowledge rather than reducing cost? An example of such a transition is given at the end of this chapter. The centralization of the activity may generate substantial economies of scale in the level of expenditures that are incurred but it is now the corporate leader who is deciding on which areas to spend the funds. There can be a danger that the centralized research function becomes too removed from the real opportunities in the marketplace and is excessively internally focused. Many groups have large centralized research facilities that are regarded as remote ivory towers by the business unit leaders who are supposed to use the new developments from this centralized activity.

It is therefore very important that the corporate leader at the centre succeeds in getting the high level of buy-in from the relatively few key business unit managers who are most affected by any particular centralization. Although the leader normally has the organizationally granted authority (i.e. managerial power) potentially to force the centralization of any particular activity, such centralization will not prove effective if these key business unit managers are actively opposed to the resulting level of direct intervention. Trust between the leaders at the corporate centre and their followers in the businesses is more important for the 'manager' style than for the 'shareholder' style, and the level of trust required increases as the centralization incorporates increasingly core business activities. Thus the general managers of major business units may not be too bothered if some peripheral support activities are centralized by 'diktat' from the centre, but they will want to be much more involved in any decision affecting what they perceive as a key value-adding activity for their businesses.

This is not an insuperable problem as the corporate leader can give the business units their desired involvement and still achieve their own objectives. The dominant general skill of the directing style leader is supply chain expertise so that the leader should be able to identify those areas where their direct intervention can generate significant savings. These tend to come from the removal of duplication and the standardization of practices across the group as well as the increased bulk-buying power of the total group. Of course the lowest level of direct intervention is to centralize only the actual 'buying' activity but to leave the business units complete freedom as to what to buy. The next level restricts the choice of suppliers to those that are approved by the centralized buying function. Then the corporate centre takes more direct control of what is being bought, and then what is done with it when it is bought. Thus the corporate leader also needs appropriate skills in 'managing' each area that has been centralized.

However, this skill will be focused on improving the operational efficiency of each centralized activity and this need not include the ability to set the longer-term objectives and strategic focus for this area. The directing style corporate leader can get this more externally market-focused input from their business unit managers if they are likely to have much more relevant insights. Thus the business units could still set the priorities for any centralized key business activity (which may be R&D, information systems development, logistics, manufacturing or even sales and marketing) and the corporate leader would then deliver these agreed priorities but at a lower cost than could be achieved by any individual business unit.

Indeed, in some cases the directing style leader may delegate the actual delivery to one business unit if that business unit already possesses most of the specifically relevant skills. This happens quite frequently in the case of R&D projects and major information systems activities, where one business unit takes on the prime development role and therefore works for the corporate leader at the centre. An example may make this clearer.

The European Human Foods Division (the division's title sounds strange but the group is also the world's largest producer of pet food) of Mars Inc. had identified a very exciting new product development idea that could potentially have a global market. Arising out of its R&D activities for its new UK-based processed meat products business (mainly convenience canned products sold through retail, catering and industrial channels), the division had started preliminary work on an artificial meat product made out of soya protein. This basic concept was not revolutionary as soya-based, textured vegetable protein products had already been introduced to a relatively poor consumer response. Masterfoods used a completely different approach based on spinning technology (similar to that involved in producing artificial fibres such as nylon) to create a much finer spun vegetable protein. Each individual fibre could be coated with an appropriate meat or other flavouring and the fibres then woven together to form a meat-textured end product. This product did not require specialized storage and could have a dramatically longer shelf life than 'the real thing'. Of course, there was a massive amount of work to do to bring such a completely new idea to an actual product launch and the division was not sure that its profit potential justified the scale of investment that would be required.

The group's corporate leadership agreed that the project looked interesting and had potential outside the European division's area of control. Accordingly the corporate centre directly funded the project so that this expenditure did not affect the short-term performance of the division, on which its top team was incentivized. If the project was successful, the division would get what it had wanted anyway in terms of being able to sell the resulting products, but it did not have to bear the entire project risk itself. The company would obviously have the ability either to make any resulting products available to other divisions around the world, without them paying Masterfoods a royalty or licence fee, or it could itself license the product to external third parties. Also the corporate leadership could ensure that there was no duplicated effort being input elsewhere in the group by centralizing all the appropriate resources in the one division and it could effectively direct the pace of the project through the resource allocation process.

This type of 'delegated centralization' tries to avoid the corporate leaders at the centre becoming too distant and remote from the real competitive environment of the underlying businesses. However, there is another potential remoteness issue that can be caused by a strongly centralizing corporate leader who is totally focused on reducing costs. This can be illustrated by comparing, in general terms, the differing approaches of the automotive industries of the USA and Japan. This was explicitly highlighted by the well-documented experiences of NUMMI, which was a joint-venture operation set up in the USA between GM and Toyota.

The US-based car companies were primarily following a cost-reduction strategy in their operations activities. This meant that all new in-house component designs were sent out by a centralized sourcing team to a number of potential suppliers for competitive tendering. Some of these 'suppliers' could be other parts of the same group. These companies maintained flexibility through only granting short-term contracts to the successful bidders. The role of the suppliers was therefore seen to be to deliver exactly what had been ordered and any departures from the tightly defined group requirements and procedures would normally result in severe sanctions on the defaulting supplier.

The usual Japanese approach was to work closely with a more limited number of suppliers. These suppliers were supposed to contribute to the development of new products and this capability for innovation by the supplier was a key issue in developing a close and long-term relationship with the major auto manufacturer. Once selected for such a relationship, the supplier went through a quality certification process that meant their customer could do away with goods inwards inspections. Also the car company worked with its suppliers to develop joint designs and developments and was willing to give these suppliers long-term contracts to supply these parts. This enabled the suppliers to commit to investments in highly specific assets that could ultimately result in lower costs to its customers. The selling price to these customers also reflected the lower required rate of return that resulted from the reduced risk perception generated by the long-term contract and high volumes. Thus the higher level of trust that is generated from this closer working relationship means that it does not necessarily lead to higher costs. In many cases, the adversarial approach can cause a substantial increase in the total governance costs needed to manage such a relationship. This is still true even if the adversarial relationship is completely within the group, so that corporate leaders must be clear as to the type of relationship that they want to see following any centralization decision.

Service-level Agreements

The most common way to regulate these relationships between any centralized activity and its internal customers (i.e. the business units that are required to take the output from the centralized function) is by establishing a service-level agreement (SLA). The SLA should set out very clearly the agreed responsibilities of each party to the agreement. This enables full accountability to be associated with each party's responsibility. Where all the specific responsibilities are clearly identified it is much easier to gain the required high level of buy-in from the business unit managers who are most affected by the centralization.

Thus, if the production activities of a manufactured goods group are being centralized, the SLAs between the sales and marketing-focused business units and this centralized production area must clarify how the relationship will work. This means that the frequency of ordering, the order-to-delivery lead times, the delivery schedules, the quality specifications, the responsibility for defective products, as well as pricing levels, must be explicitly stated to the satisfaction of both parties. If the relationship was being set up with an outside third party it would be automatic that such a contractual agreement was reached prior to commencing working together. Yet in many large groups there are a multitude of informal, unspecified commercial relationships that can lead to significant problems as soon as things start to go wrong. It is very common to find a culture of blame apportionment between the business units and the corporate leadership in directing style-led groups, and this is often exacerbated by the absence of the clearly defined responsibilities that can be created by the design of appropriate SLAs.

Designing these SLAs obviously requires some skill as they should not become excessively bureaucratic and over-detailed, but as the directing style corporate leaders should have substantial supply chain expertise they should be able to develop practical, value-enhancing agreements for the group. One major issue that the SLA should cover is the internal pricing mechanism that will be used for each centralized activity. It is important that this is seen by both parties as a 'pricing' arrangement and not a method by which the centralized area simply apportions its total costs across the business units. A key risk for this style of leadership is the demotivation of business unit managers and this is easily achieved if they are held accountable for things over which they can exercise no control. The business units may often still be primarily focused on their own divisional financial performance and the level of costs that are transferred to them from centralized parts of the group can have a material impact on the profit performance of these business units.

The corporate centre in the directing style, of course, has a more complex role in that it has to lead and motivate not only the business units and the centralized activities and processes, but also the relationship between these discrete areas. The primary performance measurement metric for all the centralized resources will be their relative cost performance, as this should be demonstrably lower than could be achieved by the individual business units. However, the actual cost savings generated by such centralized facilities will obviously depend upon the utilization levels achieved through the demand that comes from the group's business units.

Therefore the group planning process needs to consider the appropriate scale of the centralized resources and this requires that the internal business unit customers are involved so that a properly integrated and coordinated plan is produced. Thus the planning process for this style of leadership can be described as driven from the corporate centre (as they are looking for cost-reduction opportunities) but with shared responsibilities for the actual usage levels of centralized resources. There are many examples of corporate centre-driven initiatives that create very large centralized facilities that remain extremely underutilized by the group's businesses. This is clearly disastrous for the company as the economic justification for this type of centralization is to reduce the total costs of the group. The directing style leader should only therefore be centralizing activities that are essential to the business units and for which they have obtained their commitment. This required commitment by the business units to use these 'essential' centralized resources can be reflected in the transfer pricing system that is used within the group. If business units are prepared to guarantee to take a specified level of output from a centralized activity, the transfer price should be appropriately reduced to reflect the greater certainty that this provides for this centralized resource.

This means that transfer prices should be structured to reflect the real business decisions that the group faces in deciding whether to centralize any particular activity, exactly as would be done if the group was negotiating an outsourcing contract with an independent third-party supplier. Unfortunately, in most large multinational groups, the only factor that is taken into consideration in designing a group-wide transfer pricing system seems to be gaining approval from the tax authorities around the world. Hence the most common transfer pricing system is 'cost plus 10 per cent' (or some similar add-on to the basic cost). In any group where the focus of the corporate leadership is on cost reduction, it is bizarre that the 'return' generated by an internal centralized activity should increase if its costs actually go up.

A Strong Leadership Role

This type of externally focused, tax-driven transfer pricing system would seem more appropriate for the much less involved, incentivizing style corporate leader. The directing style has a significantly greater strategic leadership role within the group, although it may adopt a lower external profile in some cases. The focus of this leadership is on achieving the greatest economies of scale possible for the group. This can result in acquisition-led growth strategies if the existing portfolio of businesses does not generate a sufficiently large critical mass for certain activities and processes. It can be perceived that 'the tail is wagging the dog' if new businesses are acquired solely so that the corporate leadership can increase the level of economies of scale. However, these increased economies of scale should also reduce the costs of all the existing business units, as well as benefiting the newly acquired business. Also the main economic justification for the group remaining as a group is this economies of scale driven, value-adding role of the corporate leaders.

Indeed, the overall objective of the directing style leader can be stated as being to achieve volume leadership in at least one core business activity that has relevance across the entire group. As already discussed, it is important that the corporate centre selects very carefully both the core processes that are to be centralized and the business units that will be involved. The negative impacts on the business units of any required standardization in these processes could more than offset the economies of scale achieved by the centralization. Alternatively, this can lead to those business units that have more specialized requirements opting out of the centralization process and destroying the potential economies of scale savings.

This gives the corporate leader a critical challenge of gaining acceptance of their planned centralization changes from those managers most highly affected, e.g. those with the specialized requirements. These most important managers must give high commitment to the centralization strategy rather than merely reluctantly complying with a change that is mandated by the centre. They need to be involved in developing the SLAs that will be implemented and should also have input to the proposed transfer pricing system. A relatively simple ploy to increase the level of buy-in is to guarantee that their costs will fall after centralization. The level of guaranteed cost reduction that is needed will be related to the amount of change that the business unit will need to make because of any standardization in the centralized process. If this cost reduction cannot be guaranteed, given the technical management expertise and supply chain skills in the group, the corporate leaders probably should reconsider their plans to centralize this core process.

Changing Leadership Style

This discussion of the directing style of corporate leadership has indicated that, while the aligning leadership activity can be significantly value creating, it also can have a finite life as a highly value-enhancing style. This means that companies may need to change their leadership style if value creation is to be sustained over time. An example of how this can be achieved may make this clearer.

Supermarkets in the UK, and in most other major markets, started their rapid growth phase by operating very clearly with directing style leadership. The corporate leaders intervened very directly in the operation of the stores by centralizing most core business processes and almost all support activities. The focus of this intervention was to reduce costs through maximizing the level of economies of scale generated by the group. A critical area was obviously the centralized buying department that enabled the supermarkets to negotiate not only significant volume discounts but also generous settlement terms from suppliers. These suppliers became increasingly subservient to the buying power of these dominant supermarket chains as they grew their market share by opening more and larger stores. Thus the initial maxim of the supermarkets can be described as 'pile it high, sell it cheap and pay for it tomorrow'. Indeed, a financial analysis of the published financial statements of a once leading discount supermarket chain, such as Kwik-Save, during these early, rapid-growth years would highlight that the group actually only broke even on its retailing activities and made its total net profit margin by investing the substantial cash mountain generated from its negative working capital.

The next stage in this strategy was to strengthen its negotiating power still further by putting its own name on an increasing proportion of the products that it sold. These 'own labels', as they were originally known, turned their suppliers into more commodity manufacturers than the branded goods companies that they had previously been. Indeed, several new manufacturing groups grew up that specialized in producing only retailer-branded goods, but many of the previously high margin branded manufacturers saw their profits dramatically squeezed by this increasing retailer power.

At the same time, the centralized support activities were finding new ways to reduce costs in the stores. Point of sale automation removed the need for individual product price marking in the store and for checkout operators to key in price data. However, this computerized database system had several even more important benefits. It obviously provided real-time information on what was being purchased by customers. This could be used to make inventory management and even store layouts more dynamic but, much more importantly, it could give detailed information on who was buying what and how frequently they did it. Of course, in order to capture this potential information the supermarkets needed customer details and these could be obtained from some form of loyalty card, store card or in-house credit card.

As a result, the supermarkets developed very detailed information about their customers in terms of shopping frequency, purchasing habits, product combinations, etc. This information could then be added to through direct communication with their 'loyal' customers so that tailored special offers could be designed in order to increase this 'level of loyalty'. This increased level of 'knowledge' about who their customers were and what they really wanted further tilted the industry playing field towards the supermarkets and away from the manufacturers. Originally the fast-moving consumer goods (FMCG) manufacturers were the experts on consumers as they did all the research on potential consumer demand, etc. However, now the retailers were able to collect real factual information from every transaction that took place; this is known as biographic segmentation, or 'you are what you buy'. This has forced the FMCG companies to upgrade their consumer research to consider more fundamental reasons for buying (e.g. psychographic segmentations).

The generation of this in-depth customer information and increased focus on customer loyalty is inconsistent with the cost-reduction focus of directing style leadership. These enabling corporate leaders are now seeking to add value to the group by leveraging its knowledge about consumers and their shopping habits and preferences. This has been consciously reinforced by the leading supermarket groups through repositioning their retailer brands. These are now seen as perfectly acceptable quality products in their own right and, in some cases, they are even themselves being segmented into different positionings, such as 'value', 'simple', 'finest', 'organic', etc. Such new propositions have also enabled the supermarkets to broaden their product ranges dramatically and to move away from their previous dependence on their store outlets.

The competitive advantages that the supermarkets initially brought to many of the services that they now sell (e.g. insurance, banking and utilities) was their trusted branding and their customer insights, rather than their buying power. This knowledge could be leveraged by the corporate leadership through entering into partnerships with established companies in each of these new product areas. Undoubtedly this new trend has *transformed* the way in which these groups will develop in the future. Of course the retail stores will remain important but increasingly they will be only one part of the group as directly sold services (e.g. banking and insurance) and goods (e.g. internet-based retailing) grow much more rapidly in the future. It is therefore helpful that we now move on to consider the implications of changing corporate leadership style in Chapter 8.

Conclusion

The directing leadership style focuses on the aligning activity in order to make the organization as structurally capable as possible of achieving the overall corporate vision. It is therefore very important that all companies have directing leadership at some level if they are to achieve and sustain extraordinary levels of financial performance. However, the potential for value creation from this style of leadership at the very top of an organization is more limited. It can be appropriate for businesses that need to focus on standardizing activities in order to generate substantial economies of scale. Once these cost savings have been achieved even these companies may need to migrate to a more sustainable value-creating leadership style at their very top.

PART 3

The Leadership Model in Practice and Theory

8

Leading change and changing leaders

Throughout the book, we have tried to maintain a very clear distinction between the roles of managers and leaders. This differentiation is especially important for the issues considered in this chapter. As already stated, ideally all managers will also be regarded as leaders by their subordinates who have become their willing followers. Unfortunately, this is often not the case.

A significant blockage to this transition from organizationally empowered manager to personally authorized leader can be the manager's need to be totally in control; the term 'micro-managing' is often used to describe such a need. This can most readily be seen when an organization is going through a period of substantial change. The problem is that most companies are now continually going through such periods of change. Many managers, not surprisingly, want to 'manage' these changes and this desire for control is normally, given the focus of management that was discussed in Chapter 1, translated into detailed plans for, and controls over, the changes that are to be made. For this 'change management' concept to make any sense, it must be possible to predict, in quite specific terms, what the outcomes from these potential changes will be. This may require the preparation of a number of contingency plans or detailed scenarios to take account of alternative, but less probable, out-turns. However all such potential outcomes should be capable of prediction so that the possible new organizational strategies and structures will already have been foreseen. Only in such cases can managers be said to be in control of the change process and, hence, to be 'managing change'.

Quite clearly there are many transformational changes, particularly in the external competitive environment, where it is impossible to predict with any clarity what the company will look like after the change. All that can be stated with certainty is that the organization will be significantly different after going through such a transformational change. The company therefore needs leadership, rather than management, during such periods of fundamental change. It is critical that the corporate leaders maintain the trust and respect of their followers, notwithstanding the unavoidable feelings of uncertainty and doubt that these followers will have about the future. This will be achieved in different ways depending upon the particular leadership style that is being used, as is shown in Figure 8.1. An inspiring leader who is focused on the visioning leadership activity can re-emphasize their belief in, and commitment to, the company's long-term vision, despite any short-term upheaval caused by such transformational changes. The enabling style leader can reinforce the need for the various parts of the organization to continue to work together, albeit potentially in quite dramatically different ways.

Even when the potential future changes could be classified, in our terms, as transactional changes the company may still require leadership rather than management. As already stated, it is not possible to

Enabling style	Inspiring style
Leader changes the focus of knowledge shared across the business	Leader lives the desired change, i.e. 'walks the talk'
Incentivizing style	**Directing style**
Leader changes the performance measures used in order to refocus followers	Leader changes the focus of centralization/standardization, e.g. from support to core activities

Figure 8.1 How leaders achieve clarity of changes required

'manage' truly unpredictable changes as the organization cannot, by definition, know in advance what the results will be. Thus for transactional changes with such uncertain outcomes, the key role is still 'leading change', rather than trying to manage the change. This can be seen quite clearly in the directing leadership style, even though these leaders primarily change 'where' certain activities are carried out within the organization, rather than transforming 'what' is done. These leaders may stimulate a significant transactional change within the organization, but they should not attempt to dictate in detail how this changed activity should be carried out. It is important that their followers are given the discretion to exercise their own initiative, i.e. to implement their own leadership style, in the detailed implementation of this change.

Similarly for the incentivizing leadership style with its focus on the delivering activity, the leader can refocus the energy of their followers by devising new performance metrics that are much more relevant to the changed competitive environment. However, they should not try to micro-manage how this new expected level of performance is achieved. Once again their followers should be allowed to select their own leadership style and develop their own strategies to deliver the new stretching targets agreed with this leader.

This issue is acknowledged by many writers on leadership and management but, in the same way as many continually refer to leaders and their subordinates, most still then go on to talk about 'managing change'. As individuals progress up the organizational hierarchy, their managerial roles alter significantly as they become 'managers of managers', i.e. they have subordinates who themselves are managers with their own subordinates. One of the critical behavioural changes that is required for a successful transition to this new managerial level is that the manager of managers backs off sufficiently to allow their direct reports enough space so that they can act as managers in their own right. A very common initial failing of people when they are promoted to this level is that they persist in jumping in on every problem, and try to take every decision. They are obviously not acting effectively for the role that they now have in the organization.

The negative impact generated by leaders behaving in a similarly inappropriate way can be very much greater due to the potentially much wider spread of any leadership role. The adverse consequences from such excess interference by a manager of managers are normally limited to the development of their direct reports and the performance of their own departments. Leaders can have followers who do not directly report to them and thus can have an impact across the whole organization.

It is therefore critically important that both leaders and followers approach all such significant changes in a positive and, wherever possible, a proactive way. Such changes are rarely smooth and easy transitions but our research has found specific issues that can make an organization more successful both in responding to externally enforced changes and in proactively stimulating changes themselves. These issues are particularly relevant when the scale or nature of the change means that a change in leadership style is also required. Figure 8.1 showed that this clarity can be achieved in different ways by each leadership style. Followers, by definition, look to their leaders for a sense of direction and it is therefore critical that the leader does indeed 'lead' the organization into any significant changes. How well this message is received and responded to by their followers is obviously influenced by the change capability of these followers.

The 'clarity of required change' dimension of Figure 8.2 refers to the articulation of both the need for change and the type of change that is required. As already stated, the leader will often not be able to describe in any detail what the changed organization will look like, but they must state clearly in what ways they expect the business to change. The key dimensions of these changes are the scale of change, the pace

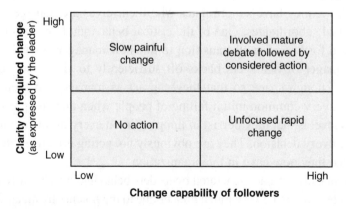

Figure 8.2 Leading change: the leader's perception

of change, the type of change, the impact of the change, the complexity of the change, as well as the reason for the change. These multidimensions mean that the perception of any change by the leader may not completely match with the perceptions of their followers. Indeed, perceptions may differ among followers and any such differences can impact the willingness to change.

In some cases the need for change may be identified by followers before it is seen by their leader. This can cause frustration and resentment when the leader eventually seeks to create change. Even worse is where the leader seeks to implement a different change from that already identified by their followers. This often results in an unwillingness to implement the required changes as the followers rapidly remove the personal authority that they had granted to the leader. If the ex-leader tries to force through these changes by reverting to their organizationally granted managerial authority, some form of guerrilla warfare may be waged by the now very disenchanted ex-followers. Guerrilla warfare can also result if there is disagreement on the effects of the proposed changes. If there was no *real* agreement between the leaders and their followers regarding the existing strategy or positioning of the company, there may be no clarity and agreement about the need to change. This is particularly true where the change required involves altering the leadership style that is being implemented, as is discussed below.

The change capability of followers is made up of their ability and willingness to change. Long-serving, senior managers can become very averse to almost any change and can effectively block even very well-articulated changes proposed by a leader at the top of an organization. Any progress achieved will be slow and relatively painful for all concerned. If the leader is not sure exactly what sort of change they want, then the high resistance to change will ensure that the status quo is preserved. Where potential followers are quite willing to change but the leader does not clearly and consistently articulate the required change, the result can be a series of unfocused, often mutually inconsistent, rapid changes. The followers are responding very quickly to what they think their leader wants, except that the leader appears to keep changing their mind.

Any organization that is facing the need for substantial change obviously wants to be in the top right-hand box of Figure 8.2, because this leads to an open constructive debate about what changes should be made and how these changes should be implemented. In other words, followers will feel maturely involved in this process. The detailed processes for moving into this consistently value-creating box can be developed from this model.

As shown in Figure 8.3, if followers are quite capable of changing but have not been given the clarity they need, their leader must focus on improving their communications of the company's vision and/or long-term goals and objectives: the 'why and where' of Figure 8.3. If the current leaders cannot provide this clarity or achieve the required level of buy-in, these leaders may need to be changed. Alternatively, if the key followers lack the ability to change, the leader must help them by showing how the changes can be achieved in their areas of influence: the 'what and how' of Figure 8.3. If these followers are extremely unwilling, rather than unable, to change then, as an ultimate sanction, the leader may need to replace some of these people in order to clear the blockage. However, these blocking key followers are probably the very long-serving, senior managers referred to earlier; the introduction of an early retirement programme is a common solution.

However, when applying our leadership model within organizations, the start point can be in the bottom left-hand box of Figures 8.2 and 8.3. There is neither change capability on the part of followers nor clarity of the change required by leaders. In such cases we have found it very helpful to change the descriptions used on both dimensions of the matrix. It appears that top teams often see these issues as being the

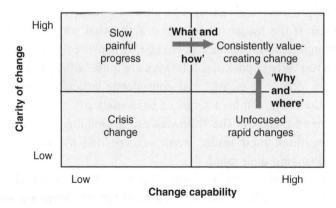

Figure 8.3 Leading change: improving communication

differences between agreeing on the interpretation of strategy (the causes) and agreeing about the implementation of the strategy (the consequences), as shown in Figure 8.4.

Restating the earlier discussion, followers in a particular business unit could agree with their corporate leaders about their long-term vision, the aims and overall objectives of the business, but fundamentally disagree about how to achieve them. The result is that followers in this business unit, who are of course themselves supposed to act as leaders within their business unit, may develop strategies that are, in the view of the top-level corporate leaders, completely inconsistent with the long-term corporate strategy. These followers need help with developing competitive strategies that are more fully aligned with the needs of the overall corporate vision and strategy: the what and how of Figure 8.4. Conversely, followers in a specific business unit may implement a rapidly changing array of very detailed competitive strategies but these have almost no relationship with the corporate vision as espoused by the corporate leader. In other words, there may be agreement on the implementation of strategy but not on how the vision and strategy is being interpreted. In this case, the corporate leader needs to focus on clearly communicating the corporate vision and values, as well as the aims and objectives in order to increase the agreement on the 'why and where' of Figure 8.4. If this is achieved, the followers in

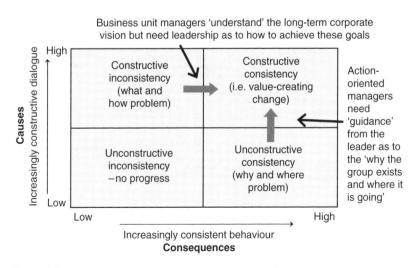

Figure 8.4 Leading change: changing the description of issues

the business unit can be left to implement their own appropriately tailored competitive strategy.

The practical implementation of this process clearly differs depending upon the leadership style at the top of the organization and the resulting leadership framework that is being implemented. However, the changes that are being experienced may themselves necessitate a change in this leadership style and framework. The current leadership style may have been very successful in the previous competitive environment, but it may be inappropriate for the environment in which the business will find itself in the future.

As we have argued before, leadership effectiveness is determined by the degree of alignment, shown as the overlap of the circles in Figure 8.5, among the needs of both followers and the business and the specific strengths of the leadership style that is being implemented. In the very best led companies there is a high degree of overlap between the needs of the business and the needs of the critical people who can make this business achieve its full potential. Thus the proportion of this full potential that is actually achieved is largely dictated by the degree of alignment between the leadership strengths and these business and people needs.

If the externally stimulated changes have significantly modified the needs of the business and/or these critical people, the current leadership style may no longer be the best fit with these amended needs.

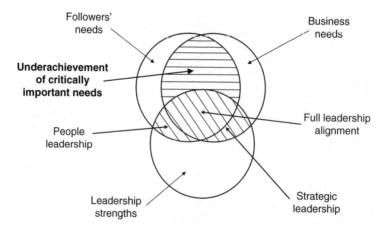

Figure 8.5 Level of full potential achievement

This means that the current leader should either change their style or the organization may need to find a new leader with a more appropriate style. In Part 2 we also argued that, in any case, the value-creating potential of each leadership style within any particular context is finite and that value-creating corporate leadership therefore needs reinventing or reinvigorating from time to time. Again this can result in the need for a change in leadership style if the value creation is to be continued. If this change in leadership style takes place right at the top of the organization, our leadership frameworks highlight that corresponding changes may be needed at lower levels as well.

Changing Leaders

One of the classic statements about organizational cultural change is that you either 'change the *People*' or you have to '*Change* the people'. In other words, if the existing people are completely resistant to the changes in behaviour that are perceived to be needed within an organization, the only other option is to bring into the organization new people who already exhibit these desired behaviours. A similar logic can be applied when a different leadership style is required within an organization.

Either the existing leader has to change their leadership style or the organization needs to find a new leader. This new leader may come from within the organization or may be brought in from outside, normally from another organization where they have already been a successful leader. Such external appointments are commonly made in response to a perceived crisis within the organization, so that the new incoming 'leader' is definitely expected to 'lead change'. However, it is critically important that this incoming top executive can successfully identify and implement the leadership style that is most appropriate to the changing needs of the business and its people.

Using the willing follower view of leadership highlights that any newly appointed, externally sourced chief executive officer or business unit head must be regarded initially as a 'potential leader'. They only become actual leaders, as opposed to very senior managers, once they have gained the required level of trust and respect from the potential new followers within their new organization. In many cases new appointees attempt to accelerate this process by bringing with them loyal willing followers from their previous leadership roles. These existing followers will immediately display high trust and respect for their leader, which may influence other potential followers, but they will also normally try to develop their own appropriate leadership roles to complement the new leadership style at the top of the organization. In Chapter 2, we discussed the two outsiders who were brought in to IBM during times of crisis. The second of these, Lou Gerstner, dramatically and rapidly changed the top team of the group as he developed his leadership role within the business during a period of substantial transformational change. It is very difficult to see how an insider, who would have been steeped in the very strong IBM culture, could have achieved so much change so rapidly.

However, dramatic changes in leadership style can be achieved by internal appointments, as was demonstrated by Jack Welch's leadership role in GE which was discussed in Chapter 4. The previous chairman and CEO had very successfully implemented an incentivizing leadership style with its focus on the delivering leadership activity through agreeing stretching financial targets with his followers. These people were themselves the heads of the many business units comprising the group. This emphasis on financial performance had resulted in a very diversified and increasingly fragmented group. Jack Welch implemented a seemingly very different leadership style that created a much more coherent group vision and led to a significant number of disposals by the group. However, as is discussed later, the changes required to move from one style to the other are logical, and he had already been implementing this complementary style in his role as a lower-level leader in the group.

The challenge faced by an internal appointee, in such a successful group, is highlighted by the statement that the previous leader is 'a hard act to follow'. This may suggest that the business is still highly successful because the existing leadership style is still highly relevant and should not be changed. If true, the new potential leader will probably need to change their style. Our leadership frameworks demonstrate that the leadership style of a willing follower, which an internal appointee would normally have been if the current leader was still successful, will be different from that of the leader who they have been willingly following. As already discussed, amplifier leadership, which is where leaders and their followers all implement the same leadership style, does not normally work, not least because it assumes that the needs of followers at all levels in the organization are exactly the same.

Such a change in personal leadership style is possible, but it can be more difficult if the current style has gained a large number of very willing followers. They may struggle to understand why their leader, upon moving to a new level within the organization, starts to behave very differently. This will not be a problem for those within the business who were not previously followers, as they will not perceive any change. Thus it is easier to make a significant change in leadership style when moving from one organization to another, or when promoted from a relatively low profile role, with few followers, to a much larger leadership role within the business. Common examples of this are promotions from technical roles, such as research and development director or even finance director, to more general roles, such as chief executive officer. A change in leadership style will probably be expected, even by previous willing followers, as the spread of the new role is so different.

Leaders are also followers

There are therefore a number of reasons why leadership styles may need to be changed. These include the changing needs of a business without a compensating change in the actual leader, as well as a change in the leadership role of a particular leader. In this section, we will consider changes in leadership roles, by examining the relationship between an individual's needs when acting as a follower and their simultaneous role as a leader. Leaders should understand the needs of their potential willing followers and their selected leadership style should appropriately address these needs. The ideal leadership style for given combinations of followers' needs are shown again diagrammatically as Figure 8.6. The arrows on this figure show how, by changing only one dimension, a follower with specific needs can become a leader who can appropriately address the needs of a different group of followers. Each of these moves is explained in this section, as is the much greater challenge of trying to change both dimensions simultaneously which can be thought of as trying to leap diagonally across Figure 8.6.

The ideal follower profile for an incentivizing style leader is the high personal achiever, as shown in Figure 8.7. These followers have a high

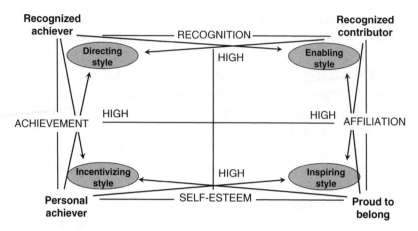

Figure 8.6 Possible leadership styles for given combinations of followers' needs

need for both achievement and self-esteem. Therefore they are likely to respond very positively to the stretch targets and related high incentive payments that are integral to this leadership style. Such people do not have strong needs for recognition by others or for a sense of affiliation to something greater than the area in which they directly work. Consequently group awards dinners and group-wide team-building sessions are not important to them as followers, but they may make use of them in their own roles as leaders.

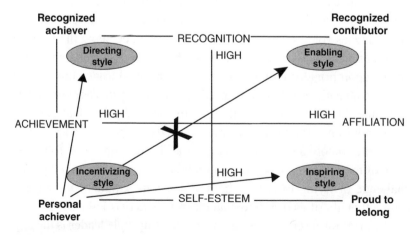

Figure 8.7 Possible leadership styles for a 'personal achiever' follower

This is because it is logical for them to play to their strengths in understanding followers' needs when they themselves look to take on a leadership role. Clearly the simplest way for them to do this would be to adopt the incentivizing leadership style to which they have themselves positively responded. Unfortunately, this is what we have already described as amplifier leadership in which successive levels of leader adopt exactly the same style; as we have argued before it is not value creating to have the same style of leadership at all levels in the organization.

The next logical option is to change as little as possible so that the leader is most likely to have a good understanding of their followers' needs. For our high personal achiever follower this can be done by building on their own need for self-esteem but allying this to potential followers' needs for affiliation: the 'proud to belong' follower of Figure 8.7. The most appropriate leadership style for such followers is the inspiring style with its focus on the visioning activity. This fits with our out-to-in leadership framework where the incentivizing style of leadership at the top of the organization is complemented by the inspiring style at the business unit level. The message from the high personal achiever to their potential followers is effectively 'we can do it together, as long as we believe we can', thus positively using their own record of achievement to create a powerful sense of wanting to belong to something exciting.

The other logical leadership style for such a follower is to build on their own record of and need for achievement while granting their potential followers a high level of recognition for their achievements. The appropriate leadership style for such recognized achievers is the directing style with its focus on aligning the organizational structure. This can create significant value if it is done below the incentivizing leadership style. In Chapter 5, we acknowledged that a potential weakness of having this style at the top of an organization is the challenge of how to achieve the cross-business economies of scale that can result from the directing leadership style.

A key element in implementing each of these leadership styles is that personal success in fulfilling their individual needs as a follower helps to build the trust and respect that is so essential as a leader. Thus a record of high achievement is important to the potential followers of a directing style leader, as is a high level of self-esteem critical to followers of an inspiring style leader. This building of trust and respect from personal strengths also explains why it is very difficult to leap diagonally right across this followers' needs model. For the high personal achiever follower, this would involve implementing the enabling leadership style. This style appeals most strongly to followers who have a high need to be a recognized contributor to the organization. As a follower, this potential leader had neither the need for recognition nor affiliation. Hence they are unlikely to understand such potential followers and, equally importantly, they cannot display the characteristics that will build trust and respect from these potential followers. In our terms, this is a step too far for most potential leaders. This can create a problem when the incentivizing style of leadership is at the top of the organization and the enabling style is implemented across the group in the functions headed by members of the group top team.

The ideal followers' needs for the inspiring leader style are a high level of self-esteem and a strong sense of affiliation: what we have described in Figure 8.8 as 'proud to belong'. As the inspiring style, with its focus on the visioning leadership activity, is often found right at the top of the organization, it is important that the followers of such a leader can find their own successful leadership styles. As already discussed, this is not done by simply repeating the inspiring style.

By building on their own strong need for affiliation, e.g. by being seen as a very strong team player themselves, this 'proud to belong' follower can implement the enabling leadership style. This requires them to give recognition to potential followers who are willing to share

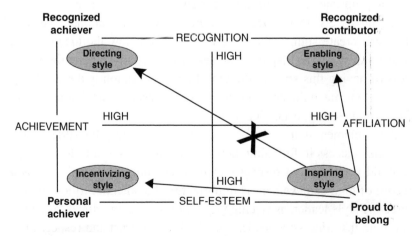

Figure 8.8 Possible leadership styles for a 'proud to belong' follower

their knowledge widely across the organization. Alternatively, as they understand the need for high self-esteem, when implementing the incentivizing style they can attract high personal achievers as willing followers. This is done by setting stretching targets that enable such people to feel personally fulfilled through delivering against them. The more problematic leadership style for followers of inspirational style leaders is the directing style as its ideal followers' needs are for acknowledged achievement. Once again the people trying to make the leap across do not necessarily fully understand these needs as they do not have them themselves. Also they cannot automatically demonstrate the personal qualities that will build the required level of trust and respect with their followers. This means that, in an organization that has the inspiring style at its top, there needs to be another leadership style in between this and the directing style that may be appropriate in some of the group functions. As already discussed in our in-to-out leadership framework, this is often the enabling style of leadership as this can be successfully implemented by a willing follower of an inspiring style leader.

An enabling style of leadership is most appropriate to followers who have high needs for recognition and affiliation: what we describe in Figure 8.9 as a recognized contributor. Willing followers of this leadership style can themselves therefore adopt either the inspiring leadership style, through leveraging on their own strong sense of affiliation to create the desire to be part of something really exciting, or more

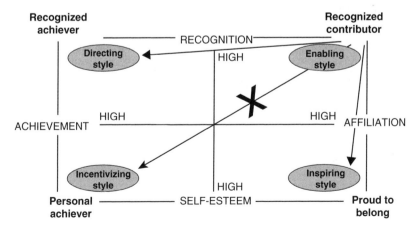

Figure 8.9 Possible leadership styles for a 'recognized contributor' follower

normally the directing style. This uses recognition as a means to motivate the acknowledged achievers who are the ideal followers of the directing leadership style. The fact that this potential leader is already a recognized contributor to a large part of the whole organization should build trust and respect from their prospective followers to whom recognition is important.

The problem leadership style for followers of enabling style leaders is the incentivizing style. The followers' needs of high personal achievement are unlikely to be fully understood by an individual who personally values being seen as a recognized contributor to the greater good of the total organization. Thus, if the enabling style of leadership is being implemented at a high level of the organization, direct followers of this style will find it difficult to implement the incentivizing style successfully at, say, the business unit level. As with the movement from inspiring style follower to directing style leader, there needs to be a complementary intermediary style of leadership to make the linkage practically achievable.

This could be the directing leadership style as willing followers of this style can themselves become successful incentivizing style leaders, as is shown in Figure 8.10. These recognized achievers can also implement the enabling style but will often struggle if they try to become inspiring leaders. This problem was mentioned in Chapter 7 when directing style

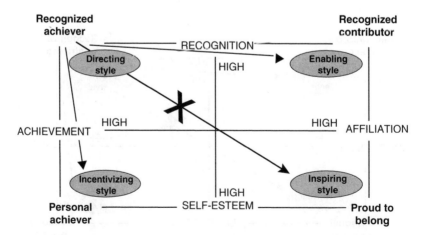

Figure 8.10 Possible leadership styles for a 'recognized achiever' follower

leadership creates the momentum to create shared service centres. Within the shared service centres, a complementary style of leadership is required and an obvious candidate would appear to be the inspiring style. This would enable the shared service centre leader to create an appropriately tailored vision and set of values with which to motivate and inspire their direct followers. However, it is very difficult for a willing follower of a directing style leader to understand fully the needs of followers of inspiring style leadership.

These relationships between followers' needs and leadership styles can obviously be used to analyse the likely success of changes in leadership styles by any leader. Clearly any dramatic changes in style involving simultaneously changing both dimensions of followers' needs, such as from directing to inspiring style, are less likely to be successful. This is due to the potential damage to the trust and respect built up with existing followers, who do not have either of these new needs, and the lack of credibility of the leader with potential followers that they are seeking to acquire. However, moves that only involve changing one dimension of followers' needs at a time, such as from inspiring style to enabling style or vice versa, are more likely to be successful for the reasons just discussed.

Of course, if the possible change in leadership role is caused by a promotion to a more senior managerial level in the same organization the decision by the promoted individual is whether to change their style or to try to make their new potential followers accept and willingly follow their existing, and presumably, successful style. As already discussed, this has been done in many cases, with Jack Welch on his promotion to Chairman and CEO of GE being a classic example. What increased the probability of success in this case is that the previous leader had been implementing the incentivizing style so that the change to the inspiring style of Jack Welch only required the acceptance of a greater degree of affiliation than had been emphasized before.

Another factor, that is also common to many other examples of promoted leaders maintaining their current style and thus requiring their new followers to adapt, is that several followers of the previous leader are likely to leave once the new 'leader' takes over. Certainly most of Jack Welch's rivals for the top job at GE left to become CEOs and potential leaders of other very large US-based corporations.

They therefore faced the challenge of being the externally appointed 'potential leader'.

From Leader to Follower

The previous discussion considered the issues of a willing follower when they seek to become a leader in their own right. However, these issues also occur in reverse when an existing leader becomes the willing follower of their own leader. Great leaders automatically and willingly become positively committed followers of other leaders when appropriate. No ego issues or status concerns are allowed to get in the way of realizing the maximum potential performance from the organization.

In a truly team-based organization this can result in rotating leadership, where different leaders are readily accepted by the rest of the team depending upon the particular challenge facing them. We have already described this as 'standing together' so that there is no need for a 'single leader' to whom the organization always turns. Obviously this depends upon a very high level of mutual trust and respect among these rotating leaders and followers. However, much more importantly, it also requires that these alternative leaders implement different leadership styles. There is no extra value created by passing leadership from one enabling style leader to another. The best enabling style leader should stay as the leader of this group. The value creation is achieved by changing to the most appropriate style of leadership for the challenge facing the organization. Once this challenge has been surmounted, leadership can be passed back to the ongoing leader or passed on to a new temporary leader with the next most appropriate style.

At its extreme, this can almost become 'leadership without a leader'. An organization can become known as the leader in its field, e.g. Oxford and Cambridge Universities in the field of academic research. As a result of its reputation it therefore attracts the best people, i.e. the best academic researchers, and this reinforces its reputation as the best in its field. However, these people are often self-motivated and work relatively independently in their own fields of expertise. Hence they do not require strong leadership to motivate them to put in discretionary effort. In essence they are inspired by the reputation of the organization itself, rather than by any current individual leader within the organization.

Even externally there is often no strongly visible leader who is the personification of the organization in order to attract the best talent. The role of leadership at the top of this type of organization is therefore about preserving the freedom of these highly talented people to work in their own way on their particular area of expertise; in other words, to allow them to become real leaders in their field. In this sense, organizational leadership can be about preserving the status quo, in a low key way, rather than stimulating change. The changes, in the form of new ideas and breakthroughs, will come from the lower-level leaders attracted to the organization. This low profile leadership is clearly important to many organizations where knowledge creation is the major source of competitive advantage.

Conclusion

Most leaders are also followers of another leader. Therefore it is important to understand how their needs as followers are linked to their own most relevant leadership styles. Leaders need to understand the needs of their potential willing followers and this is most easily achieved if they share some of these needs themselves. Hence there are logical relationships between any individual being a willing follower of one leadership style and this person then implementing a complementary leadership style. Further, if there is no commonality between these two sets of followers' needs it is more difficult to develop the trust and respect that is essential to becoming a value-creating corporate leader.

9

Theoretical underpinnings of the model

The research that resulted in our leadership styles model developed out of earlier cross-functional work into the value-creating or value-destroying roles of top teams at the centres of large companies. Utilizing a configurational approach, this research highlighted four ways in which a corporate centre can create value in a large multi-business organization. However, when we sought to apply this configurational approach to the potential leadership roles of the senior executives located within these various top teams, we were disappointed with the relevance of existing corporate leadership models. Our configurational model of shareholder value creation by corporate centres had been built up from a theoretical grounding in transaction cost economics and resource-based theory. By contrast, any economic benefits derived from corporate leadership seem to be largely implicit or assumed within these leadership theories. Leadership should not be done simply because it is a 'good thing' to do. It should be done because it enables a corporation to produce extraordinary results from an otherwise ordinary group of employees.

One of our key objectives of this research was therefore to see if we could find an explanatory and causal relationship between specific leadership activities and any 'resulting' sustainable improvement in business performance. A fundamental problem with some current management and leadership research is that it looks for any common factors among several successful companies and then interprets these common factors as being the causes of the success of these varied businesses. We set out to try to develop a theoretically sound explanation of cause and effect between leadership and improved performance.

Another objective was based on our definition of the terms leadership and particularly leading. As stated in Chapter 1, we regard leading as an activity and therefore we wanted to examine the potential value-creating activities of leaders. Further, in our view to be 'a leader' carries the connotation of being extremely good at something, if not the very best that there is. Hence we were trying to identify if value creation could be increased by leaders focusing their own energy in order to get better at a more limited range of activities. Most existing leadership models seem to require leaders to be expert at all the many different aspects of leading and to be capable of switching among various styles and capabilities as specific situations demand. Many years of research into this area at Cranfield School of Management had already demonstrated to us that a critical element in corporate leadership was developing trust and respect from potential followers, and that this was built up through consistency in behaviour over time.

Therefore in this chapter we try to set out some of the key theoretical underpinnings of our leadership styles model. We start with a very brief discussion of how transaction cost economics and resource-based theory inform the value-creation potential of each of our leadership styles, as these were fundamental building blocks of our earlier work on corporate strategy. We then consider a few key elements from theories of corporate strategy before looking at specific leadership theories. Given the vast literature on leadership, we are not attempting to provide a comprehensive précis of this whole subject area. We have selected certain key areas so that our model can be both related to and contrasted with existing concepts and theories.

Value Creation through Leadership

At the beginning of the book we distinguished leadership from management in terms of the extra, unspecified, discretionary output that can be achieved by leaders from their willing followers. These additional or, in our terms, extraordinary outputs result from the additional efforts that these followers willingly input into the business.

Transaction cost economics (TCE) theory has developed from its origins in the 1930s (Coase, 1937) when it questioned the existence of frictionless, i.e. truly efficient, markets. It argued that there are costs incurred in using the market price mechanism, e.g. discovering what the relevant prices are. Thus these transaction costs can make it more efficient to carry out a specific activity within the firm rather than through the external market. This fundamental idea was developed to incorporate governance structures within the firm and to introduce the idea of asset specificity (Williamson, 1975, 1985). Thus TCE sees firms and markets as alternative means of coordinating economic activities; firms coordinate through authority relationships while markets use the price mechanism as their means of coordination. A fundamental tenet of the original TCE theory is that common ownership of two activities (i.e. in-house activities) is economically beneficial only if contractual hazards (i.e. the risk of opportunistic behaviour by the external supplier) and the associated, but consequently, required governance costs are significant. In other words, the market is assumed to be more efficient than the firm unless it can be proved otherwise.

However, the theory has been developed (Ghoshal and Moran, 1996; Simon, 1991) with the view that the modern world is really an organizational economy not a market economy, where markets begin where organizations fail. Clearly, this is the reverse of traditional TCE as firms replace markets where non-market means of coordination and commitment are superior (Rumelt et al., 1991) whereas, as already stated, traditional TCE sees markets as the natural choice for activities. Importantly, opportunism as an attitude is also separated from opportunistic behaviour. According to the theory of reasoned action, volitional behaviour is caused by behavioural intentions. These are determined by attitudes and subjective norms. This would make opportunistic behaviour, which can be defined as self-interest utilized with guile and unconstrained by morality, positively influenced by opportunism.

Opportunism itself has causal factors, one of which is opportunistic behaviour. However, the other two are feeling for the organization and prior conditioning caused by both conscious and unconscious stimuli. Thus, feelings and prior conditioning could create a dissonance effect on opportunistic behaviour, particularly if such behaviour is accompanied by high commitment and freedom of choice. Strong governance may have a positive effect on the cost of opportunistic behaviour but it normally has a negative impact on the feeling for the organization through the removal of trust. The dissonance effect could itself lead to modifications in behaviour, without strong governance.

In a managerially dominated organization, excellent governance may be needed to control opportunistic behaviour because employees have no strong feelings for the company and are motivated only to do their prescribed jobs. The role of the corporate leader is to achieve high identification with, and positive feelings for, the company from a wide range of willing followers. Excessively strong governance could erode any positive attitudes so that 'consummate cooperation' turns to 'perfunctory compliance'. There is also a distinction between rational control, the basis of TCE, and social control. Rational control is the normal, relatively formal governance process, whereas social control is based on people, their preferences, and informal mechanisms to build motivation and commitment. Social control can actually influence behaviour with or without a change in attitude. Its advocates seek to induce individuals to internalize the values and the goals of the organization; such internalization implies a change in attitude.

Social controls are increasingly important as the strength and influence of leadership, as distinct from management, grows within an organization. Rational controls work best where performance can be objectively measured and evaluated against agreed targets, such as with incentivizing style leadership and, to a degree, the directing style. However, with inspiring style leadership, social controls only are best as the vision and values of the organization must be totally bought into by the vast majority of employees.

This logic can also be applied to the development of organizations. Companies can adapt autonomously in response to external market signals but this 'autonomous adaptation' is directionless, so that it is biased towards static efficiency (Hayek, 1945). This is the transactional leadership focus of our incentivizing and directing leadership styles. However, firms are capable of 'purposive adaptation', i.e. coordinated but with a shared purpose. The shared purpose gives the adaptation direction and this has several advantages. It can work in the absence of prices and markets so that formal service-level agreements, transfer pricing agreements, and other rational control processes are not essential. Companies can create new options and activities, and this can transform the institutional context in which relationships are embedded.

This represents the transformational leadership focus of our enabling and inspiring styles. It is particularly relevant for highly innovative companies, as innovative activities are often characterized by missing prices or markets, by strong uncertainty and high ambiguity. Companies may thus beat markets in this area of innovation but, to do so, they need strong leadership rather than merely strong management.

Resource-based theory (RBT) of the firm (Wernerfelt, 1984, 1994; Barney, 1991) emphasizes the resources or capabilities of the firm, enabling firms to generate enduring sources of competitive advantage through distinctive ways of utilizing their resources and capabilities. Resources are viewed as a strength of the business, and these resources are both tangible and intangible assets that are tied semi-permanently to the organization. Thus they include brands, customers, processes as well as knowledge and skilled personnel.

RBT considers multi-business companies as portfolios of resources rather than portfolios of products. This means that a group can be exploiting one resource to deliver super profits while it develops the next. Both RBT and industrial organization economics, on which Michael Porter's work is based (Porter, 1980, 1985), focus on explaining the achievement of super profits, i.e. the profits above the required rate of return that generate shareholder value. The source of this excess rate of return is located within the company's transformation process, what Porter referred to as the value chain. RBT highlights the human or 'cultural' resources as being critical to this value-creation process. In other words, inert resources cannot, by themselves, create shareholder value; they need human input.

This has led to the more recent development of the concept of the dynamic capabilities of the firm as being the processes by which resources are created and utilized (Teece et al., 1997; Eisenhardt and Martin, 2000). In this development of RBT, the term 'resources' is used only for inputs into the production process whereas, in normal resource-based theory, 'resources' are used both for inputs (assets) and processes (Barney, 1999; Dierickx and Cool, 1989). A key element of RBT is that it sees resources and dynamic capabilities as distinctive competences of firms, i.e. firms can do better than markets at carrying out certain activities. Inter-firm collaborations enable a firm to access complementary resources in order to overcome resource constraints.

Then it can apply its specific dynamic capabilities to these resources in order to create shareholder value.

RBT gives precision to the analysis of shareholder value creation. We can distinguish between new value creation (increasing the total value created by an industry value chain) and value capture by an individual company. The transformation of input resources by an organization produces a use value for the final output. This use value is, by definition, subjective as it is the use value 'perceived' by the customers in relation to their specific needs. However, this can only be realized by producers through the exchange value paid by customers that actually buy this output. Logically the customer's perceived use value of a purchase should exceed the exchange value paid. Indeed, the concept of consumer surplus is exactly this gap between perceived use value and exchange value paid. The perceived use value can therefore also be thought of as the total monetary value of the output produced, but there will normally be a value gap between this total monetary value and the exchange value captured by the producing organization.

This means that there are two potential sources of additional value capture for an organization because most organizations act as both suppliers (receiving exchange value for their use value produced) and customers (paying exchange value for perceived use value supplied to them). One source of value capture for the company is to focus on its role as customer and try to pay less exchange value for a given use value acquired, i.e. increase the value gap by reducing input costs. This cost-reducing emphasis does not affect the use values delivered to their external customers. These same use values are simply produced for lower input costs. However, the other source of value capture does impact on the final customer because it focuses on the organization's role as supplier. Here the supplier is trying to deliver the same (or something better) to the customer for a greater share of the total monetary value of the (changed) output. This is the value-creating, transformational side of our model, while the other emphasizes the cost-efficiency, transactional elements. Thus the two sides of our model utilize different sources of bargaining power within the total industry value chain.

The organization can further seek to increase its value capture by creating 'intermediate' use values that exist outside of the people who created them, e.g. brands, reputation, software, and other forms of relational capital. This knowledge can then be leveraged across the group, as is done by our enabling style leadership. However, these 'differential' labour inputs can also create quite enduring human capital that leads to enhanced use values through the development of truly innovative products. Human use capital can take the form of informal networks, team working, and communities of practice that occur in open, sharing cultures, where there are very high levels of mutual trust and respect, as are required for our inspiring leadership style.

The inert inputs of RBT can also be split into two categories: normal inputs (raw materials, generic labour) and the enduring inert capital (fixed assets) of the business. The directing leadership style focuses mainly on the exploitation of the enduring inert use values within the group, while the incentivizing leadership style tries to minimize wasted and unproductive expenditure. This includes minimizing the exchange value paid to suppliers and what RBT refers to as maintenance activities. Thus these cost-efficiency focused styles emphasize 'bought' inputs while the enabling and inspiring styles emphasize the inputs built internally within the group. These ideas are summarized in Figure 9.1.

As shown in Figure 9.1, it is also possible to identify distinct dynamic capabilities that are relevant to each leadership style. Activities and processes that are directed at the creation of future RBT resources can be regarded as dynamic capabilities. The incentivizing style of leadership has the lowest requirement for trust and respect between the leader and their followers. Hence this leadership style can utilize more of the rational controls of TCE theory that are more commonly associated

	Enabling style	Inspiring style
Resource Dynamic capability Extraordinary output source	Intermediate use values Explicit knowledge Releasing psychological energy	Human use values Tacit know-how Increasing total energy
	Incentivizing style	Directing style
Resource Dynamic capability Extraordinary output source	Inert use values Input cost reduction Redirecting existing energy	Enduring inert use values Improved asset utilization Releasing physical energy

Figure 9.1 Applying resource-based theory to the leadership model

with management rather than leadership. If these governance processes result in very low levels of wastage on unproductive resources and minimal expenditure on firm maintenance activities, this would be a dynamic capability that creates cost-reducing resources. This is totally in line with our value-creating concept for this style of redirecting the existing energy inputs of followers.

With the directing leadership style, the centralization of activities and processes that maximizes the utilization of fixed assets is also a dynamic capability that creates a cost-saving resource. Again this matches with the release of physical energy for this style in our model. The enabling leadership style takes existing group intermediate use values and codifies them so that their value-creating capability across the group is optimized. The dynamic capability is the process by which the critical knowledge is made explicit so that others in the group can utilize it. This enables the release of psychological energy, as these others do not have to reinvent the wheel.

The human capital-creating activity of the inspiring leadership style creates new value through the use of more tacit know-how rather than explicit knowledge. Tacit skills are a process because they are about how to do things. Deeply ingrained tacit skills can be very difficult to communicate to outsiders. Therefore they are a dynamic capability of the inspiring leadership style in that they increase the total energy available to the organization. They also completely match the RBT definition of a valuable asset, i.e. valuable, rare, inimitable and non-substitutable. This is why inspiring leadership is the most sustainable value-creating style.

Links to Corporate Strategy Theory

As already stated, the leadership styles model developed from a deep interest in the value creation or destruction (Goold et al., 1994) of corporate top teams, in other words corporate-level strategy rather than the more widely researched competitive strategy. Henry Mintzberg is the leading researcher in this field and has, with others, analysed a comprehensive range of the strategy development processes used over the years (Mintzberg et al., 1998). In addition to the configuration process that we developed for multi-business groups of companies (Ward et al., 2005), two of these processes are of particular interest to any discussion of corporate leadership.

Most of the strategy development processes considered by Mintzberg are rationally-based, analytical processes as a result of which *the* corporate strategy should be developed. However, the Learning School regards strategy development as an emergent process. Strategies are still being developed as they are being implemented so that the process becomes evolutionary. The organization develops routines that evolve as the environment changes and learning takes place. Thus the organization does not develop *the* deliberate corporate strategy but a series of strategies emerge. Deliberate strategy emphasizes control in the sense of making sure that senior management's intentions are realized. Emergent strategy emphasizes learning so that the role of corporate leadership is to stimulate and drive the process of learning.

Another of Mintzberg's schools of strategy development, the Cultural School, emphasizes the collective nature of the process. As already discussed, culture binds a group of individuals into an integrated entity and is, by definition, a collective and social process. Indeed, some would argue that businesses do not have a culture, the business is a culture, as culture represents the life-force of the organization. A true company ideology can therefore be described as a rich passionately shared culture. The implications of this are clearly that the corporate strategy will be significantly influenced by both the nature and the relative strength of this commonly held culture. We have tried to incorporate this into both our individual leadership styles and the leadership frameworks, which show how the different styles can be made to work together at the various levels within a large organization.

Another body of corporate strategy research that highlights the value-creating role of leadership within corporate top teams is that of Jim Collins and others (Collins and Lazier, 1992; Collins and Porras, 1994; Collins, 2001). Collins identifies great leaders as requiring a paradoxical blend of personal humility and professional will; they do not need to be personally charismatic. The key role of these leaders is to create a clear vision that is both bought into and actively pursued by the employees of the company. This is greatly facilitated if the group has clearly identified what is critically important to it, what Collins calls the company's 'hedgehog concept'. The hedgehog concept represents the intersection of the company's core values, its core competences and the key drivers of its super profits.

One of the very important elements in this framework of 'building and maintaining a great company' is that the vision not only incorporates the core values and beliefs together with the fundamental reason for the existence of the company (the core ideology) but also has a measurable mission statement. This mission should be challenging and compelling but have a measure of risk, if it is to create the stretch that is required for greatness: what Collins and Porras (1994) called Big Hairy Audacious Goals (BHAGs). As one mission comes close to being achieved it needs to be replaced by a new BHAG so that the organization is always stretching itself to reach new goals. Thus everything but the core ideology can and should change as required by the external environment. This is reflected in the standards applied by these companies. The values standards are very rigid and non-compliance should result in expulsion from the company. The performance standards are also very high, because great performers get very fed up if the organization tolerates poor performance, but they are less rigid. Indeed learning failures are encouraged, as long as the learnings are shared across the group.

Not surprisingly, we have no problems with any of these elements of corporate leadership but find it incredibly challenging to expect any single leader to do it all. Most of Collins's leadership roles fit within our inspiring leadership style but the stretch targets and spreading knowledge are, we believe, more appropriately given as the focus of separate leaders located at other complementary levels in the organization.

Fitting our Model into the Existing Theory

As we have set out in detail earlier in the book and as summarized in Figure 9.2, each of our leadership styles focuses on one value-adding leadership activity and therefore needs excellence in one related key capability. We believe that only one key capability, communicating for success, is common across all the leadership styles as all leaders need to be able to motivate their followers, albeit to differing degrees. The idea of leadership capabilities, or competences, is neither new nor contentious. What is new is the concept of different leadership styles requiring different capabilities. Yet we would contend that this is the logical consequence of much previous research.

Enabling style	Inspiring style
Key leadership activity	**Enabling style**	**Inspiring style**

	Enabling style	**Inspiring style**
Key leadership activity	Connecting	Visioning
Key capability	Engaging through dialogue	Crafting the future
	Communicating for success	
Type of leadership	People/transformational	
	Incentivizing style	**Directing style**
Key leadership activity	Delivering	Aligning
Key capability	Handling paradox	Exhibiting staying power
	Communicating for success	
Type of leadership	Strategic/transactional	

Figure 9.2 Summary of leadership model

In his books, *Working with Emotional Intelligence* (Goleman, 1998) and *The New Leaders* (Goleman et al., 2002), Daniel Goleman identifies a range of leadership competences. These can be grouped into the two main categories of personal competences and social competences. Personal competences relate to how you 'manage' yourself in terms of self-awareness and self-management. Self-awareness encompasses a true sense of emotional self-awareness and an accurate, honest, self-assessment from which can be gained a soundly-based level of self-confidence. The main point is that any potential leader needs a very good understanding of their own personal characteristics before they can attract and retain willing followers.

In addition, the potential leader needs competences in several aspects of self-management. One of these is emotional self-control to which is added a sense of optimism; few followers would want to be led by a pessimist who regularly loses all self-control. Two other of these self-management competences are transparency and adaptability but, in our terms, the most important attributes for a leader are a need for achievement and a willingness to exercise initiative.

The required social competences are also divided in two: social awareness and relationship management. The social awareness headings are a good ability to empathize with followers (which is very similar to our communicating skills attributes and our resulting communicating for success capability), organizational awareness and a strong sense of service. It is with the relationship management competences that we have the most concerns. These include inspirational leadership, influencing skills, developing others, building bonds and teamwork and collaboration. The remaining two are acting as a change catalyst and conflict management. Our concern is partly that this list yet again seems to blur the roles of leadership and management but, more importantly, that many of these competences are as important for those acting as willing followers as they are for their leaders.

It is because of the confusion that we believe is caused by this approach that we have tried to distinguish between personal attributes that are needed by potential leaders and the capabilities that they must show. As stated in Chapter 1, we do not focus on the resulting extensive list of personal attributes as many of them are equally required by their followers and some even by those senior managers who are without any leadership capabilities. We totally agree therefore that self-awareness and a knowledge of one's impact on others are important personal attributes, but have difficulty in classifying this as a competence or, in our terms, a capability. We prefer Zenger and Folkman's approach (2002) where they identify six potentially fatal flaws that would stop someone from becoming a leader. These are a lack of integrity, an inability to learn from mistakes, a lack of core interpersonal skills, a lack of openness to new ideas in the form of arrogance and/or compla-cency, a lack of willingness to be held accountable and a lack of initiative. We agree that any of these would make leadership impossi-ble, but they would also have a severe impact on the value-creating contribution of someone fulfilling the role of a willing follower of another's leadership.

Zenger and Folkman treat leadership as a combination of attributes and the results that are achieved and have developed what they term a leadership tent. This has five leadership building blocks; these are personal character, personal capability, a focus on results, interpersonal skills and leading organizational change. From their research they have made 20 insights into leadership and identified 16 leadership competences or behaviours that come out of their five leadership build-ing blocks. What they do state is that personal character, i.e. high integrity and honesty, is a necessary but not sufficient condition for great leadership. Further, personal character and personal capability (which covers knowledge, problem-solving skills, innovation and initiative, professional skills, etc.) must be in place before the remaining building blocks will start to work.

However, our concern with their conclusions is that they state that an individual must be in the top quartile for each of their competences to be a great leader. This effectively requires someone to be great at almost everything, although they acknowledge that developing leaders is about developing complementary capabilities. Indeed, displaying strength in only one of their competences has the biggest impact in improving an individual's ranking as a leader. Having five strengths out of their 16 gets over the ninetieth percentile in their ranking structure. They then identify ten very powerful combinations of two or three leadership competences that have the most impact on improving leadership performance. At this level their conclusions become quite aligned with our leadership styles model. This is reinforced by their strong recommendation to focus on developing strengths, rather than reducing weaknesses. It has to be clearly understood that any of their potential fatal flaws must, however, be fixed.

Another leading researcher and writer in this area is John Kotter (1990, 1999) and he has focused a lot on distinguishing leadership from management. Once again, he identifies 20 attributes shared by effective leaders, some of which are fixed early in life, such as the level of integrity, as well as drive and ambition, and intelligence or intellectual skill. Others can be developed, particularly by giving potential leaders real challenges early in their careers, so that they gain broad experience and learn to fail. He has also argued that leading change, as discussed in Chapter 8, is a critical role for many leaders; indeed, he states that leadership is about coping with change whereas management is about coping with complexity.

However, there is still an emphasis on the personal attributes of leaders rather than on their leadership activities. As already stated we believe that most of these personal attributes are required by those many willing followers, who will never take on a leadership role, if they are to make their maximum contribution to the performance of the organization.

This is well borne out by the work of Robert Kelley as set out in his book *Star Performer* (1998). His original research highlighted 45 potential factors that could explain star performance at work by people at all levels in the organization. These were grouped into three sets of factors: cognitive factors, personality factors and social factors. The detailed subsequent research highlighted *no* actual differences in performance that could be explained by any of these original 45 factors.

The conclusions from this research were that *how* an individual works is the critical determining issue of the level of relative performance. Nine key work strategies were identified; in addition cognitive ability and technical competence were required hygiene factors but were not sufficient on their own for star performance.

The most important characteristic was the willingness to exercise initiative, which was linked to the creation of a mutually beneficial network of contacts. Next came an ability to link one's own work effort to the critical path of the organization, which is linked to a sense of perspective. By this Kelley means 'getting the big picture' in terms of recognizing patterns and exercising expert judgement. However, the next two are particularly important because they are, in order of importance, followership and then leadership. Star followers willingly participate in teams led by others but are actively involved followers who contribute independent critical thinking to these teams. For star performers, undertaking leadership roles is more important than becoming permanent leaders so that leadership may rotate within a team as appropriate. As with Collins, Kelley's work emphasizes the need for a lack of ego irrespective of whether an individual is acting as a leader or follower.

The remaining key work strategies for star performers are a good sense of teamwork, but only to those teams that are necessary and where the individual is adding value to the team, organizational 'savvy' in terms of building important relationships and the ability to persuade the right audience with the right message: what Kelley calls 'show and tell'. The important thing about this work is that it highlights the need for great value creators to operate as both leaders and followers and indicates that many characteristics often referred to as essential for leadership are equally relevant to any willing followers who are going to be able to deliver their maximum potential performance for the company.

This is reinforced by Daniel Cooper in *Leadership for Follower Commitment* (2003). He compares and analyses several definitions and attitudes to different levels of commitment to organizations and the leaders within them. As with many other writers, he distinguishes managers as having strategies based on imposing control while leaders base their strategies on eliciting effective commitment. In Cooper's terms the highest level is 'affective' commitment, which is the positive, energetic commitment shown by willing followers who are granted 'natural recognition' by their leaders. He argues that leaders and followers both have responsibilities within these relationships. If followers do not respond positively to their leader's efforts to improve the relationship, the leader may revert to managerial behaviour and impose authority-based structures. He argues that high self-esteem in a positive response organizational environment is important if psychological energy inputs are to thrive. Social acceptance or at least acknowledgement of social worth also satisfies a need for recognition; without this, it is argued that followers' commitment will decay.

We do not disagree with these arguments but hold that the needs of followers can differ significantly so that not all followers have high needs for both self-esteem and recognition. Hence our different leadership styles will be more relevant to some followers than others. However, we do not believe that it is either possible or practical for a single leader to tailor their leadership style to fit, and hence attract and retain as willing followers, all the potential varying needs that can exist across all employees in a major multinational corporation. Hence we have developed our leadership frameworks that enable differing, but complementary, leadership styles to be implemented at various levels within an organization. We totally agree with Cooper that all potential followers should be positively committed to one leader. We just do not necessarily believe that they all need to follow the same leader.

Conclusion

This brief review of the relevant theory has tried to indicate how our leadership model fits in and what its new contribution is. We believe that it makes the development of potential leaders within an organization a more practical proposition. It also highlights the possible problems that can be faced when leaders are changed or when the competitive environment, in which a particular style of leadership is being implemented, changes. We hope that our own energy input and commitment to this research proves to be value creating for those organizations that take up the concepts and ideas generated by it.

References

Barney, J.B., 1991, 'Firm resources and sustained competitive advantage', *Journal of Management,* **17**(1), 99–120.

Barney, J.B., 1999, 'How a firm's capabilities affect boundary decisions', *Sloan Management Review*, Spring, 137–45.

Coase, R.E., 1937, The nature of the firm, *Economica,* **4**, 386–405.

Collins, J.C., 2001, *Good to Great*, Random House.

Collins, J.C. and Lazier, W.C., 1992, *Beyond Entrepreneurship*, Prentice Hall.

Collins, J.C. and Porras, J.I., 1994, *Built to Last*, Random House.

Cooper, D.J., 2003, *Leadership for Follower Commitment*, Butterworth-Heinemann.

Dierickx, I. and Cool, K., 1989, 'Asset stock accumulation and sustainability of competitive advantage', *Management Science*, **35**(12), 1504–11.

Eisenhardt, K.M. and Martin, J.A., 2000, 'Dynamic capabilities: What are they?' *Strategic Management Journal*, **21** (10–11), 1105–21.

Ghoshal, S. and Moran, P., 1996, 'Bad for practice: A critique of the transaction cost theory', *Academy of Management Review*, **21** (1), 13–47.

Goleman, D., 1998, *Working with Emotional Intelligence*, Bantam Books.

Goleman, D., Boyatzis, R. and McKee, A., 2002, *The New Leaders*, Time Warner Books.

Goold, M., Campbell, A. and Alexander, M., 1994, *Corporate Level Strategy*, Wiley.

Hayek, F., 1945, 'The use of knowledge in society', *American Economic Review*, **35**(4), 519–30.

Kelley, R., 1998, *Star Performer*, Times Books.

Kotter, J.P., 1990, *A Force for Change: How Leadership Differs from Management,* The Free Press.

Kotter, J.P., 1999, *What Leaders Really Do*, Harvard Business Review Books.

Mintzberg, H., Ahlstand, B. and Lampel, J., 1998, *Strategy Safari*, The Free Press.

Porter, M.J., 1980, *Competitive Strategy*, The Free Press.

Porter, M.J., 1985, *Competitive Advantage*, The Free Press.

Rumelt, B.P., Schendel, D. and Teece, D.J., 1991, 'Strategic management and economics', *Strategic Management Journal*, **12,** 5–29.

Simon, H.A., 1991, 'Organisations and markets', *Journal of Economic Perspectives*, **5**(2), 25–44.

Teece, D.J., Pisano, G. and Skuen, A., 1997, 'Dynamic capabilities and strategic management', *Strategic Management Journal*, **18**(7), 509–33.

Ward, K., Bowman, C. and Kakabadse, A., 2005, *Designing World Class Corporate Strategies: Value-Creating Roles for Corporate Centres*, Elsevier Butterworth-Heinemann.

Wernerfelt, B., 1984, 'A resource-based view of the firm', *Strategic Management Journal*, **5,** 171–80.

Wernerfelt, B., 1994, 'The resource-based view of the firm – ten years after', *Strategic Management Journal*, **16,** 171–4.

Williamson, O.E., 1975, *Markets and Hierarchies: Analysis and Antitrust Implications*, The Free Press.

Williamson, O.E., 1985, *The Economic Institutions of Capitalism*, The Free Press.

Zenger, J.H. and Folkman, J., 2002, *The Extraordinary Leader*, McGraw-Hill.

Index